James P. Kirkwood,   Making of America Project, Saint Louis Water
Commissioner

Report on the Filtration of River Waters for the Supply of Cities

as practised in Europe, made to the Board of water commissioners of the city of St.

Louis

James P. Kirkwood,   Making of America Project, Saint Louis Water Commissioner

Report on the Filtration of River Waters for the Supply of Cities
as practised in Europe, made to the Board of water commissioners of the city of St. Louis

ISBN/EAN: 9783337399375

Printed in Europe, USA, Canada, Australia, Japan

Cover: Foto ©Andreas Hilbeck / pixelio.de

More available books at **www.hansebooks.com**

REPORT

ON THE

FILTRATION OF RIVER WATERS.

FOR THE SUPPLY OF CITIES,

AS PRACTISED IN EUROPE,

MADE TO THE

BOARD OF WATER COMMISSIONERS

OF THE

CITY OF ST. LOUIS.

BY

JAMES P. KIRKWOOD,
CIVIL ENGINEER.

PUBLISHED BY PERMISSION OF THE BOARD.

ILLUSTRATED BY THIRTY ENGRAVINGS.

NEW YORK:
D. VAN NOSTRAND, PUBLISHER,
23 Murray Street and 27 Warren Street (up stairs).
LONDON: TRÜBNER & CO.
1869.

CONTENTS.

REPORT.

To the Board of Water Commissioners
of the City of St. Louis. Geo. K. Budd, *President.*

Gentlemen : In obedience to instructions received from the Board of Water Commissioners in December, 1865 (see Appendix), I have visited Europe for the purpose of understanding the modes in practice there for the filtration or clarification on a large scale of river waters, where these are made use of for domestic purposes in the supply of cities.

To this end I have visited the cities of Genoa, and Leghorn, in Italy ; of Marseilles, Toulouse, Lyons, Tours, Angers, and Nantes in France ; of Berlin, Hamburgh, and Altona in North Germany, and of London, Leicester, York, Liverpool, Edinburgh, Perth, and Dublin in Great Britain.

I submit herewith statements descriptive of the modes of filtration in use at each of these places.

The obtaining of this information has occupied much more time than I had anticipated. In many places it was found impossible to get at all the details and statistics which were desirable, without a larger expenditure of time and money than your instructions, however liberally construed, would have warranted. What may be wanting, however, in the description of one place will generally be found in another. No one but the superintendent or engineer of each work, who had watched the process of filtration from year to year, could give minutely all the experience which each place learns for itself. The process, however, unless where the areas were incommensurate with the service, was in England everywhere successful. The conditions were simple, well recognized, and easily understood ; and when, as in two instances particularly, they were violated, it was but temporarily—the increase of area required being acknowledged, and being about to be corrected.*

---

* January, 1869. At each of these places the enlargement of the filtering area has since been made.

In France, while what is called the natural filter is successful, the artificial filter is usually a failure, for reasons which are sufficiently explained in the descriptions of the several places.

In England, where the rivers rarely carry as much sediment as the Mississippi, except in floods, I found the arrangements for filtration very general and very manageable, and that, so far as my knowledge extends, wherever a city derived its supply from river or stream, unless where large storage reservoirs intervened, filter beds were used as a matter of course, to render the water in every case as unobjectionable and satisfactory to the consumer as might be practicable.

In England and France, where the winters are usually mild, the ice seldom forms so thick as to require any extra attention on the filtering basins. I visited Northern Germany, where the climate is as severe as our own, to understand whether the formation of thick ice impeded or interrupted the filtering process.

In the description of each place,* while the special object is to give an account of its filtering works, I have noted such other information as incidentally came within my reach, in order that the general scheme of each place might be understood.

Instead of giving a synopsis illustrative of the varying experience of the different places described, it will be more useful probably to explain the principles in practice, which govern the construction and operation of filter beds in England and elsewhere.

The accompanying sketches of a filter bed suitable for St. Louis, will serve to illustrate the details of this practice.

It will be obvious, however, that the pertinency of what I may say cannot be judged of without that kind of preliminary information which the statements referred to are intended to convey.

We are accustomed here to consider the filtering arrangements on European works, as having in view simply the removal of the fine sediments which discolor river waters; but the filter bed equally intercepts and removes the fine vegetable fibres and the minute organisms, vegetable or animal, which in all river waters prevail more or less during certain of the summer months. The removal of this class of impurities is getting to be considered in England, and elsewhere, as of as much importance as the removal of the sedimentary uncleanness which is more apparent. During certain of the summer months, when the rivers usually carry but little sediment, this forms the chief duty of the filter beds. The surface of the sand becomes occasionally as much

---

* Since this report was written, the London journal called "Engineering" has published descriptions of the London Water Works, in which will be found minute descriptions of several of the London pumping engines. The "Encyclopedia Britannica," "Bourne's Specimens," and "The Engineer," may also be consulted for similar details.

impeded then with this matter as with the earthy sediments which more usually clog it, and it is of a nature to taint the water under certain conditions more offensively than the other. The sand filters are therefore considered very important instruments of purification in this relation. They become, indeed, screens of the greatest delicacy, intercepting all material impurities, not the least of which are the very small fish with which all waters are crowded at certain seasons. Most of the European rivers, however, pass through lands where manure is used more extensively, and where a higher state of cultivation prevails than on the lands bordering our Western rivers; and where also a denser population usually exists. Our rivers, therefore, will not probably for a long time carry at any time the same amount of organic matter in suspension.

In some of the places visited by me, what is called the natural filter is in successful use; I will refer to this again, and confine myself first to the artificial filter.

The filter bed was designed to get rapidly rid of that very light portion of the sediment carrried by river waters, which takes some time (a fortnight or more) to subside under ordinary circumstances. This clayey discoloration, though trifling in weight, renders the water very objectionable in appearance, very objectionable in its application to any of the arts or manufactures, and no acquisition certainly either as regards health or cleanliness; although custom, as on the Western rivers, may reconcile persons to its presence, especially when its absence is associated, as there, with the hard and unpalatable waters of the lime-stone springs. That portion of the sediment which, from its greater weight, subsides rapidly, say within twenty-four hours, can be more economically got rid of in subsiding reservoirs. The successful use of the filter bed presupposes the preparation of the water in a subsiding reservoir. Wherever the attempt has been made to use filter beds without that preliminary aid, they have either failed altogether, as in France, or rendered the water but partially clarified, as in one of the London works. On the London works the aid of subsiding reservoirs is being more and more availed of of late years, both as rendering the filtering process more economical, which they seem to have been slow to perceive, and as a necessary auxiliary in time of flood, to the efficiency of the other. They have become besides, valuable expedients, especially on the Lea, for the storage of water. In some places as at Liverpool, Leicester, Edinburgh, and Dublin, the large valley reservoirs required for compensation and flood storage, perform for the filter beds the functions of a subsiding reservoir.

I will refer again to the size and arrangement of these.

The materials used for filtration on a large scale are very simple. They are sand, gravel, and broken stone or shingle—the depth of the whole varying from five to six and one-half feet; a layer of shells has sometimes been used, placed within the stratum of gravel, but this is not found essential, and is now generally omitted.

It will be convenient to consider here the most appropriate size for a filter bed before giving the arrangement and thickness of its materials. The sizes in practice will be found to be very variable, and seemingly to have followed no regular standard. The first filter beds at Chelsea proved inconveniently large, and have since in practice been divided. The new filter beds at Stoke Newington (London), the filter beds at Liverpool, and those now under construction at Dublin, are fair specimens of modern practice, as applied to large cities. For small cities it is found convenient to make the dimensions proportionally smaller.

The areas of these are 45,000, 30,000 and 22,550 square feet each, respectively. Their forms are rectangular, 300 × 150, 300 × 100, and 205 × 110.

At Stoke Newington, with a delivery of 12,000,000 imperial gallons daily, there are 5 filter beds in use now, and two projected, making 7 in all when complete.

At Liverpool there are 6 now, for a delivery of 9,000,000 to 12,000,000 imperial gallons.

At Dublin, for an assumed delivery of 12,000,000 imperial gallons, there are 7 filter beds in process of construction.

Each filter bed, at short intervals varying with the condition of the water, must have the deposit which accumulates on the surface of the sand cleaned off or removed, and while any one is undergoing this cleansing process, the other remaining filters must be competent to deliver the required supply without overstraining their functions. If, then, there are six filters, five of them must be competent to the full duties of the service, and if eight filters, seven of them must be competent to this duty, on the supposition always that not more than one filter will at any time be off duty. Should the circumstances in effect render two unserviceable, the remainder must have area enough to meet the requirements of the case.

We see, then, that the smaller the filter beds—with the condition, however, that not more than one shall be off duty at a time — the smaller will be the total area of filtering surface required for the particular duty. The materials available for construction, and their cost, will also measurably influence the dimensions to be adopted, and it must always be borne in mind that although there may be but one filter off duty, it will frequently happen that another is nearly unserviceable. It is, therefore, found best to give a liberal area of filtering surface, to be prepared for all the contingencies of the service. For a city of the population and prospects of St. Louis, I will for the present assume 260 × 150 as convenient dimensions, giving an effective area of 37,450 square feet for each filter bed. See Plates 1 and 2.

The bottom of the filter bed is prepared to suit the circumstances of its position. It must be made practically water-tight. This is sometimes insured by laying concrete on the bottom (*a* Plate 2), but quite as often by a layer of hard clay puddle 18 to 24 inches thick, over which a flooring of brick is laid ; where the ground is more than usually bad, both the clay and the concrete may be used with advantage ; when concrete is used the brick paving is not essential. Upon this flooring a central drain (*b*) running lengthwise is laid, with which are connected on either side small tubular drains (*c*) of 6 to 9 inches diameter, prepared for this purpose, the sides being pierced with holes to facilitate the entrance of the water. These side drains are laid nearly at right angles to the central drain, and from 8 to 12 feet apart. The central drain referred to as arranged in Plate 2, and as in use on many of the London filters, is a double drain, performing two offices—the lower part (*b*), which is covered, gathering the filtered water, and the upper part (*d*), which is open, delivering the unfiltered water upon the sand, when refilling a filter bed immediately after cleansing, and in use then only for that special purpose. This central drain is sometimes of brick, and sometimes of stone covered with stone flagging, the side walls of the lowest twelve inches of the drain being in either case laid dry ; the water-way for this size of filter should not be less than 30 inches wide by 15 inches of height.

A little reflection will show that the lateral drains can hardly be placed too close together, for it is desirable that the filtered water should flow to the collecting drains with as slow a velocity as possible ; and the further these drains are apart, the greater must be the amount of water running through each drain.

In the latest constructed filter beds of the New River Works at Stoke Newington, the lateral pipe drains are dispensed with, and over the brick flooring, dry brick are laid instead ; forming a series of small drains not more than six inches apart from centre to centre. The filtered water finds its way into these through the open joints of the bricks. This forms the most perfect arrangement for collection that I have met with ; but it is also, probably, the most expensive. These small drains deliver there into two central drains.

This drainage skeleton rests on the base of the filter bed, and becomes the means provided to collect the filtered water and deliver it to the outer passages or wells. Upon the flooring of the filter beds, and covering the gathering drains as well as filling up the intervening spaces, a layer of broken stones is laid, large shingle or quarry spauls (*e*).

The stone should not be larger than will pass through a 4-inch ring, nor less than will pass through a 2-inch ring, and they must be clean and free from earth or quarry rubbish.

The shingle so called is obtained in England from coarse gravel or beach deposits, and is screened to the size wanted.

This layer of broken stone wants to be 24 inches thick to cover efficiently the pipe drains. Upon this layer of stone properly levelled off, from 18 to 24 inches of gravel is laid (f), say 18 inches. This gravel is usually screened into two or three sizes,—the larger of walnut size, the next of the size of a hazel nut, and the third between that and pea size. The largest size lies upon the broken stone, the smallest size at the top, the layers six inches thick each. Over this gravel there wants to be laid not less than 30 inches of fine sharp sand (g). The sand to be screened to insure the requisite degree of fineness and uniformity. The lower 12 inches may be a little coarser than the upper stratum of 18 inches, but it is important that the two layers should be of uniform fineness and quality throughout, otherwise there will be danger of the water passing through more rapidly at one point than another. The whole depth of these materials amounts to *five feet eight inches*,—a depth which will appear at first sight unnecessarily great, since we know that the upper stratum of sand performs apparently the whole duty of cleansing the water. The different degrees of fineness in the materials beneath the sand and their several thicknesses, were intended first to prevent the fine sand from following the water downward into the drains, and next to insure the presence of such a body of clean water below the surface of the filter, as would penetrate the numerous joints and openings of the drains, and keep them full, without creating anywhere currents or veins of water of any perceptible difference of velocity.

With the drains much nearer to the body of the sand, it will be understood that the tendency of the water would be to flow through the filtering material more rapidly just over the pipe than at 5 feet on either side of it. The distance through which it had to travel might be so short as to induce its concentration. The low velocity at which the water flows through the filter, the uniformity of fineness in the sand, and the distance of the collecting drains from its surface, all work together to produce that regularity of action over the entire filter bed upon which its perfection depends. The large gravel and the broken stone covering the lateral drains, presents in fact by the voids or spaces existing in such material, an innumerable collection of crooked tubes conveying the water in as many threads to the collecting drains, and rendering as well its concentration impracticable.

All the clear water underlying the surface of the earth, from which our springs and wells derive their supplies, has been filtered into the clearness in which it is found, by passing through earthen strata, where the muddy impurities which it held on the surface after heavy rains, have been intercepted and separated by a process precisely similar to that of the sand filter, so far as its limpidity is concerned.

From the ends of the pipe drains referred to, as well as from the end of the central drain, small cast-iron pipes (h), of 4 inches diameter, rise to the surface of the ground to enable the air to escape while the water is being first let on upon the filter bed.

In England the sides are usually paved with brick or stone to slopes of from 1 to 1 to 2 to 1. In this climate as in North Germany the side walls would have to be vertical on account of ice (see Plate 2), and the depth of the water over the filter beds should not be less than 4 feet. With vertical walls as at Berlin and Altona, the attendant, with proper tools, readily keeps the ice separated from the walls, and although it frequently forms 18 inches thick, and occasionally 24 inches, it does not interfere with the filtration, nor has it damaged the side walls, to which the floating cake of ice is never allowed to become attached. The water of the river Spree at Berlin, and of the Elbe at Altona, is usually clearer in winter than in summer. The filter beds on that account will operate for a longer period during the winter months than at other times without being uncovered. At Berlin and Altona, as I was informed, the filtering had never been interrupted in winter nor had the works been damaged by the ice. In our Western rivers the winter waters usually present the same character of greater clearness during the winter than during the summer months. But some winters are exceptional in this respect, and during such winters it would be desirable and might be necessary to uncover and clean off, as in summer, any filter that should become, from an accumulation of sediment, unserviceable. The proposed roofing in of the filter beds, to defend them from the hot suns of midsummer, would come into play here to defend the beds on occasion from frost, and admit of their being uncovered for cleansing. Practice would speedily indicate how best to meet any exceptional difficulty of this kind; and what had succeeded so well in the severe climate of Northern Germany, would not probably fail here from want of the required ingenuity or intelligence to meet the case.

In the worst stages of the English rivers a filter bed has to be cleansed once a week, rarely oftener.

The stuff, whether sediment or otherwise, intercepted by the filter, is found collected on the surface of the sand; in the process of its removal, a thin paring of sand is necessarily taken with it, not exceeding from half an inch to three-quarters of an inch in thickness. The impurities carried by the water are not found to have penetrated the sand. The paring of sand is usually cleansed and laid aside for future use, except when fresh sand can be procured at less cost than the washing of the old sand. The thickness of the sand bed is allowed to be reduced by these repeated parings from 8 to 12 inches before it is renewed.

The original thickness of 30 inches of sand becomes then but 18 or 22 inches before it is replaced and brought up to the original lines. The renewal is usually made once in six months, sometimes but once a year, as the convenience of the service may permit.

At each cleansing of the filter bed the sand is loosened by forks for some 6 to 8 inches in depth, and afterwards raked smoothly over.

The sand is liable to pack close if the cleansing is too long delayed. In such case the weight of the water is felt upon the sand ; in the usual state of the filter it is not so felt.

The filter bed is usually filled with water from above by flowing it slowly upon the sand either from one point in connection with an overflow drain (as in Plate 2) or from several points on the side of the filter. It would be safer and more convenient as regards getting rid of the air, to fill it from below by means of the drains there ; but if this were done with the uncleaned water it would distribute its impurities all through the filter. The filtered water may, however, by suitable arrangements, be made available for this service. When the filter has been once filled it is not necessary to empty it entirely at each cleansing of its surface.

The lowering of the water 12 to 18 inches below that surface will afterwards be sufficient to admit of the workmen removing the crust of sediment collected upon it.

To insure the perfect cleansing of the water by the filters as well as to prevent any disarrangement of the materials of which they are composed, the velocity of movement of the water must be very slow. There is but little difference of opinion among English engineers as to the best average rate, although in some places that rate is exceeded, the consumption of water having in such cases increased more rapidly than was anticipated , and the works fallen temporarily behind the necessities of the service.

Mr. Charles Greaves, Engineer of the East London Water Works, limits this rate to an average of one-half gallon per minute for each square yard of sand surface, which is equal to $3\frac{1}{2}$ gallons per hour for each square foot of sand area of the filter bed. Mr. James Simpson, Engineer of the Lambeth and Chelsea Water Works, who may be said to be the originator of the method of filtering now in such general use in England, gave me as his opinion that the filtering surface should be predicated on a rate of 72 gallons per diem for each square foot of sand, which is equal to 3 gallons per hour per square foot. Mr. Henry Gill, Engineer of the Berlin Water Works, considered that the rate should not exceed half a cubic foot of water ($3\frac{1}{2}$ gallons) per hour per square foot of sand. Mr. Thomas Duncan, Engineer of the Liverpool Water Works, who is a close observer, gave me his opinion that the works should have in view a rate of filtration of from half a cubic foot ($3\frac{1}{2}$ gallons) to one-third cubic foot ($2\frac{7}{10}$ gallons) per hour per square foot of sand.

The gallons mentioned above are imperial gallons. It will be convenient to give all the measures in feet, the various gallon measures differing considerably. Referred to feet, the opinions of these engineers appear as follows :

	RATE OF FILTRATION IN CUBIC FEET OF WATER, PER SQUARE FOOT OF SAND SURFACE.	
	Per Hour.	Per Diem.
Mr. Chas. Greaves..	0.533	12.79
Mr. Jas. Simpson.	0.480	11.52
Mr. Henry Gill...........................	0.50	12.00
Mr. Thos. Duncan......................	0.50	12.00

I will assume half a cubic foot of water per hour per square foot of the sand floor as a fair exponent of the best English practice, and as a rate which with the usual attention will be certain to insure satisfactory results. This rate is equivalent to 75 imperial gallons, or 89¾ United States gallons, per foot square per diem.

When the flow of water through the system of filters during the 24 hours cannot be made uniform, that is to say, when, as is sometimes the case (in the absence of an intermediate clear water basin), it varies with the consumption, being greater during the day hours than during the night hours, the combined area of the filter beds in that case should be made to meet the maximum or daylight consumption of the service per hour.

The average rate of half a cubic foot per hour pre-supposes a maximum and a minimum rate, both of which have their working limits. When the filter is clean the water is allowed to pass through more rapidly than the average velocity of six inches per hour, and when it becomes clogged with sediment it cannot be made to pass through it at that rate. So far as I can judge, the rate should not exceed 8.8 inches per hour (110 imperial gallons per square foot) when the water is clean, nor get below 3.2 inches per hour (40 imperial gallons per square foot) when it becomes obstructed by the deposit. Mr. Hack, of the West Middlesex Water Works, stated that it varied on their filter beds from 11½ inches to 2.9 inches per hour ; but these appear to me to be extremes, rather to be avoided than copied.

The objection to the very low velocity of 2.9 inches per hour may not be apparent without explanation. The most obvious objection refers to the work done ; the delivery at that rate is trifling and incommensurate with the cost of the machine ; but the low velocity indicates another source of danger growing out of the compression or packing induced upon the sand by the scaling of

2

its surface, and the risk of this almost impervious coating being of unequal thickness, and of the water venting itself unequally at the thinner spots.

The filtered water from each filter bed should be delivered into a small well (as at *m*, Plate 2), whence it escapes into the proper conduit, and is carried either to a common clear water basin, or directly to the pumps. The sluices at this well can be so arranged, by operating downwards instead of upwards, as to adjust the head of water actually in action upon the filter bed. When the filter is clean, nine inches of head will produce the required flow through the filtering material ; according as the sediment becomes deposited on its surface, this head has to be increased to 2 or 2½ feet, varying a little with the character of the sand. If the head be allowed to exceed 3 feet, it is because the surface is being rapidly closed ; the weight of the water comes then into play upon the sand, induces the packing already referred to, and leads to the labor of loosening up the material during the process of cleansing. Sometimes when this amount of head is exceeded, the pressure leads the water to break through at points where some slight difference in the material gives it opportunity. It will then flow through in veins, damaging the filter bed. Such overstraining of the filters is rare. I observed but one instance of it, but the effect can readily be brought about by overworking the filters.

The English filters are all deficient as regards any arrangement for measuring the precise flow from each filter, or the precise head of water on each filter while it is in action. A simple arrangement, involving very little cost, admits, as our sketch shows, of this knowledge being rendered certain where it is now guessed at. In London, where the service of each company is effected by steam power, the daily or hourly delivery of the pumps forms the measure of the amount of water passing through the filters. The engineer knows by this means when the filtering area is too small, because in that case the pumps are insufficiently supplied ; and he would know if the water was passed through the filters too rapidly, by its want of that perfect clearness which an efficient filtration always produces. But of the separate action of each individual filter bed he is ignorant, except by guess. The attendant can see when the filter bed has ceased to operate, by its ceasing to pass the water thrown upon it, and he can see when it passes the usual amount too rapidly, and can check this tendency by lowering his stopcocks and allowing the water to lower upon the filter bed ; but his judgment may frequently be in fault in both cases, and there ought to be something more than the instincts of an intelligent laborer to regulate points of so much practical bearing on the proper working of these filter beds, as the varying amount of water delivered upon them, and the constantly varying head required to pass that water under the changing conditions of the sand bed.

The small well at the terminus of the centre gathering drain, with the iron sluice shown there (Plates 2 and 3) operating downwards, will enable the attendant to know at any time the head in action upon each filter, and the amount of water passing, for the top of the sluice becomes then a weir. He will thus learn, without guessing, when the delivery of any filter is so low as to render cleansing essential, and will throw it out of action and have it cleansed accordingly, and he will learn precisely, as the sand bed becomes gradually clogged, the head of water under which it will continue to deliver sufficiently—beyond which amount of head it is needless, and it might be dangerous to go ; and he can always at the sluice regulate precisely the amount drawn from the filter per hour, so that the flow through it shall never be too rapid, nor the water permitted to be imperfectly cleansed. He will learn by this means, in fine, what the safe maximum flow really is ; and as it becomes less and less notwithstanding the increased head produced by his lowering of the sluice, he will ascertain the least flow under which it is advisable to work it, and will know exactly when to throw it off and prepare it for cleansing.

The best size of filter bed for such a city as St. Louis has been assumed to be 260 × 150, giving a sand area of 37,440 square feet. This area, at the rate of one-half cubic-foot of water per hour per square foot of bed, gives a filtration 18,720 cubic feet of water per hour, which is equivalent to 449,280 cubic feet, or 3,360,847 United States gallons in twenty-four hours.

To filter twelve millions of gallons daily, five filters of this size would be necessary, on the supposition that the flow of water through four of them is continuous through the twenty-four hours. To insure this condition the clear water basin should be large enough to receive the water passing through the filters during the night hours, accumulating it there for the day service.

This clear water basin need not be large. The ability to store up one-third of the calculated daily consumption would meet the case.

I have very little information in regard to the precise cost of filtration in England, no separate account being ordinarily kept of its particular expenses. At the Chelsea Water Works, London, the extra charge for filtering, Mr. Simpson informed me, averaged 4 shillings and 6 pence per annum per tenement. If each tenant consumed 300 imperial gallons per diem, this charge would be equal to one cent (specie) for each 1,314 United States gallons. The charge probably includes some profit.

At Liverpool, Mr. Duncan found the cost of filtering (exclusive I presume of the capital invested in it) to average nearly £100 sterling per annum for a million imperial gallons filtered daily, or for each 365,000,000 imperial gallons.

This is equal to 1.14 mills per thousand United States gallons or $1.14 (specie) per million United States gallons.

For a delivery of 12,000,000 United States gallons daily, this would make the cost of attendance, repairs, and maintenance, equal to $4,997 (specie) per annum.

Mr. Hack, the Engineer of the West Middlesex Water Works, London, stated the cost of filtering as about 10 shillings, ($2.40 specie) per million imperial gallons. These works are very economically managed, and this amount includes the capital invested. On the supposition, as before, that each tenement used 300 imperial gallons per diem, or 109,500 per annum, equal to 131,435 United States gallons, the cost per tenement is in this case but 13 pence, equal to 26 cents (specie).

The first cost of such works varies with the nature of the ground, the cost of material at the particular place, and the character of the construction. We cannot therefore infer from any one place, except in very general terms, the expenditures to be encountered at another for the same extent of water supply.

I have already said that the use of settling basins forms a necessary and an economical preliminary to the use of the filter bed in all cases, and especially during those months of the year when the water is very turbid.

In a temperate climate, such as England, it is of little consequence how large these settling basins are made, provided that the depth of water is not less than 8 or 10 feet, and that it is not held unchanged for any great length of time.

But in our warm climate it will be advantageous to have the settling basins as small as practicable consistent with the due preparation of the water for the filters.

This preparation, our experiments upon the Mississippi water have shown, can be secured in 24 hours. Within that time, in still water, the heavier portion of the sediment in suspension sinks to the bottom, leaving the water thoroughly discolored still, but holding, as respects weight, a very small part of the original matter. This part, which even in still water settles and disappears very slowly, is intercepted and separated readily and speedily by the sand filter, leaving the water invariably clear and limpid.

Under this arrangement we have the water but 24 hours still ; during the rest of the time it is in motion.

To make the arrangement efficient under all circumstances there should be four settling basins, each of capacity to hold 12 millions of gallons with not less than 12 feet in depth of water when full. When a greater capacity is required the walls could be carried up, and a greater depth of water obtained.

With the four basins, there would be one filling, one in which the water was still undergoing settlement, one in which the water was being drawn off, and one upon which the process of removing the stuff deposited on the bottom could be going on without interrupting the duty required of the others.

Waste pipes from each settling basin to the river would enable the attendants to scour or flush off at intervals the lowest three feet of the water, and by some manipulation to pass off with it more or less of the accumulated sediment. It never was supposed that this deposit would flow off without this kind of assistance, and it can only be determined by experience whether it will be cheaper to run it out by wheelbarrows or to carry it off by mixing it with water.

If it should be desired to use settling basins without filters, they ought to be much larger than indicated above to secure approximately the same results. They would not be so economical in first cost if of sufficient size, but they might be more economical in attendance ; but it is to be remembered that in this connection, having in view their probable dimensions, they would be an experiment which it might be interesting to have made, but which could not be advised, that I know of, on the faith of its having succeeded elsewhere. Even where very large gathering reservoirs have been available, as at Liverpool and at Dublin, filter beds have been constructed on the usual scale, to get rid of that slight discoloration which frequently remains in large bodies of water, and to meet the turbid character of such water when the reservoir is low, as well as to intercept the organic impurities referred to elsewhere.

It remains to speak of the natural filter, of which we have specimens at Genoa, Toulouse, Lyons, Angers, and Perth.

The descriptions of the works at these places will show that this mode of obtaining a supply of clear water has been eminently successful, as regards the quality, if not always as regards the quantity. The character of the water at the places referred to is indeed unobjectionable, the slight increase of hardness at Lyons as compared with the Rhone water being too small to be of any moment. The water, indeed, in this case, is not made clear and pure by any artificial process ; it is received from the underground flow as from springs, and has not been exposed to light or to surface contamination of any kind.

Bordering upon all rivers there are found at intervals narrow plains of gravel or sand brought down and deposited there by the river under the varying positions of its channel way. When these beds of gravel extend to a depth below the bottom of the neighboring stream, they will always be found saturated with water mainly derived from that stream, and however turbid the water of the river, this underground flow will always be found clear, provided that we tap it at a reasonable distance from the channel way. The cities referred to derive their supplies of water from gravel accumulation of this kind—Genoa at a considerable distance from the city, but the other places in the immediate vicinity of the several cities.

Covered galleries have been carried through these beds of gravel at depths sufficiently below the channel of the neighboring stream to insure a supply of water within the gallery during the lowest stages of its water. The water in these gravel beds rises and falls with the height of the water in the river, and unless the galleries were placed below its lowest water they would obviously become dry and would cease to deliver at its lowest stage. These galleries are of various sizes and of various widths, eight to thirty feet in width being the latest practice. But the experience of one place will seldom be applicable to another. The character of the neighboring stream and the fineness or coarseness of the gravel or sand in which the galleries are placed, influence importantly the rate of supply.

As regards St. Louis, although I have already in a former report, expressed an unfavorable opinion in regard to the applicability of this method here, it seems to me important that an experiment should be made upon the river plain above Bissell's Point, to ascertain whether the material of that bottom is sufficiently open and gravelly to secure a supply of water in this way, what length of gallery would probably be necessary there, and whether the water would be of the same character as the Mississippi water.*

If clear water could be obtained there by underground galleries at a reasonable cost, it would be more satisfactory to the inhabitants probably, than if the river water were rendered equally pure to them by filtering or settling reservoirs operating above ground. The experiment should be on a sufficiently large scale to give some confidence as to the ultimate results.

Although the filtering galleries of the Genoa Water Works give larger results than any others that I am acquainted with, no conclusion can be drawn from them which would be applicable to our case, the circumstances being so very different.

At Toulouse, Lyons, Angers, and Perth, the circumstances bear a closer resemblance to our own, though I fear that the materials of the plain above Bissell's Point may prove finer and closer than the sand and gravel deposits of the places above mentioned.

These galleries are all of stone masonry, open at bottom. The water in all these cases enters principally from the bottom, and the estimated rate of delivery in these galleries is generally referred to the area of the bottom.

The flow into them must be at a velocity which shall not carry sand or any kind of material with the water. There is, therefore, no danger of undermining the side walls.

The first galleries built at Toulouse and Lyons were two small in size to give the best results there. The latest galleries have been made larger. At Toulouse 7½ feet wide, at Lyons 33 feet wide. The galleries at Angers and Perth are too small for your purpose.

---

* This recommendation was not carried into effect, the Commissioners not feeling warranted, from such information as they could obtain, in risking the delay which a sufficient experiment would necessarily entail.

The minimum deliveries of these underground galleries per diem per square foot of their bottom areas is as follows :

	Cubic Feet.	U. S. Gallons.
Toulouse, the new gallery	38.50	288
Lyons, the new gallery	19.64	147
Angers, the latest gallery	40.10	300
Porth	24.32	182

The lower the gallery can be carried below the lowest stage of the river the more safe and abundant it is said will be the supply.

If we suppose the galleries to be 20 feet in width, and that a rate of 200 United States gallons per square foot of bottom could be obtained from them at low water of the Mississippi, the length of gallery required to give 1,000,000 gallons daily would be 250 feet, and for a supply of 12,000,000 it would require a length of 3,000 feet.

In other words, the bottom area, to produce this last quantity, would be 60,000 square feet. The filtering galleries and basins at Lyons have an aggregate of 57,706 square feet, giving, at low water of the Rhone, a daily delivery of about six millions U. S. gallons, but the galleries of the other cities give much higher results, as you have seen, than the Lyons galleries.

The river water which finds its way into the deposit of sand or gravel where the galleries are placed, must have deposited somewhere the sediment held by it in suspension while in the river channel. I could not learn, however, that the filtering galleries became unserviceable from any such cause. The deposit which takes place upon the river bottom in the ordinary and in the low stage of its water is removed, it is asserted, in time of floods, when the bottom is scoured of all its light matter, and the coarser earths composing it become in this way periodically exposed. This, and the fact that the water drawn from a gravel bed of this description percolates into it from a very extended face as compared with any artificial filter, may account for the continued regularity of flow into the natural filtering galleries.

In the accompanying descriptions there will be found some other modes of filtering in practical use, but I refrain from alluding to them here, as they are not applicable to your case, nor can they be recommended for similar works. The two modes of sand and gravel filtration to which your attention has been specially directed—the natural filter and the artificial sand filter—have each of them met the test of long and successful use ; and when the natural filter is not available, the artificial filter may always be safely depended on in connection with subsiding reservoirs as competent to render any river water, however turbid, entirely limpid and satisfactory in that respect for domestic use.

Respectfully submitted by

JAMES P. KIRKWOOD.

NOTE.—April, 1869.—New works for the supply of the city of St. Louis with water are now in the course of construction under the charge of Mr. Thomas J. Whitman as chief engineer, the undersigned being connected with them only as consulting engineer. These works include settling reservoirs, but the public mind of St. Louis, so far as it has been expressed, does not yet seem to consider filtration important.

I will take advantage of this note to mention the works now under construction (May, 1869), for supplying the city of Newark with water, as presenting the only instance in the United States that I know of where provision is made for the filtration of the river water from which the supply is derived. In this case two basins, 350 feet by 150 feet each, have been constructed alongside of the Passaic river, above the village of Belleville. They have eight feet depth of water in them now. The flat or bottom land on which the basins are placed is understood to consist of sand and gravel, resting on a sandstone rock. The river is distant about 200 feet from the basins. The water which fills them is evidently dependent mainly on the river as its source of supply, not drawn exclusively from that part of the river immediately bordering the basins, but as well from the plain above and below, which must be saturated with the same water. These basins collect the water on the same principle as the filtering galleries at Lyons and Toulouse. They are, however, open basins, while the French filtering galleries are all covered. The basins are bordered by vertical stone walls of excellent masonry, very neat and substantial in character. Mr. Bailey is the engineer of the works.

At the Hamilton Water Works, in Canada, built after the designs of Mr. Keefer, another instance occurs of this kind of surface filtration. The water there is not drawn directly from the lake, but from an artificial pond bordering the lake. The lake water finds its way into this pond through the intervening beach of gravel which acts as a filtering medium. The pond, however, is not so elaborately finished as the Newark basins.

J. P. K.

DESCRIPTIONS OF THE FILTERING WORKS REFERRED TO IN THE REPORT.

LONDON, *June*, 1866.

The metropolis of London derives its supply of water at present from the Thames, the river Lea with certain springs in the valley of the Lea, and from a series of chalk wells in the valley of the Ravensbourne, sunk on the upper side of a fault which occurs in the chalk basin there, in the neighborhood of Deptford. The proportions are nearly as follows :

From the Thames...................... 49 parts of the whole.
From the Lea........................ 44 "   "
From Chalk Wells in the Ravensbourne
   Valley........................ 7 "   "
                                   ———
                                   100

The present condition of the supply is in a measure due to the legislation which followed the visitation of the cholera in 1849, and the result when compared with what was tolerated before that time must be admitted to be very satisfactory.

The past history of the waters delivered to, and submissively endured by, the populations of London and Paris, may be studied as instances of how much discomfort and filth in this direction communities will suffer before being roused to insist upon the remedial measures within their reach.

Previous to 1852, when the Parliamentary investigations following 1849 ended in a bill to provide for and insure the improvement of the water supplied to the city, the Thames Companies drew their supplies from the river within the city lines, where the water, besides being turbid more or less at all times, was contaminated by the sewerage of the largest city population in Europe.

After 1852 the Thames Companies were required to get their water from a point on the Thames above the city influences and above the tidal flow ; they were also all required to filter the water intended for domestic use, including in this term all water except that used for street or fire purposes ; but as the latter, when delivered separately, involves a separate pipe distribution, the filtered water is, with most of the companies, applied to the entire service of the district.

3

   Although my visit to the London works had reference simply to the modes of filtration in use there, and any details outside of that subject might seem to be in this connection superfluous, I have thought that a general knowledge of the schemes of supply would be interesting, and in some measure necessary to a proper appreciation of the filtering arrangements.

The population of the metropolis was estimated in 1849 at 2,000,000 ; in 1861 the census gave 2,803,034 ; in 1865 it was estimated by Mr. Bateman at 3,000,000 ; in June, 1866, the Registrar-General gave it as 3,067,538 ; at this date, June, 1866, it is generally supposed to exceed somewhat three millions of souls, say, 3,060,000.

The waters delivered to the metropolis are supplied by eight different companies to as many separate districts.

The following table is in large part prepared from a return made in 1866. It shows the reported deliveries of water then by each company, to which I have added the aggregate areas of the filtering basins provided at the different works and some other statistics :—

	Totals.	Lambeth.	Chelsea.	Southwark and Vauxhall.	Grand Junction.	West Middlesex.	New River.	East London.	Kent.
Average total consumption per diem, 1866, gallons	95,406,192	......	......	......	......	......	......	......	......
From Thames, 1864, daily average, imp. gallons	46,977,423	8,950,000	8,000,000	12,502,000	9,317,255	8,206,168	......	......	......
From Lea and its springs, 1865, imp. gallons	42,278,769	......	......	......	......	......	22,898,769	19,380,739	......
From Springs in the chalk, 1866, imp. gallons	6,150,000	......	......	......	......	......	......	......	6,150,000
Quantity for house supply daily, imp. gallons	......	7,699,000	6,807,000	9,425,288	8,124,359	7,652,168	18,536,804	14,380,000	5,794,000
Hardness as given by Dr. Letheby, 1867, degrees	......	15.5	15.5	14.3	13.5	13.	13.5	14.4	18.1
Hardness after boiling, by Dr. Letheby, 1867, degrees	......	5.8	5.6	5.5	5.	4.8	4.2	6.	8.
Hardness as given by Dr. Frankland, 1868, deg.	......	18.7	19.3	19.3	19.7	19.1	18.4	20.4	26.5
In each case 1 degree = 1 part carb. of lime in 100,000 parts of the water.									
Aggregate areas of the filter basins, 1868, sq. feet	......	66,000	174,000	432,000	225,000	358,000	460,950	522,720	0
Aggregate areas of settling basins..........acres	......	3.10	4.5	13.41	7.62	25.	47.	115.	0
Estimated population supplied	3,064,738	125,000	201,000	449,540	238,050	255,500	800,000	658,570	237,068
Rate per head, per diem..............gallons	......	34.23	33.86	21.	34.	30.	23.17	22.	24.4
Number of houses, 1866, excluding trade business premises and public buildings	......	37,203	26,000	70,983	26,450	36,500	112,964	90,174	33,864
Rate per house per diem	......	207	253	182¾	307	210	169¾	161	171
Daily average per year, 1868..............gallons	99,892,478	9,707,300	8,386,533	14,483,241	9,834,179	8,831,400	23,265,000	18,118,972	7,263,578

If we take the given population supplied at three millions, and the average daily delivery at ninety-seven million gallons, we have a rate of daily consumption per head of 32⅓ imperial gallons, this amount being inclusive of all water used for manufactories, shipping, fires, streets, and other purposes.

The Thames, at an unusually low stage of the river, in August, 1868, as measured by Mr. Hamilton N. Fulton, near Tottenham Lock, was delivering 256,000,000 gallons in 24 hours. In 1867, its lowest state was mentioned by Mr. Simpson as being at no time less than 300,000,000 gallons per diem. The water companies, it will be seen farther on, withdrew a little over one-fifth of the lowest of 1858, or 57,900,000 imperial gallons.

The drainage area of the Thames above Hampton is stated to include 2,352,640 acres, or 3,676 square miles.

The drainage area of the river Lea at Fields Weir, near to where it is tapped by the New River Company, is stated to measure 444 square miles, and the entire drainage of the river at the point above Lea Bridge where the river is tapped by the East London Water Works Company, I estimate as equal to 640 square miles. I find it difficult to get at the minimum flow of this river, but it seems plain that it has more than once fallen below the amount which the two water companies are entitled to draw from it, making a recourse to storage reservoirs therefore indispensable.

I visited the works of all the Metropolitan Water Companies, and, although my object was to obtain the required information in regard to their filtering processes especially, I was permitted at the same time to take notes of the general dimensions of their pumping engines. The information thus collected, however, is necessarily incomplete. Neither the time at my own disposal nor the time of the officials, to say no more, permitted me to acquire that fulness of detail that was desirable. Such as it is, however, it may prove to others, as it has done to myself, useful as a basis of reference.*

All of the water delivered to London undergoes a process of filtration through beds of sand and gravel, with the exception of a portion of the water used for fire purposes and for street washing, and with the exception of the water delivered by the Kent Water Company.

This last water is obtained from wells sunk in the chalk, and does not require filtration.

Allowing for these deductions, the amount of water filtered daily must reach about eighty million gallons. The aggregate area of the filter beds at the works of the seven companies herein described amounts to 2,239,010 square feet, or 51.10 acres. If we take six-sevenths (⁶⁄₇) of this area as in daily use, the other seventh being under repair, it would give, as compared with the eighty million gallons filtered, an average rate of 41½ imperial gallons per

_____

* See Appendix.

square foot of sand area per diem ; but at least three-fourths of the London supply is delivered during the day hours (6 A. M. to 6 P. M.), and for a certain portion of the mid-day hours in summer, the consumption may be taken at double the average which refers to the diem of 24 hours. The rate of filtration, therefore, during the day may at times reach an average rate of 83 gallons per square foot—a rate which exceeds by 11 gallons the average (72) which the best authorities recommend as the proper limit.

All the companies deriving their supplies from the Thames are required by law to take the water from the river above Teddington Lock ; in other words, above tidal influence, and above the influence of the sewerage of London, Teddington Lock being the first lock on the river above its tidal flow. The law also requires that all storage reservoirs for filtered water situated within five miles of the centre of London (St. Paul's), shall be covered. All of them are, therefore, arched over. The storage reservoirs, probably on account of the great expense attending their construction and the cost of property within the city, are most of them comparatively small, and, while they assist to meet any extraordinary increase of consumption, as in the case of fires to which the pumping engines of the night service might not be able to respond at once, they are rarely sufficient to enable the entire engine power of any company to be at rest during the night hours, far less to admit of one or more days' intermission of the pumping operations to meet any extraordinary emergency.*

August, 1868.—Since the above introductory remarks were written and this report presented to the Board, a short visit to England, in July, 1868, has permitted me to visit again most of the pumping stations of the different London water companies.

Since my former visit in 1866, the Chelsea Company has added a new settling reservoir at Thames Ditton, and is now constructing two additional filter beds there; the Lambeth Company has more than doubled its filtering area, and has provided for three settling reservoirs in connection with these, one of which is finished and the other two under construction.

The Grand Junction Company is constructing three new filter beds and an additional settling reservoir at Hampton, and has also under construction an additional storage reservoir at Camden Hill ; and the New River Company has constructed two new filter beds at Stoke Newington. I crave leave, therefore,

---

* The Metropolitan water acts prescribe as follows :

From and after 31st August, 1865, no company to take any water from the Thames below Teddington Lock, except the Chelsea Company.

From and after the 31st August, 1856, no water to be taken by the Chelsea Company below Teddington Lock.

From and after 31st August, 1855, every reservoir within a distance in a straight line of five miles from St. Paul's Cathedral shall be roofed or otherwise covered over, except storage reservoirs for collecting the water before filtration, and except reservoirs for water used for street cleaning or fires, and not for domestic use.

From and after the 31st December, 1855, every company shall effectually filter all the water supplied by them within the metropolis for domestic use, excepting any water which may be pumped from wells into a covered reservoir or aqueduct without exposure to the atmosphere.

to revise that part of my report which referred to the London Works so as to meet more nearly the present condition of things there, and with the permission of the Board of Water Commissioners, the changes and improvements referred to are now incorporated accordingly.

To appreciate the present situation of the London water supply in a sanitary point of view, the report of Dr. Parr on the cholera epidemic of 1866 should be read. The sewerage of the many villages within the valleys of the Thames and the Lea finds its way into these streams now. When the rivers are as low as they have been this season, this cannot but affect the purity of the water, which, while it can be clarified and made perfectly limpid by sand filtration, cannot by that process be dispossessed of any noxious gases which it may have from such sources absorbed, nor of some of the very minute organisms due to such causes. A law passed recently for the defence of river waters against such sources of contamination, will, to some extent, it is hoped, correct the evil referred to, though it cannot entirely remove it.

In this place it may be well to keep in mind that the water which will satisfy a chemist will not always be a safe water for public use. Chemistry cannot always detect the nicer shades of impurity which should render a water objectionable to the consumer. Impurities which the sense of smell or of taste can detect, the researches of chemistry fail to expose, and for that reason are apt to ignore.

Dr. Letheby, the Professor of Chemistry in the London Hospital, and Medical Officer of the city, has acknowledged "that we have not at the present time any absolute test for discovering organic matters in water, much less the nature of those organic matters." "We cannot distinguish absolutely vegetable from animal substances in water unless they are in so large a quantity as to be able to show us their marked properties, when they can be tested; but under common every-day circumstances of organic matter in water, we cannot say whether it is vegetable or animal organic matter." The General Board of Health in their report of 1850, speaking of the Thames river, makes the following remarks to the same effect: "High up the river the water is so transparent that the bottom is visible more than eight feet deep. As the examiner proceeds downwards the transparency diminishes, and the water becomes turbid until it reaches the metropolis, where nothing is to be seen within a few inches beneath the surface. It was the task of Dr. Angus Smith to follow the river and ascertain by analysis more closely than had hitherto been done, the nature and quantities of these variable additions. This he has done carefully with all the aid which chemistry is capable of affording. But as yet chemistry has failed to determine the qualities of much animal and vegetable, and above all, gaseous matter, that is perceptible and offensive both to the taste and to the smell."

The works will now be described as shortly as practicable, in the order in which they were visited.

THE CHELSEA WATER WORKS

The water supplied by this company is derived from the river Thames. The filtering works are situated on the right bank of the Thames, close to the river at Seething Wells, near Thames Ditton.

The original works of the company were situated at Chelsea ; they were removed in 1852, to Seething Wells.

The accompanying sketch will explain the form of these works (Plate 4).

The narrowness of the strip of ground available, controlled the arrangement here, and has obliged the engineer to place the engine-houses rather inconveniently away from the filter beds. There are three settling reservoirs and two filter beds. The settling reservoirs have each a water area of about one and a half acres. The filter beds have each a sand area of about one acre or very nearly 44,000 superficial feet. Two new filter beds were being constructed during the summer of 1868, of the same capacities very nearly with those now in use.

The settling basins have a depth of water in them of six to ten feet, varying with the water in the Thames. The first and second from the filters, are each 272 feet long by 226 feet wide at the top of the banks, with inside slopes of 1 to 1.

The third has about the same water area, but is a little differently shaped, to meet the situation of the ground. The water passes into each freely from the Thames through a sluice-way, and stands at the same level as the river water.

In the sluice-way there are screens. At the side of each reservoir opposite to the sluice-way, the water passes to the filter beds by means of a 24-inch pipe controlled by a stopcock. A rough semicircular filter of gravel and small stones, shown on the sketch, intervenes between the pipe mouth and the water of the basin, and intercepts any floating grasses or other impurities that may have passed the screens.

The condition of things here does not admit of the water remaining at absolute rest in either basin. It enters at one side in each case and passes slowly through to the other side, the movement being more rapid during the day than during the night.

This slow passage admits of a sufficient amount of deposition in the present state of the Thames (June, 1866), when its water is but very slightly turbid; but when the river is in flood and carrying much sediment, the preparation here for the filter bed must be insufficient.

The settling basins are said to be cleaned out twice a year. To effect this the water is drawn off through an 18-inch pipe into a silt well, whence it is pumped off by two small pumping engines appropriated to this service, the mud at the bottom of the settling basin being stirred up during the process of pumping, so that the greater part of it flows with the water into the drain-well of the pump. The dirty water and slush pass into a sewer which has its outlet on the Thames, about half a mile below the works.

The pipe (24-inch) which takes the water from the settling basins to the filter beds, passes round to the extreme side of the beds, and delivers the water upon each bed by 6 branch pipes, of 6 inches diameter each.

After a filter bed has been cleaned, and while its surface of sand is bare, the covering it again with water is an operation requiring considerable circumspection. The sand will be rutted into channels if the water is let on rapidly, or blown, if the process is not effected so slowly as to admit of the escape of what air may be lodged within the filter bed.

After the filter is well covered and in use, the water may be delivered upon it as rapidly as it can use it.

The branch pipes above mentioned do not deliver the water directly upon the sand surface, but they deliver it into wooden troughs 10 feet long, 12 inches wide inside, and twelve inches deep. From these troughs, which are imbedded in the sand, the water flows over their edges upon the filter beds without disturbing the sand.

When a filter bed is bare here, it is filled from the surface, and the attendant says that he finds no difficulty in effecting this and getting rid of the air, except that the operation must be begun slowly.

. There are air pipes along the two ends of each filter bed, connected with the clear water drains, but these air pipes can be of little service, except when the water is entirely drawn off from the filtering materials, which seems rarely to be the case. Usually the water when drawn off is not lowered more than two feet below the surface of the sand.

. I saw one of the filters bare in February, 1866. At the time of my last visit they were both covered. The depth of water in each was 3½ feet.

The water delivered into London from these works in June, 1868, was reported to average daily 9,333,900 imperial gallons, and in July, 1868, 9,748,100 imperial gallons.

Assuming 550,000 gallons to consist of the unfiltered water delivered for street and fire purposes, there remains say 9,200,000 of filtered water delivered per diem in July. Had this been an ordinary year as regards temperature, the delivery of filtered water would not probably have exceeded a per diem of 8,000,000.

This Company, as well as each of the other four Thames Water Companies, has a right to take from the river twenty millions imperial gallons per diem. At this date the five companies take a little exceeding fifty million gallons daily from the stream.

To avoid to some extent the excess of duty thrown upon one of these filter beds by the disuse of the other (during the process of cleansing), a low earthen bank has been run across each of the filters, dividing each into two, and making practically four filter beds. This earthen division being but a make-shift of not more than 2½ feet in height, the water is partially drawn down when it is brought into play. The effect, however, is to secure the use approximately of three-fourths of the entire filtering surface, leaving but one-fourth necessarily in disuse.

The two filter beds have a joint area of 88,000 square feet. Assuming three-fourths of this to be always in service, there are 66,000 square feet of sand area to filter ordinarily 80,000,000 gallons of water. But although the larger portion of this amount is pumped during the day hours, the day rate of filtration cannot be more than 393,000 gallons per hour, because two pairs of engines cannot deliver above this rate. This is equal to 6 gallons per square foot of filter per hour, or 144 gallons per square foot per diem ; with the whole filtering area in use, the flow is reduced to 107 gallons per square foot per diem. Both of these very much exceed the rate which the Engineer considers best, a rate namely of about 72 gallons per square foot per diem, but the increase of the population of the district has exceeded the anticipations of the Company, and the filtering works have fallen behind the necessities of the service.

When the new filter beds are completed, this condition of things will be entirely corrected.

The outer walls of the filter beds are slope walls of brick on edge laid at an inclination of 1 to 1.

On two sides of each filter bed, appearing at the top of the slope walls, are rows of 3-inch cast-iron air pipes, communicating with the drains on the bottom of the filter beds.

The pumping power at work during the day is about double of what is at work during the night.

The additional charge made for filtration, Mr. Simpson stated to be about four shillings and sixpence (one dollar) per house per annum on the average.

The materials of these filters consist of sand, gravel, shells, and small stones, in the following proportions :

4

Fine sand...................................30 inches.
Coarse sand............................ .... 6 inches.
Shells... 4 inches.
Fine gravel................................... 6 inches.
Large gravel.................................24 inches.
                                           ———
                                           70 inches.

Perforated clay pipes are imbedded in the large gravel.

The thin layer of shells was intended to intercept any sand which might follow the water.

On the bottom there is a central drain, into which the water is collected by these earthenware perforated pipes, branching from it across the bottom on either side. These drain pipes were given me as of 9, 8, and 6 inches in diameter on each branch, the smallest being placed furthest from the central drain. A circular well of about 12 feet diameter receives the filtered water; it is transmitted thence by a cast-iron pipe to the pumping engines, which are situated on the opposite side of the Kingston road, as shown on the sketch. At the time of my last visit, the water in the well (at noon) stood 3 feet below the water on the filter beds, both of which were then in full use.

The water in the well varies from 2 to 4 feet below the level of the water on the filters, according to the condition of the beds.

The filter beds are cleaned off from once in six to once in twenty days each, according to the condition of the river. The amount of sand taken off does not exceed half an inch, and this is washed and used over again. A circular sieve (kept in motion by one of the small engines) into which the water is poured from perforated iron pipes, is used for cleansing the sand.

The position of the engine-house is shown on the sketch.

There are six double-cylinder rotative beam engines here, working in pairs, having one fly-wheel to each pair. The engines, however, can be uncoupled and worked separately. Of these engines the first and second pairs are known as the "A. B." and "C. D." engines; the third pair, furnished in 1867, as the "E. F." engines. Each pair is given as of 300-horse power, or 150-horse power for each engine.

The steam cylinders of each are: the small or high-pressure cylinder, 28 inches diameter, and 5 feet 6 inches stroke; the large cylinder, 46 inches diameter, and 8 feet stroke.

The pump is in each case a plunger and bucket pump; the barrel 24-inch diameter, the plunger 17½-inch, and the stroke 7 ft. 1 inch.

The delivery pipes of the pumps unite on one pipe main. There are two air vessels to each pair of engines, connected with the delivering pipes.

Any dimensions or details given by me of engines in this report, were derived from the foreman or the engineman in charge. The precise forms and plans of these pumping engines must be sought for in other works. The general characteristics only are aimed to be given here.

These engines cut off on the small cylinder at half stroke—steam 38 to 40 lbs. The engines make 12 to 14 revolutions per minute, varying with the city consumption. The pumps were stated to deliver 120 to 126 gallons per double stroke.

The beam of each engine is double, composed of two flitches, 32 feet in length between end centres, and five feet in depth at its bearings. The first built engines were not precisely balanced. To remedy this in the pair just built, the beam is made heavier on the side towards the steam cylinders than on the other side. The beams of the other engines are having balance plates added to them inside, at the same end, to perfect their adjustments.

The one fly-wheel to each pair has a diameter of 18 feet, weight 14 tons. The suction valve of the pump is a two-ring valve. It is in fact a four-beat valve of the same character as the Harvey & West valve, except that in this case the beats are upon the same plane, and the facilities of emission for the water are therefore not so good ; the two rings are not connected, but act independently of each other. The delivery valve is a flap valve, consisting of two, and sometimes three, inclined iron flaps, hinged at the upper end, and beating on leather linings.

For the first two pair of engines (A. B. and C. D.) there are 13 boilers in one house. One of these pairs was at work to-day with six of these boilers under steam.

The steam carried varied from 40 to 42 lbs. pressure. The boilers are all of the Cornish type, single-flued, the shell 5 feet 10 inches diameter, the flue 39 inches, length 30 feet. Ten boilers are used when both pairs of engines are at work. The steam pipe connecting all these boilers, and running into the engine-house, was of 14 inches diameter.

The fuel used is the slack of Newcastle coal (bituminous).

The last built pair of engines (E. F.) has a battery of seven boilers. Five of these were in use to-day. They are Cornish boilers, single flue. Shell 5 feet 10 inches diameter, flue 38 inches ; length 32 feet, carrying 42 lbs. steam.

There are two large square chimneys here of 110 feet in height ; I was not able to ascertain the sizes of the flues.

This class of engine has now been long and well tried at these works, and its performance, so far as duty trials are comparative evidence, has proved to be at least equal to that of the best Cornish engines.

At the time of my visit two pairs of engines were at work (A. B. and E. F.) pumping into the same rising main, which is of 30-inch diameter, and conveys the water to the Putney reservoir, distant six miles. It is not considered safe to work the three pairs of engines into the same main, and until a second main is laid, one pair of engines will always be at rest.

The Company is laying a second 30-inch main at this time.

' The filtered water is all pumped into the Putney reservoir, with the exception of a small portion which is drawn from the rising main to supply the intervening villages.

From the Putney reservoir, the City district pertaining to the Company is supplied by gravitation.

The Putney reservoir stands 181 feet above the pump well; at the time of my visit the gauge in the engine-houses showed a pressure of 220 feet.

The A. B. engines were making 14 to 14½ revolutions per minute, and the E. F. engines, 12 revolutions. Both pairs of engines were stated to be working continuously through the 24 hours, and every day of the week. It has been usual for two pairs to work during the day, and one pair at night, but the increased demand for water this season must lower the Putney reservoir during the day much more than heretofore.

Under any circumstances the water in the rising main is never supposed to come to a state of rest, but the rate of flow during the day is generally much more rapid than during the night.

During the night hours the supply of water is cut off from the city tenements, with the exception of factories or other works, where the necessary supply of water cannot be continuously maintained by cisterns. The main pipes must, therefore, be always charged.

The Putney reservoir, which is covered, has a capacity of 8,300,000 gallons. There is a small open reservoir near it for unfiltered water, with a capacity of about 1,250,000 gallons.

The water for fire purposes, and for street-washing, is not filtered. Two small engines deliver this water into the small open reservoir above mentioned, whence it is passed into the city by a separate system of distributing pipes. The engines for this service are single cylinder rotative engines, with a flywheel to each. They are arranged, however, so as to be coupled, and generally work in connection. The steam cylinder of these engines is 20 inches diameter, with a stroke of 36 inches. The pumps are plunger and bucket pumps. The pump barrel is 11¼ inches diameter, with 30-inch stroke.

The delivery of unfiltered water is very light in winter, but may sometimes reach 500,000 gallons per diem in summer.

The pipe main conveying the unfiltered water to the Putney open reservoir, is of 15 inches diameter, and 5¾ miles in length.

There are a pair of small engines (15-horse power) for the drainage service —that is, for pumping off the low refuse water, when required, from the settling basins, and we presume, also, for draining off the water from the sand of the filter beds, when they require cleansing.

These works have been constructed from the designs and directions of Mr. James Simpson, Civil Engineer, under whose charge they continue now. Mr. Simpson is understood to be the originator of the very simple and manageable sand filter which has been so successfuly used at the London Works and elsewhere.

LAMBETH WATER WORKS.

The Lambeth Works are situated on the right bank of the Thames, immediately above the Chelsea Water Works. They are under the charge of the same engineer, Mr. James Simpson.

There are four filter beds here, each of the same size and form, as may be seen in the accompanying sketch (Plate 5), where they are marked a^1, a^2, a^3, a^4.

The outer walls of these filter beds are vertical brick walls, thrown into the curved forms for strength.

The central wall, which appears to divide each, is a buttress wall, built to receive the thrust of the horizontal arch walls, and arranged so as not to interfere with the free passage of water from the one half to the other.

These filter beds have been doubled in size within the last two years. The sand area of each filter bed is 16,500 square feet, now making for the four beds an aggregate of 66,000 square feet.

These works were reported in July, 1868, to be delivering that month an average of 11,210,400 per diem), the whole of this water passing through the filter beds.

Two pairs of engines were at work on the day of my visit, making 15 revolutions per minute.

At this rate I calculate their delivery to be about 453,000 gallons per hour, which, applied to the filtering surface, gives a flow through the filters of 6.86 gallons per square foot per hour, when the four beds are in use, and in a serviceable state.

The average, as already stated, should not exceed 3.12 gallons ($\frac{1}{2}$ cubic foot) per square foot per hour.

The rate here is therefore more than double the usual velocity, but this defect is to a certain extent compensated by an auxiliary filtration which the water undergoes at the settling reservoirs.

These works, which at my previous visit in 1866, possessed no settling reservoirs, have now one settling reservoir in use, and two under construction.

The three when finished will have a water surface of 3.1 acres. The subjoined plan (Plate 5) will show the position of these, and of the filter beds. To remedy the inadequate surface area of the latter, a vertical filter of fine gravel, designated on the plan as "rough filter," is constructed across the lower end of each settling reservoir. This gravel is held in place by two brick walls, bolted together at intervals. The walls are 4 feet apart, and the screen of gravel is, therefore, 4 feet thick, by about 15 feet in height, and 150 feet in length. The bricks are laid slightly apart at the joints, to permit the water to reach the gravel and to escape from it on the other side.

The arrangement will be understood on inspection of the plan.

That this rough filter was operating to some purpose seemed evident from the fact that the water stood 18 inches lower on the one side of this filtering wall than on the other.

Doors are arranged on the upper side for drawing off the gravel at intervals and cleaning it.

The bottom of each settling reservoir consisted of a layer of concrete resting on clay, over which was a paving of brick on edge, laid in mortar. The side slopes were 1 to 1, laid in the same way.

The water is drawn directly from the river into these settling reservoirs, at the upper end of each, passing through the whole length in each case, before reaching the filtering walls. There are screens and sluices in the entrances from the river.

Three of the filter beds were in use at the time of my visit (7th August, 1868), the fourth had just been cleansed. One of the filters was said to be cleaned every ten days. There was 4 feet of water on the beds.

The materials of the filters are the same as on the Chelsea bed, and the relative arrangement the same, but the mode of collecting the clean water is different. On the floor of the new portions of the Lambeth filter bed a series of small brick arches is built, as shown on the cross section (Plate 5).

These arches have vertical openings in them across the axis of each, of 1 inch in width on every 27 inches in length of each arch. This allows the water to pass through, without drawing with it any of the shingle. The water has thus but a short distance to travel, to reach a collecting drain.

These small drains deliver into a larger drain communicating with the outside conduit to the pump wells.

On the original portions of these beds (the halves on the river side) small square drains are in use, covered with slabs of slate 3 feet long, 8 inches wide, and 3 inches thick.

The slabs are kept an inch apart and covered with large shingle. These drains, as in the other case, deliver the water into the central collecting drain. Some fine sand, I was informed, would occasionally get through the shingle into the collecting drains, before the enlargement of these filter beds, probably caused by the unusual rapidity of flow through the filtering materials, which prevailed then.

The depth of water on these filters, which formerly varied with the stage of the river, can now be controlled from the settling reservoirs, and made uniform or otherwise at discretion.

The sand removed from the surface of the filter-bed ($\frac{1}{2}$ to $\frac{3}{4}$ inch in thickness) during the process of cleansing, is washed and replaced at intervals. The washing here is done by using hose connected with a pipe, from the rising main.

Eight per cent of the sand is said to be lost by the washing process. Twenty-four inches of sand is taken off in twelve months, by the various cleansings. It is ordinarily replaced but once a year. The labor of attendance and cleansing of the filters was stated (1866), to be nearly £1,000 per annum.

There are six double-cylinder rotative pumping engines working in pairs (3 pairs), with one fly-wheel to each pair. The third pair was added in 1866–7.

The engine-houses are situated about 600 feet from the filter beds. The water is conducted by a conduit to the pump wells.

The engines are all represented to be of the same dimensions, viz. :

The small steam cylinder, 28 in. diameter, with 5′ 6″ stroke.
The large　　　"　　　　"　　46 in.　　"　　　　8 feet　"

The pumps are plunger and bucket pumps ; the pump barrel 24 in. diameter, with 6′ 11″ stroke ; the pump plunger $17\frac{1}{2}$ inches diameter.

There are two air chambers to each pair of engines, 10 feet high, by 38 inches diameter, of cast-iron ; they are connected at the top. There is no stand pipe here. The beams are all double. The length between end centres on the new engines, was 26 feet ; the depth of the beam at the gudgeon, 5′ 6″; diameter of gudgeon 15 inches. These last beams were made heaviest at the steam end, sufficiently so to balance the engine. The diameter of the fly-wheel is 21 feet, 4 feet cranks, weight 15 tons.

The engine was cutting off at one half on the small cylinder, and making 15 revolutions per minute.

The suction valves are 4-beat valves, in two rings ; these valves are weighted to make them work well. The valves of the new engines were striking hard, and were said to be out of adjustment as regards weight. The delivery valves were flap valves in two parts.

For the six engines there is provided a battery of 19 boilers, all connected. Twelve boilers were in use to-day for the four engines at work.

There are never more than four engines at work at present, but when the second force main is laid, the three pairs of engines will be able to work simultaneously, if necessary ; the second main, also of 30-inch diameter, is now being laid.

The boilers are all Cornish boilers, each 6 feet diameter of shell, and 31 feet long, with one flue 39 inches diameter. The fire grates 6 feet in length. Every boiler has a large drum 5½ feet high, and 39 inches diameter. The steam pipe runs over the drums, and is 15-inch diameter.

The chimney is a large square chimney, 100 feet in height, and apparently 8 feet square inside.

The coal used is Newcastle slack.

Four engines were at work during my visit, and work at present continuously, I was informed, night and day. They all pump into the Brixton reservoir, through a rising main of 30 inches diameter, and 10½ miles in length.

The Brixton reservoir is situated 103 feet above the pump well. The gauge showed a pressure against the engines of 190 to 192 feet. At night the pressure shows 200 to 210 feet, the difference arising from the relief afforded by two or three branches from the rising main, delivering into the country district, which are not in operation during the night.

From the Brixton reservoir the water is distributed to that portion of the district which it controls, the remainder being pumped up from that point to meet the requirements of the higher grounds within the district. The reservoir is covered and has a capacity of 15,000,000 gallons, with 12 feet depth of water.

The reservoir falls during the day hours, showing the consumption of water to exceed the ordinary rate of the pumping power. It is filled up by the pumping engines during the night hours.

At this reservoir there are three sets of supplementary pumping engines moving portions of the water received here from the river engines to higher altitudes.

The first set, consisting of two engines, pumps the required supply for the Streatham reservoir, situated 82 feet above their pump well, and also into Salthurst reservoir, situated 103 feet above their pump well. An 18-inch main connects the pumps with both reservoirs, the length to the Streatham reservoir being about one mile, and to the Salthurst reservoir about 5 miles. The Streatham reservoir has a capacity of 3,672,000 gallons; the Salthurst reservoir, of 3,400,000.

The two engines are each double-cylinder rotative engines, but the large cylinder is annular, enveloping the small one, and the length of stroke is the same for both. The dimensions were given me as follows :

Small cylinder....................16 in. diameter and 5′ 6″ stroke
Annular " ....41 in. " · " 5′ 6″ "

The pump is a plunger and bucket pump, the barrel 17½ inches diameter, plunger 12½, stroke 4 feet 7½ inches.

5

But one engine was at work.

During the night the two engines are at work, filling the reservoirs. The engine at work during the day is pumping directly into the appropriate portion of the district, the reservoirs delivering then into the same distribution pipes.

There is no delivery of water to the district during the night except for fires, and for any manufacturing works that may require a continuous delivery. The day delivery is intermittent, the turnkey letting on the water so many hours to one portion of the district, and so many hours to another. The same practice prevails in the Chelsea district.

Two smaller engines, 16 years old, deliver into the Rockhill reservoir, which controls and supplies the highest portion of the district.

The Rockhill reservoir (covered) has a capacity of 1,250,000 gallons. Its water, when full, stands 247 feet above the pump wells of the engines which supply it (or above the Brixton reservoir).

An iron tank is built within the grounds of the Rockhill reservoir, raised 18 feet above its level, and with a capacity of 120,000 gallons.

To supply a small portion of the district situated above both of these last-mentioned reservoirs, there is a stand-pipe on the Rockhill grounds, which, when in use, carries the water 50 feet above the Rockhill reservoir. The water is pumped over this stand-pipe by the Brixton pumps so many hours every day.

The engines referred to are rotative beam engines, usually working coupled, but capable of working independently. There is a fly-wheel to each. But one of the engines was at work at the time of my visit.

The steam cylinder is 21½ inches diameter, with 36 inches stroke. The pump is a plunger and bucket pump, the barrel 12 in. diameter, plunger 8½ inches, and 31 in. stroke. The engine makes, according to circumstances, 22 to 26 revolutions per minute.

Another pair of new and novel engines pump into the same high service main for the Rockhill reservoir.

These are rotative beam engines coupled to one fly-wheel, the steam cylinders arranged so that the pair forms, in effect, one double-cylinder engine.

There is a plunger and bucket pump to each engine. The engines and cylinders stand about 6 feet apart, centre to centre. There is a small air chamber to each engine. The pair were making 30 revolutions per minute. The gauge showed a pressure of 316 feet.

The one engine has a steam cylinder of 12 in. diameter, with 36 in. stroke ; the other a cylinder of 21½ in. diameter, with the same stroke. The pump barrel in each case was 7½ in. diameter, with 31¼ in. stroke.

The engines were said to work very economically as regards fuel.

The delivery of water by the Lambeth Works was stated to average in 1866 9,000,000 gallons per diem, exceeding this amount considerably during the summer months. All of this water passes into the Brixton reservoir, with the exception of the small portion distributed between that reservoir and the river pumps.

In 1849 the delivery of this Company is reported to have averaged 3,077,260 gallons per diem ; in 1855, 6,109,000 gallons per diem ; while in June, 1868, it is reported at 10,607,300 per diem.

SOUTHWARK AND VAUXHALL WATER WORKS.

The water for the district supplied by this company is taken from the left bank of the Thames at Hampton, in accordance with the law which requires all the Thames water companies to take the water from the river above Teddington Lock. But the principal works of the Company, which originated when London lay entirely to the east of them, are situated at Battersea, on the right bank of the Thames, upwards of 13 miles from Hampton. Previous to 1855, the Company drew its water from the Thames at Battersea. The pipe main connecting the two places crosses under the river near Richmond.

At Hampton the Thames water is first drawn into two subsiding reservoirs of 45,000 superficial feet, or a little over an acre each. Three sets of vertical iron strainers intercept all coarse floating matter.

The level of the water on these reservoirs corresponds with the water in the Thames. They are calculated to hold from six to eight million gallons, according to the height of the river. The water does not remain at rest in either reservoir, nor are they large enough to admit of much subsidence taking place at any time. The slow movement, however, of the water through them admits of a certain amount of deposition, and, together with the screens, separates the grosser floating matters which would otherwise reach the pumps. The existence of two divisions admits of the one being cleansed while the other is in service.

A 36-inch cast-iron main, 13.07 miles in length, transfers the water from this point to the works at Battersea. To equalize and relieve the action of the engines, the water is pumped into a stand-pipe, the rising leg of which is 135 feet in height above the reservoirs, the other (the down leg) 65 feet where it connects with the longer leg. The pressure on the pumps, therefore, cannot at any time be less than 65 feet; at the time of my last visit (5th of August, 1868) the gauge showed 130 feet. In other words, the head required at that time to produce the required flow in the long pipe main was 130 feet.

For this duty there are three Cornish engines of the variety called "bull engines." Two of these are usually at work night and day, but at this time, in consequence of the great demand for water, the three engines were at work through the 24 hours.

The engines have the following dimensions:

1. Steam cylinder 70 inches diameter, stroke 10 feet; plunger or pole 42 inches diameter, stroke 10 feet.

2. Steam cylinder 66 inches diameter, stroke 10 feet; pump pole 39 inches diameter, stroke 10 feet.

These two engines were (11th of June, 1865) making 10 strokes per minute.

3. Steam cylinder 60 inches diameter, stroke 10 feet; pump pole 35 inches diameter, stroke 10 feet.

Engines Nos. 1 and 2 have air vessels on their branches to the stand-pipe. All the engines pump into the stand-pipe. The three engines when working together (as they were in August, 1866) were controlled by one cataract, and averaged then 9,780 strokes in 24 hours each, equal to about 7 strokes (6.8) per minute.

At the time of my first visit they were making from 9 to 10 strokes per minute; during the day hours the velocity is usually greater than at night. The engines were cutting off at two-thirds.

The suction valves, and also the delivery valves, were four-beat valves, of the Harvey & West pattern.

For the three engines there is a battery of nine boilers, all of which were under steam to-day, the pressure carried varying from 38 to 39 lbs.

They are all Cornish boilers with single flues; shell 5 feet 10 inches, length 28 feet, flue 44 inches. The fuel used was large Welsh coal (bituminous).

At Battersea, the water pumped by these engines through the long 36-inch main pipe, is received into two subsiding reservoirs, one of 270,000 square feet (6.20 acres), the other of 140,000 square feet (3.31 acres). In both, 9.41 acres; their joint capacities, 32 million gallons. The small basin was empty at the time of my visit, undergoing a cleaning out. The large basin was full of water, the depth being about 10 feet. . These settling basins were stated to be cleaned out once in two to four months.

The water from Hampton passes into these receiving basins, one or both, as may be convenient, and from thence is distributed to the filter beds, of which there are five. The water has no opportunity of remaining at absolute rest in these settling basins, but the slow movement through them admits of a certain amount of deposition, and as the Thames water carries but little sediment in suspension, except in floods, the process, in addition to what occurs in the Hampton basins, is ordinarily sufficient to prepare it for the filter beds. Under the best summer state of the Thames water, the filter beds would operate efficiently without this previous preparation. But besides that, in times of high floods, when the river is very turbid, this previous process of deposition of the grosser matters is most important; it is at all times valuable, as lengthening the time during which the filters continue efficient, and economizing the process of cleansing the sand beds and the cost of attendance. The history of the different works shows a growing appreciation of the advantage of large settling basins, and the great value (in insuring at all times a perfect filtration as well as in economizing its annual cost) of this preliminary process.

The forms of the settling basins and filter beds are shown in the accompanying sketch (Plate 6.)

The settling basins are marked B^1, B^2. The filter beds c^1, c^2, c^3, c^4, c^5.

The following are the sand areas of the filter beds :

c^1, 31,000 square feet.
c^2, 65,340   "   "
c^3, 130,000   "   "
c^4, 58,080   "   "
c^5, 94,000   "   "

The borders of the filter beds and settling basins, with one exception, were sloped at the rate of 2 to 1, and covered with shingle. One of them has a brick vertical wall on two sides. When the filters are bare the water is let on slowly from above, that is, upon the sand surface ; and the attendant averred that he had no difficulty in refilling the beds in this way. There were numerous air-pipes along the tops of the slopes communicating with the clear-water drains below.

A shallow open drain extended from the one end to the other of the filter, which lay bare, the tops of the side walls of which were level with the sand surface of the filter bed. In refilling the filter, the water is let into this drain and flows slowly over its two sides upon the sand ; it is obvious that if the sand surface rose slightly from the drain towards the outer slopes, the filling would take place without producing any current upon the bed of sand.

The materials of the filters were stated to be as follows :

Sharp river sand.................................36 inches.
Fine gravel....................................12 inches.
Screened gravel................................. 9 inches.
  Do.   rough gravel........................... 9 inches.
Coarse large gravel.................... ....12 inches.
                                              ——
                                              78 inches.

These materials rest upon a floor of concrete.

Small drains collect the water in some of the beds into a large central drain, and perforated pipes in others. The collected water is conveyed by a conduit to the pump wells of the several pumps.

There is no reservoir to receive and store up the filtered water. The rate of filtration must therefore vary with the rate of consumption.

The quantity of water (all of which passes through the filters) pumped into the proper district, averaged in 1867 about 13,000,000 gallons daily, but during the months of June, July, and August of this year (1868), it has increased to a consumption of about 15,000,000 imperial gallons daily. Assuming 11 of the 15 millions to be delivered by pumping between 6 A. M. and 6 P. M. (there being no high storage reservoirs connected with these works), the rate of filtration with one-fifth of the filtering surface unemployed, amounts to 3.03 imperial gallons per square foot per hour, a rate of velocity through the filters which corresponds with the best practice; during the night hours the rate will be very much less. Each filter bed was stated to be cleansed off once in two months, in the ordinary state of the river, and once in two to four weeks when the river is in flood.

There are six pumping engines at this station, all of the Cornish stamp ; two of them, however, being mongrel in that respect, having double-acting pumps. All the engines are beam engines except one. The quantity of water pumped daily, all of which passes through the filter beds, exceeds at this date (August, 1868), 15,000,000 gallons.

There are two separate services in this district—a high and a low service. The mass of the water goes to the low or London service of the district.

For the low service, four engines are used, and were all at work. Towards night two are kept partially at work, and sometimes three.

The four engines appropriated to the London service work through two stand-pipes, one with four legs and the other with three legs.

In the absence of any one at the works who could explain to me the necessity of so many pipes or legs, I have had to assume that the object was to give stiffness and to avoid the use of guys, neither set of stand-pipes being enclosed in masonry.

Both sets of stand-pipes have but one up leg, the others are down legs ; the junction of these with the up leg is at the same height in both cases, viz., 150 feet above the pump well, but the pressure gauges in the engine-rooms showed the water to be standing at 165 feet in the up leg, or 15 feet above the junction. On the four-legged stand-pipe the up leg was of 48-inch diameter, the principal down leg 42-inch, the other two legs of 28-inch each. The foreman of one of the engines stated that the large down leg only was in use ; the other two were shut off, but could be connected if desired.

In the three-legged stand-pipe the up leg is of 28-inch diameter and the principal down leg the same ; the other leg is of 12-inch diameter, and whether used or not, did not appear. In the cases of both stand-pipes, the legs are at intervals tied together by rods.

The general dimensions of the four engines referred to are as follows :

No. 1.—*Single-Acting Beam Engine.*

Steam cylinder 64 inches; stroke 10′ 6″, making eight strokes per minute.
Pump plunger 33 inches; stroke 11′ 6″; double beam, unequal, 5 feet
deep at gudgeon.   Pumping over the largest stand-pipe.
Small air chamber between engine and stand-pipe.
Working against 165 feet head.

No. 2.—*Single-Acting Beam Engine.*

Steam cylinder 112 inches; stroke 10 feet, working close to 9′ 9″.   6th
August, 1868.
Cutting off at one-half; 8 strokes per minute.
Pump plunger 50 inches; stroke 10 feet.
Double beam—length 32 feet between centres; depth at gudgeon 8 feet;
diameter of gudgeon 18 inches.
The flitches three feet apart and very heavy.   Working over the large stand
pipe.
There is a small air chamber outside, of 48-inch diameter.
Pressure by gauge showed 175 feet.

No. 3.—*Single-Acting "Bull" Engine.*

Steam cylinder 70 inches; stroke 10 feet; cutting off at one-half to one-
third; making 8 to 9 strokes per minute.
Pump plunger 33 inches; stroke 10 feet; working over the smaller stand-
pipe; pressure about 165 feet.
This engine usually works from 6 A. M. to 5½ P. M., and also from 12 P. M.
to 3 A. M.

No. 4.—*Single-Acting Beam Engine.*

Steam cylinder 68 inches; stroke 10 feet; working about 8 strokes per
minute.
Pump plunger 33 inches; stroke 10 feet; working over the smaller stand-
pipe.
There is a low air chamber outside, through which this pump probably
works.
Double beam, equal, length c. c. 30 feet.
Pressure by gauge showed 165 feet.
The inlet or suction valves of these four engines are four-beat Husband
valves.   Two of the delivery valves were stated to be two-beat valves (Harvey
& West), the others four-beat valves.

For the high service there are two engines which I shall call No. 5 and No. 6. These work 15 hours of the day each, but not at night, unless called upon for fire purposes. They pump into the high grounds of Wimbleton and Richmond.

No. 5.—*Single-Acting Beam Engine.*

Steam cylinder 55 inches; stroke 8 feet, making 12 and sometimes 14 strokes per minute.

Double-acting pump, 14½-inch diameter; stroke 8 feet. The pump rod is heavily weighted to enable the engine to make the down stroke.

Double beam, length c. c. 25 feet.

This engine is not connected with either of the stand-pipes, but there is a weighted plunger on the main, outside of the house, which is intended to afford the same kind of relief. There is also an air chamber 20 feet high, and 5 feet in diameter.

The suction valve and the delivery valve are both four-beat valves.

The pressure by gauge showed 285 feet, and runs up at times to 305 feet.

No. 6.—*Single-Acting Beam Engine.*

Steam cylinder 55 inches; stroke 8 feet; making 10 strokes per minute.

Double-acting pump, 16-inch diameter; stroke 8 feet.

The pump rod is weighted sufficiently to produce the down stroke.

This engine does not work into a stand-pipe.

There is a weighted double-beat valve outside to relieve the main, and there is also an air chamber between this valve and the pump. The suction valve of this pump is a four-beat valve, and the delivery valve a two-beat valve.

The gauge showed the pump to be working against a pressure of 300 feet.

The above six pumping engines were all at work. There are no storage reservoirs to meet the night service. A certain portion of the engine power is therefore always at work through the night.

To supply the requisite steam for the six engines, there are 25 Cornish boilers, all connected so as to form one battery, so to speak.

Twenty of these boilers were in use. The steam showed 32 lbs. pressure in the engine-room.

They were all single-flued boilers, the shell 6 feet diameter, the flue 42 inches, the length 30 feet.

There were three chimneys to the 25 boilers, but I could not learn their dimensions.

The average daily delivery of water by this Company was reported to be :

In 1849....................... 6,013,716 imperial gallons.
In 1855....................... 10,331,122   "   "
In 1865....................:.. 12,180,000   "   "
In June, July, and August, 1868... 15,000,000   "   "

This Company is at present (August, 1868) making important additions to its works at Hampton.

These additions (now under construction) will consist of a large new settling reservoir, three filter beds, and two pumping engines.

The water in this settling reservoir will correspond, like the others here, with the level of the water in the Thames. Screens at the entrance passage will intercept fish and floating matter, but when the river is turbid the water will not be so well prepared for the filters here as it is at Battersea. I was not able to obtain a diagram plan of the new works ; but the accompanying sketch will give an idea of the form and character of the filter bed nearest completion, without being absolutely correct in dimensions. (Plate 7.)

The sand area of the three filters I estimated at about 54,000 square feet, and the settling reservoir I should judge to be about two acres in extent.

The sketch (Plate 7) of the filter bed and cross-section will sufficiently describe its characteristics.

The water from the settling reservoir is delivered into a central drain running lengthways of the bed, having a collecting drain underneath it, to gather the clear water. On the side walls of this collecting drain. the vertical joints of the bricks are spaced an inch apart to permit the filtered water to pass into the drain. There are, besides, small drains laid on the floor at right angles to the main drain, and delivering into it.

These small drains are made of perforated brick, and have each not more than 4½ inches of opening.

The floor is concrete laid upon clay ; with no paving over the concrete. The side walls are paved with brick on edge. One of the filters was about half finished, the floor and slopes entirely so ; the floor was tight and perfectly dry, although it must have been situated nine feet below the level of the adjoining river.

The filtering material is composed of a layer of large shingle on the floor, and over the small drains, a layer of smaller shingle over that, both washed and screened ; then a layer of coarse gravel ; and, finally, a layer of fine clear river sand, at least 18 inches thick.

The thicknesses of these layers, as near as I could ascertain them, are shown in section. (Plate 7.)

There are three 12-inch air pipes rising from the central drain and apparently no others ; from which I judge that it is intended to fill the filter, when emptied, from below.

In the bottom of the upper or open portion of the same central drain are two six-inch clay pipes, with caps on them, probably used only when refilling.

From the filter beds the clear water will pass directly to the pump wells of the new engine-house. The engine-house is arranged to receive two single-acting beam engines, of 80-inch cylinder each ; they are each to work double-acting pumps with solid pistons; the pump rod to be weighted for the down stroke. There will be no stand-pipe, but a weighted valve on the branch main of each pump.

The battery for these two engines will consist of eleven Cornish boilers of the same size as those in use at this station (Hampton) now.

These pumps, when finished, will deliver the water filtered at this station directly into the high grounds of Wimbleton and Richmond, and will thus relieve the engines at Battersea now applied to this service, already described as No. 5 and No. 6. All the engines at Battersea will then be available for the low service of this district.

The high grounds of Wimbleton and Richmond lie between Hampton and Battersea ; at present the water passes these on its way to Battersea to be filtered, and, after filtration, is returned by special mains to these high grounds. The new works will save this roundabout process which must involve considerable loss of power, by new mains connecting the new Hampton engines in the shortest practicable way with the high service referred to.

I was informed that a second delivering main of 30 inches diameter was about to be laid between the Hampton and the Battersea stations.

Mr. Joseph Quick is the Engineer of this Company.

GRAND JUNCTION WATER WORKS.

The principal works of this Company are situated at Kew, but the water is obtained from the Thames river at Hampton, about 8 miles above Kew.

At Hampton there are two subsiding reservoirs and two pumping engines.

The water flows from the Thames into the two subsiding reservoirs through three sets of iron strainers arranged to intercept fish and floating matters.

The reservoirs are of the same size as those of the Southwark and Vauxhall Works, situated on the same bank of the river immediately below, viz.: 45,000 superficial feet of area each, with an average capacity of three million gallons each, more or less, varying with the state of the river.

Each reservoir has its separate communication with the Thames and can be used separately.

The water passes slowly through the reservoirs to the pumps, losing in its passage a certain portion of any matter which it may carry in suspension in times of flood.

There are two single-acting "bull" engines here (Cornish) of the same pattern.

The general dimensions of each are:

> Steam cylinder 60 inches with 10 feet stroke.
> Pump plunger 42   "   "   10   "   "

The engines were cutting off at half stroke.

Both engines are working continuously at this date (July, 1868) night and day, and have not been able at all times sufficiently to supply the filter beds at Kew, the consumption of water in the district being much above the average this season. A second pipe main between Hampton and Kew will in a measure correct this evil, but additional pumping power will also be wanted at Hampton shortly.

There is a stand-pipe with two legs, the rising leg 100 feet; the down leg connects with the other at 60 feet above the pump well. These legs are of 44 and 33 inches diameter respectively.

The engines were working to-day (July, 1868) against a pressure of 91 feet, and making 14 strokes per minute the two, or 7 strokes per minute each. The strokes were made alternating, regulated by one cataract.

There is but one air chamber to the two engines.

The engines deliver into a 33-inch main, 8½ miles in length (Mr. Mylne says 7¾ miles). The delivery was stated to average 11 million gallons daily. The Registrar's report for July gives the average as 11,121,734.

The calculated rate of these two pumps, allowing 5 per cent. for loss of action, gives a delivery of 11,515,140 imperial gallons in 24 hours. The pumps are therefore working very closely up to their capacity, with no reserve in case one of them should get disabled.

This shows a wonderful perfection in the machine, and a dangerous confidence we might add, under the circumstances of this exceptional season.

The pipe main conveys the water to the principal works at Kew, on the same side of the Thames, where it is received into two settling reservoirs, either of which can be used separately. The two reservoirs have a joint area of 245,000 square feet (5.62 acres).

The accompanying sketch (Plate 8) will explain their form and the position of the filter beds.

The water, in passing slowly through these settling reservoirs (marked d^1 d^2 on the sketch), undergoes a certain amount of deposition, and in the present state of the Thames river (11th June, 1866), is amply prepared for the filter beds. The water in the settling reservoirs is discolored and full of small floating particles, but not turbid. After filtration, as seen in a glass, it is clear and sparkling.

The settling reservoirs are said to be cleansed out once a year. They will hold 11 to 12 feet of water, but in July, 1868, they had not more than 8 feet of water in them.

There are three filter beds of about the same area each, marked e^1, e^2, e^3 on the sketch. Their joint sand area was stated to be 225,000 square feet. Two of them were in action at the time of my visit, each covered with about two to three feet of water.

Usually there is six feet of water over these filters, but the consumption of water during this hot season has during the day hours somewhat exceeded the supply from Hampton, which has the effect of drawing down the settling reservoirs, and placing a shallow body of water upon the filters. The third was uncovered and undergoing the process of cleansing.

The effect of the shallow body of water, combined with its temperature this season, which was sometimes above 80° Fahrenheit in the Thames, was to encourage a very delicate vegetation on the surface of the filter bed.

This vegetation appeared like a thin green carpet of velvet, and the workmen were rolling it off in strips, at the time of my last visit, from the uncovered filter bed. It was manifest, however, that the filter had not been cleansed immediately upon its ceasing to operate as such, but that the water had been allowed to remain upon it some time after its motion downward had ceased ; in other words, when it had ceased to change and had begun to stagnate.

The two-thirds of the filtering area in use amounted to 150,000 square feet, very nearly.

Conduits from the underground drains of the filter beds conduct the water directly to the pump wells ; there being no intermediate storage basin to receive the filtered water, the flow through the filters must vary with the variations of the service.

The average delivery of the works in 24 hours being 9,800,000 gallons, I will assume that 8 millions are delivered during twelve hours of the day. This would make the rate of filtration, at the time of my visit, during the day hours, equal to 97 gallons per square foot per diem ; when the three filter beds are in service the rate averages 65 gallons per square foot per diem. At certain hours of the day during the summer months it considerably exceeds these figures, but during summer the Thames water, except after heavy rains, is usually comparatively clear, and the chief use of the filter beds then is to separate it from all organic impurities, and from fish of all sizes and descriptions.

The service from these works is intermittent, and all the tenements receiving the water have cisterns.

There is a high storage reservoir connected with these works at Camden Hill, situated 120 feet above the wells of the pumping engines.

This reservoir by its auxiliary pumping power supplies a high district of the city above the control of the Kew engines. To this extent it loses water during the day, which is replaced during the night by the Kew engines. During the day the Kew engines are not delivering into it. It is a covered reservoir of 46,800 square feet water area, and capable of holding 22 feet of water, say 5 million gallons.

This reservoir can obviously assist in meeting any sudden requirements during the night on occasions of fires, but a certain portion of the pumping power is always held in hand besides, to meet the emergencies of that service.

The settling reservoirs and filter beds are bounded by brick slope walls, at inclinations of 2 to 1.

The filter bed, which was uncovered, showed an open drain running through its axis, the side walls of the drain being carried up to the level of the surface of the sand. In commencing to fill this filter bed with water, the water is let into this drain, and overflows from it on either side slowly upon the sand surface. The main drain for the collection of the filtered water is placed immediately underneath this open drain, and three iron 12-inch air pipes rise from it through the open drain to a height above the full water of the filter basin. From this main drain small square brick drains run either way to the foot of the slopes, and from the ends of these, small air pipes of ⅜-inch diameter rise to the top of the slope walls. These air pipes in this case were 30 feet apart.

The materials of the filter beds were stated by the attendant to be as follows:

Fine sand	24 inches.
Shells	3 "
Gravel	24 "
Pebble stones	10 "
	61 inches.

Covered and surrounded by the last are the small brick gathering drains, laid upon a floor of concrete.

In the report of a Board of Inspectors made in 1856, the filtering medium is stated differently, as follows:

Harwich sand	3 to 4 feet thick.
Fine gravel	1 foot thick.
Fine screened sand	9 inches thick.
Rough screened gravel	9 inches thick.
Coarse gravel	1 foot thick.

This gives a depth of filtering material of 78 to 90 inches. The washing of the sand was stated to cost then 8½ pence (17 cents) per cubic yard.

The filter beds are cleansed, I was told, every 8 to 20 days each. The amount of sand removed does not exceed half an inch, and this is washed and laid aside to be replaced at intervals of 6 months or more, according to the circumstances of the service. Two circular open iron tanks are used for cleansing the sand. They have each a false bottom, perforated with holes. The sand is laid upon this perforated shelf, and water under a high pressure being connected below, forces its way through the holes and through the sand, carrying the muddy particles with it, and flowing off until clear, over the sides of the tank.

There are four pumping engines at these works for the service of the district, all single-acting Cornish engines.

Their general dimensions are as follows:

No. 1.—*Beam Engine.*

Steam cylinder, 90 inches diameter; 11 feet stroke.
Pump pole   38   "   "   11   "   "   .
Weight of pump pole, 45 tons.
Walking beam 30 feet long between end centres.
Depth at centre, 5 feet.

This beam, however, has been trussed on the upper side, as have all the others, since the breaking of the beam of No. 3 engine, caused by a chisel getting upon the seat of the suction valve, which prevented its closing.

Centre gudgeon 16 inches diameter.

The inlet or suction valve is a large four-beat valve of Husband's patent; the delivery valve the same. There is an air chamber to this engine, but it was said not to be in use.

The engine was cutting off at one-third and making six strokes per minute (29th July, 1868); but this rate varies with the consumption of water.

This engine pumps over a stand-pipe, the rising leg of which is 42 inches diameter, and its down leg 30 inches. The junction of the last-mentioned with the main pipe was stated to be 170 feet above the pump well. The gauge in the engine-house showed a pressure of 165 feet; but this gauge is connected with the delivery main, at a point which I should judge to be 10 to 15 feet above the water of the pump well, or its equivalent. This would show the engine to be working against a pressure of 175 feet or thereabouts, which would make the water stand just above the junction of the two legs of the stand-pipe.

There are two stand-pipes at this station (built in 1867), both enclosed within the same tower, which is of brick, and square. This structure is 18 feet square inside, with a narrow iron stairway attached to the walls, and carried up to the top.

The stand-pipe, mentioned above, is the largest of the two; the other has a rising leg of 30 inches diameter, with a down leg of 21 inches diameter; the height of the 30-inch leg is 214 feet, and of the junction point of the down leg, 170 feet; in these respects the same as the larger one. A waste-pipe of 12 inches diameter makes a fifth vertical pipe within the tower.

The whole five are constructed from cast-iron pipes, with spigot and socket joints, caulked with lead in the ordinary manner.

The Camden Hill reservoir, already mentioned, is not connected with this engine, nor with any of the pumping engines at this station during the day, but during the night two of the engines (usually No. 1 and No. 5) pump into it and replace the water taken from it during the day. During the day these engines pump directly into the city under a head not less than 170 feet and varying to 185. One of them (usually No. 4) pumps into a higher service than the others, against a pressure of 212 feet.

The delivering main to this engine is 30 inches diameter, and its length as far as the Camden Hill reservoir, 5 miles; but its branchings and extension I have no means of stating.

The engine works at present through the 24 hours and every day of the week.

No. 2.—*Beam Engine—Cornish.*

Steam cylinder 61 inches diameter ; stroke 8 feet.
Pump pole   24   "   "   "   8   "

Double-beam 26 feet between end centres, 4½ feet deep, trussed on upper side.

Suction valve, a four-beat Husband valve.

Delivery valve, a two-beat valve.

Suction about 10 feet.

There is one air chamber to this engine and No. 3 ; height 18 feet ; diameter 5 feet.

Engines No. 2 and No. 3 work directly into a city main, but have a throttled connection with the stand-pipe to relieve them under certain circumstances, from which I infer that they are serving higher ground than No. 1.

The engines were operated by one cataract, obliging them to make alternate strokes in equal times. They were each making 11 strokes per minute and cutting off steam at between one-half and three-fourths.

No. 3.—*Cornish Beam.*

This is a duplicate of No. 2, except that the steam cylinder is given me as of 63 inches diameter.

The gauge in the pump-room showed a pressure of 165 feet on the delivery pipe.

The two engines were working at present every day through the 24 hours.

No. 4.—*Beam Engine—Cornish.*

This engine has a steam cylinder of 65 inches diameter ; in other respects its dimensions are the same as No. 2 and No. 3. It was working into a higher service against a pressure of 212 feet, having a throttled connection with one of the stand-pipes. It does not work at night.

There is an air chamber on its delivery main.

No. 5.—*Direct-Acting Engine—Cornish "Bull."*

Steam cylinder 70 inches diameter ; stroke 10 feet.
Pump pole   28   "   "   "   10   "

This engine was under repair at the time of my visit in 1868. When working it makes 10 to 11 strokes per minute. It pumps over the smaller of the two stand-pipes already described, under a head ordinarily of 175 feet, counting from its inlet water. There is an air chamber on the inlet pipe, 30

7

feet in height, 30 inches diameter at bottom, tapering to 20 inches at top. There was a value attached here to this tapering. The inlet pipe connects the pump with the clear-water well of the filter beds.

This engine, when at its routine work, pumps during the day into the city, and at night, with the No. 1 engine, refills the Camden Hill reservoir.

The water valves are four-beat Husband valves.

To furnish steam for these engines, there are twelve Cornish boilers, all connected.

Eleven of these were in use to-day, all the engines being at work. except No. 5.

Six of the boilers were of 5 feet 6 inches diameter, length 28 feet, with a single flue in each of 40 inches diameter.

The boilers were carrying 42 lbs. of steam.

The fuel used was Newcastle slack (bituminous). There was but one chimney to the 12 boilers, apparently about 120 feet in height.

At the Camden Hill reservoir, situated, as already mentioned, five miles from the Kew Works and 120 feet above their level, there are two pumping engines. These are direct-acting engines of the " Cornish bull " variety.

Their general characteristics are as follows, the one being a duplicate of the other :

Steam cylinder, 70 inches diameter ; stroke 10 feet. Pump plunger, 33 inches diameter ; stroke 10 feet.

The engine was making 10 strokes per minute. Suction valve, four-beat Husband valve. Delivery valve, double-beat Harvey & West.

The inlet pipe from the reservoir to the engines is 36 inches diameter ; the delivering main 30 inches.

The engines work over a stand-pipe, serving the highest grounds of this neighborhood.

The rising leg of this stand-pipe is 48 inches diameter and 160 feet in height ; the down leg is 36 inches diameter, and connects with the other at a point 90 feet from the ground. The stand-pipe is enclosed in a square brick tower.

The gauge in the engine-room, which is connected with the outlet-pipe, showed a pressure of 100 feet, which rises at times to 112 feet.

Both engines were at work, running 10 hours a day (9 A. M. to 7 P. M.), and every day of the week.

There are nine Cornish boilers provided for the two engines; seven of these were in use to-day (30th July, 1868). The boilers were each 6 feet diameter in the shell, and 30 feet in length, with a single flue of 44 inches diameter. They carried 42 lbs. of steam.

The fuel was Newcastle slack, and the engines were stated to be making an average duty of 70 millions to 112 lbs. of coal.

At this station a new storage reservoir was under construction, to be capable of holding twelve millions imperial gallons ; a new direct-acting engine, with a steam cylinder of 90 inches diameter, was also under progress.

Mr. Joseph Quick is the Engineer of this Company ; Mr. ——— Fraser, the Resident Engineer.

WEST MIDDLESEX WATER WORKS.

15th June, 1866.

The principal pumping-station of the West Middlesex Water Company is situated at Hammersmith, on the left bank of the Thames ; the subsiding reservoirs and filtering works lie on the Barnes side of the river, immediately opposite.

The water is now drawn from the river at Hampton, at a point six miles above Teddington Lock, as in the cases of the Southwark and Vauxhall, and the Grand Junction Water Works.

The Hampton station of the Middlesex Company is situated immediately above the Grand Junction station. There are no preparatory settling basins at Hampton for the Middlesex Works.

The water is passed through a four feet conduit from the river directly to the pump-wells ; a double set of wire screens defends the mouth of the conduit, and prevents the passage of fish and all floating impurities.

There are two direct-acting Cornish engines here (Bull engines). They are each of the same general dimensions, as follows :

Steam cylinder, 64 inches diameter ; stroke, 10 feet ; plunger, 45 inches diameter ; stroke, 10 feet.

The one engine was at work (June, 1866), making 10 to 11 strokes per minute ; the other in reserve.

When I visited the works in July, 1868, both engines were at work, operated by one cataract, so as to make alternate strokes, and making about 6½ strokes each per minute ; the pause at the end of each stroke was very marked here.

The engines were cutting off at one-third.

The suction valve is a four-beat Husband valve—a great improvement, Mr. Hach says, on the double-beat valve, which was originally in use here.

The delivery valve is a double-beat valve.

The engines work over a stand-pipe, the down leg of which is connected with the rising leg at a point 55 feet from its base. The gauge in the pump-room showed a pressure of 65 feet.

The engines work at present through the 24 hours. The delivering main, conveying the water from this station to the settling reservoirs at Barnes, is 36 inches diameter and nine miles in length.

The delivery in July, 1868, was reported to average 10,665,049 gallons daily ; in June, 1868, 9,663,274 gallons.

There is a battery of nine boilers here, but three of them were being replaced by new boilers ; there was, therefore, only six boilers in use. These were single-flued Cornish boilers ; diameter of shell, 5′ 9″, length 28 feet, diameter of flue, 42 inches.

The steam-pipe connecting all was of 18 inches diameter. There were two safety-valves and a steam alarm-whistle to each boiler.

The pipe main crosses the river at Richmond, and delivers the water into the settling reservoirs, already mentioned as situated on the right bank of the Thames, at Barnes, opposite to Hammersmith.

At this point there are three settling reservoirs of 9, 7 and 9 acres area respectively, making 25 acres in all.   And there are five filter beds—four of 1½ acres each, and one of 2¼ acres sand area, making in all 8¼ acres nearly, or 358-000 square feet, strictly, of filtering surface.

The water is delivered at option into either of the three settling reservoirs, but they are ordinarily used alternately so as to permit a deposition in still water, in each case of 10 to 30 hours, according to circumstances.   In the clearest state of the river water this settlement in still water is hardly necessary. It, however, always reduces importantly the work to be done by the filter beds, and economizes very sensibly the cost and time expended on the cleansing of the filters.   The settling reservoirs contain from 12 to 15 feet of water, but not exceeding one-half of this water in depth can be drawn off on the filter beds, and these settling basins are not contemplated to be cleansed, except at long intervals.

The basins are bounded by slope-walls of stone, sloped at 1½ to 1.

In the two first built settling basins the high water lines were but 2 to 3 feet above the full water of the filter beds ; there was, therefore, but little reserve of water held by these basins.

In the last built basin (g^2) the full water stands about 8 feet above the water of the filter beds.

The reserve of unfiltered water here is probably about 20 million gallons.

From the settling basins, or either of them, the water is drawn at discretion upon the filter beds.   The general arrangement of these, and the respective areas of the basins and beds, are given in the accompanying sketch (Plate 9), which, however, is not correct as to scale, the authorities having declined to permit me to have a tracing of the general plan.

In this sketch the settling basins, or reservoirs of deposition, as they are sometimes called, are marked g^1, g^2, g^3 ; the filter beds are marked h^1, h^2, h^3, h^4 and h^5.

The last mentioned and latest built filter bed was bare, and had but just been cleansed.

On the other filter bed the side walls are vertical. In the construction of the last filter bed a portion of the old settling reservoir (g^1) was used, and the slope-walls belonging to that reservoir were retained. This filter bed, therefore, has stone slope-walls instead of vertical brick walls, as in the case of the others. An open brick drain, of the form indicated in the accompanying sketch (Fig. 1, Plate 9), runs through the centre of this filter bed, used only in re-filling it after it has been laid dry. Its side walls correspond at top with the surface of the sand.

Immediately underneath this open drain there is a brick culvert, 2½ feet square, for collecting the filtered water. The brick side walls of this culvert are half dry; half of each brick being laid in mortar, the other half left dry to permit the entrance of the filtered water.

From each side of this culvert drain-pipes run to the foot of the slope-walls. These pipes are laid 20 feet apart c. c. They are six-inch glazed clay pipes, perforated with three rows of holes on each side, but with no holes on the top or the bottom. These pipes are bedded in the large screened gravel which forms the bottom layer of the filtering materials. The water is let on to the bed by means of the open drain above mentioned, and overflows from either side of it upon the sand.

The filtering materials are as follows:

The thickness of the top layer of fine sand varies in all filters during the season, for the half-inch taken off every two or three weeks during the process of cleansing is usually replaced but once a year.

The original thickness of fine sand may, therefore, have been reduced as much as 12 inches before it is replaced.

Fine sand .... 21 inches now—originally 33 inches.
Barnes sand 12   "
Coarse and large gravel screened to five sizes ... } 27   "

—

60 inches.

The filter beds are cleansed alternately, one in a week, or in three or four weeks, as the state of the river water may require.

The sand taken off is cleansed on sloping boards, water being freely poured on this incline. Slats are nailed across these boards at intervals, to check the flow of the sand, and allow the water to act upon it sufficiently.

The cost of filtering was stated by the engineer to be about ten shillings per million gallons (0ˢ.12 per thousand gallons, or about one quarter of a cent per thousand gallons.

While there is an average rate of filtration applicable to all the beds acting jointly, the actual rate for each will vary with the condition of the bed ; the filtration being quick comparatively when it is clean, becoming more and more slow as it gets clogged or choked with sediment or other matter.

The Engineer of these works considered the filtration to vary on any one filter from 6 gallons per foot per hour to 1½ gallons per foot per hour—that is, from 144 gallons per square foot per day to 36 gallons per square foot per day.

The daily delivery of water to this district was stated by the Engineer to average at this date 9¼ million gallons per diem ; but there being no storage basin between the filters and the pumps, the rate of filtration must vary with the service, and will much exceed at certain hours of the day the average due to 9¼ millions.

I will assume that during certain of the day hours the water passes through the filter beds at the rate of eight million gallons in twelve hours. At the time of my visit, four of the five filter beds were in use, covering a sand area of 294,000 square feet. This gives an average of 54 gallons per square foot per diem for the four filters jointly.

The clear water drains are carried to the well marked K on on the sketch.

From this well two pipes are carried across the bed of the river, conveying the filtered water to the different pumping-engines.

While the works above described lie on the right bank of the Thames the pumping-engines lie on the left bank, close to the river at Hammersmith.

At this station there are five single-acting (Boulton & Watt) beam engines, the general dimensions of which are as follows :

No. 1.—Steam cylinder, 54 inches, stroke 8 feet ; two lifting-pumps, one of 20-inch diameter and 8 feet stroke, the other 15-inch diameter and 6 feet stroke, averaging 14 to 16 strokes per minute.

This engine was at work pumping into the distributing main. The gauge showed a pressure of 160 feet. There is an air chamber on the rising main. There is no stand-pipe here to any of the pumping-engines.

No 2.—Steam cylinder, 54 inches diameter, 8 feet stroke ; pump barrel, 20 inches diameter, 8 feet stroke. The pump piston is solid, and the pump is double-acting. To make the down stroke of the pump, its rod is loaded. This engine is fifty years old. It was not at work to-day ; it works alternately with No. 1.

This engine when at work pumps directly into the distributing main during the day, assisted by the high-storage reservoir at Primrose Hill.

During the night, when the service of the district is not in action, the engine pumps into and refills the Primrose Hill reservoir.

The Primrose Hill reservoir has a capacity of 4,752,000 gallons, and an altitude above the pump-well of 183 feet.

The capacity of the Kensington reservoir is 3,500,000 gallons, and its altitude above the pump-well is 117 feet. The pipe main to Primrose Hill is 6¾ miles long, and from 30, varying to 36 inches diameter. The main to Kensington reservoir is 2¾ miles long and 21 to 23 inches diameter.

No. 3.—Steam cylinder, 64 inches diameter, 8 feet stroke.
Pump barrel, 23   "   "   8   "   "

The pump-piston is solid and the pump double-acting, the pump-rod being loaded to produce the down stroke. There is an air chamber here, but no stand-pipe.

There is a weighted safety-valve on the pipe main outside of the engine-house, ingeniously arranged so as to be weighted at will to a pressure of 130 feet or of 160 feet, according as the circumstances of the service require it.

No. 4.—Steam cylinder, 72 inches diameter, stroke 10 feet.
Pump-barrel, 23   "   "   "   10   "

This is a double-acting pump, the pump-rod being loaded as in No. 3. Not at work.

No. 5.—Steam cylinder, 80 inches diameter, stroke 10 feet.
Pump-barrel, 24   "   "   "   10   "

This pump also is double-acting, being loaded like the others.

This engine is at work, delivering into the distribution against a pressure by the gauge of 162 feet.

This pressure varies with the service from 150 to 190 feet.

The Kensington reservoir is connected with and sustains the low service of the district. The Primrose Hill reservoir is confined to the maintenance of the high service.

The reserve in these reservoirs admits of the district being supplied for a certain time without the aid of the pumping-engines, and gives time, therefore, for their careful maintenance and repair, under ordinary circumstances.

At the Primrose Hill reservoir there are two rotative pumping-engines, raising the water from that reservoir to certain small portions of the district situated above its level.

No. 6 is a horizontal engine, with crank and fly-wheel. Steam cylinder 23 inches diameter, stroke 5 feet. Horizontal pump, double-acting, 11 inches diameter, with stroke of 5 feet. This engine pumps into the main through an air-vessel; there is no stand-pipe here. The engine was making 25 revolutions per minute. It works 12 to 15 hours a day. The highest ground served is 119 feet above the engine.

The service is intermittent, the pressure varying according to the parts served from 119 feet to 40 feet.

No. 7.—In this engine the steam and pump cylinder are vertical.

Steam cylinder, 23 inches diameter, 5˙ feet stroke.
Pump, double-acting, 12 " " 5 " "

There is an air chamber on the pipe main.
This engine was not at work.
The average daily delivery of water by this Company was reported to be

In 1849 .... 3,334,054 imperial gallons.
In July, 1855 .... 6,895,368 " "
In 1865.............. 9,250,000 " "
And now, in 1868....... 10,000,000 " "

The service is intermittent, and the district served in sections ; the engines, therefore, when at work during the day, are pumping against a varying head.

In this district, there is no separate pipe service for fire purposes and street cleaning.

Mr. Wm. B. Hack is the Engineer in charge of these works.

8

THE NEW RIVER WATER WORKS.

June 13, 1866.
August 8, 1868.

THE New River is an artificial channel, constructed in the beginning of the 17th century, with the view of supplying London with water from springs in Hertfordshire.

It was begun in 1608 and finished in 1613, by Sir Hugh Middleton.

Although the New River, at the time of its construction, seems to have had in view the delivery of water from the copious springs at Chadwell only, it now derives the mass of its water directly from the River Lea. The portion derived from springs and wells at present does not exceed 22 per cent. of the whole.

In 1857 the Hampstead Water Works district was incorporated into that of the New River Company by purchase.

The Company makes the following statement of its sources of supply :

1st. The Chadwell Springs in Hertfordshire.

2d. The River Lea.

3d. Deep wells on the line of the New River, and at Hampstead Heath and Hampstead Road.

4th. Small springs taken into the river in its course.

5th. Springs at Hampstead and Highgate, collected in ponds for watering roads and other such uses.

A new well has just been sunk (August, 1868) in the parish of Wormley, near Cheshunt, from which a supply of 2½ million gallons daily is expected to be obtained.

The Company is empowered to draw water from the Thames, below Black-friars Bridge, for street and sewer uses, but it has never availed itself of this power.

The average delivery per diem was in 1866, 22,898,769 imperial gallons, of which 18,000,000 was estimated to have been derived from the River Lea.

During the month of July, 1868, the daily average amounted to 27,140,000 imperial gallons.

What has been termed the New River is a very crooked canal or feeder, leading from Hertford, in the valley of the Lea, to the centre of the metropolis.

Its length is 28 miles (originally 39 miles), of which 25½ are open cut, the remainder consisting of pipes and tunnels.

The total descent on this distance is 16 feet, the origin of this feeder near Ware being 100 feet above Trinity base, and its terminus at Clerkenwell (New River Head) 84 feet above the same base.

The greater part of the New River water is derived from the chalk district of Hertfordshire.

Comparing the analysis of this water with that of the East London Water Works, as presented in the city pipe mains, the portion of it derived from wells seems to produce no perceptible change in its general character.

The following list shows the reservoirs pertaining to the works :

Two subsiding reservoirs at		Cheshunt,	18¼ acres
Two	"	"	Hornsey,	8 "
Two	"	"	Stoke Newington,	42½ "
One	"	"	Clerkenwell,	0¾ "
Ponds at Hampstead and Highgate,		30 "

The amount of filtering area is as follows :

Three filtering beds at		Hornsey,	2 acres.
Five	"	"	Stoke Newington,	5 "
Three	"	"	New River Head, Clerkenwell,	2¼ "
Two	"	"	just finished at Stoke Newington,	
	one only in use,		2 "

There are covered storage reservoirs at Claremont Square, Maiden Lane, Highgate, and Hampstead, the joint capacity of which reaches 20 million gallons.

The drainage area of the River Lea, above the point where it is tapped by this Company, comprises 284,160 acres, or 444 square miles.

The amount of water which the Company can draw from the Lea is limited to 22½ million gallons of its natural flow, but by the construction of reservoirs to store its flood waters this amount can be increased, in the opinion of the Engineer, by 10 million gallons.

There are seven ponds at Highgate and six ponds at Hampstead Heath, from which a separate service of unfiltered water is delivered to part of the district for street watering and fire purposes.

Upon the line of the New River the Company has three stations, each sup-

plying separate portions of its large district, and each having works for settling
and filtering the water, besides the necessary pumping-engines for delivering it.
These are the Hornsey Works, the Stoke Newington Works, and the Works at
the New River Head, near Sadler's Wells.

The New River forms the feeder to each of these works; the overplus, after
supplying the lowest works, namely those at Sadler's wells, passes to the Thames
by means of a 48-inch cast-iron pipe.

1st.—The Station at Green Lanes, Stoke Newington.

At this place there are two settling reservoirs, the one of 20 acres and the
other 22 acres area.

The accompanying sketch (Plate 10) will explain the position of these, and
their relation to the filter beds.

The settling reservoirs are marked m^1 m^2. They contain an average depth
of 15 feet of water, but only 3 feet of this water is available for storage, the
remainder being below the level of the filters.

The entire flow of the New River is delivered into the further or upper
reservoir, from the opposite end of which it escapes into the second or lower
reservoir (m^2). From this reservoir, controlled by sluices, it is drawn off as
wanted, into the lower section of the New River channel, which at this place is
carried round both reservoirs, and can be used independently of them when
needful. Ordinarily this portion of the channel remains in disuse, the two
settling reservoirs fulfilling its function here, as well as encouraging the settling
of sediment by the great reduction of velocity consequent on the passage of the
water into and through them.

The channel of the New River is carried thence through the filtering
grounds, delivering a portion of the water upon the filter beds, and conveying
the remainder on to the station at New River Head. The quantity delivered
upon each filter bed is regulated by appropriate sluices. The New River water,
at the time of my visit, was quite turbid, arising from some work in progress
on its banks. This turbidity of the water was visibly diminished by its passage through the two settling-ponds.

There are five filter beds here (July, 1866), of about one acre each,
marked Nos. 1, 2, 3, 4, and 5 on the sketch. Three of these measure
300×150 feet each, and the other two 315×135 feet each.

These are the sand areas; the filter beds have brick slope walls of 2 to 1.
The water areas are, therefore, larger.

When the water is very turbid, two of the filter beds have sometimes to
be cleansed off in a week; when it is in a good state, it will suffice to cleanse
once in four weeks.

Two new filter beds have just been added (August, 1868), one only of which is in use ; these are·marked No. 6 and No. 7 on the sketch. The walls of these last have been built vertical, and therefore the sand area corresponds with the water area.

They measure each 300 by 140, very nearly, or about one acre each.

The materials of the filters were stated to be as follows :

Fine sand, originally...................... 24 inches.	
(This sand is allowed to be reduced to 12 inches before being renewed.)	
Coarse sand.............................. 12 "	
Pea shingle.............................. 12 "	
Shingle, marble size, and gravel.............. 12 "	
60 inches.	

When the filter bed is bare, there is seen a cast-iron semicircular drain 30-inch diameter, extending from the river bank to about one-fifth the length of the filter bed on its centre line. The lips of this half-pipe correspond with the surface of the sand of the filter.

When the filter bed, after being cleaned off, has to be refilled, the New River water (controlled by a sluice in the brick semicircular well shown on the sketch) passes into this half-pipe, and flows over either side of it upon the sand, slowly covering it with unfiltered water. After the bed is thoroughly covered and all the air has passed off, the water is allowed to flow on as freely as the extent and condition of the filter may require it

The iron drain referred to is supported upon iron brackets.

The water, after passing through the filtering materials, is collected by clay pipe drains into two brick drains, placed as shown on the sketch.

These brick drains, which are imbedded in the shingle, rest on the bottom of the filter, which consists of a brick paving on edge, set in mortar, and resting on a thick layer of clay puddle. These collecting drains deliver the filtered water into a brick culvert, which is carried along the river bank and across its channel to the clear-water well, gathering in its course the filtered water of all the filter beds in operation.

In the two new filter beds, built in 1867–8, the arrangements for letting on and for collecting the water differ somewhat from those of the first filters, described above.

In those last filters, the side walls are vertical ; the walling, therefore, must be more costly than the slope-walls of the old filters, but the entire space is made available with the vertical walls, while a considerable portion, when slopes are used, is useless for filtration ; there is always danger, too, of a portion of the water getting behind the slopes and reaching the lower drains unfiltered. This last result must follow, as a matter of course, where the slope-walling is laid dry. Here the slope-walls are well laid in mortar.

The bottom of these new filters consists, as in the others, of a thick layer of clay puddle, over which is laid in mortar a paving of brick, on edge.

There are two brick drains upon this floor (running longitudinally), to collect the filtered water; but, instead of having clay pipe drains at right angles to these, and delivering into them as in the other filters, the whole floor is covered with a series of brick drains, laid dry, the separating walls of which are one brick thick, and the opening of each drain precisely the size of a brick, or about 4½ by 2¾ inches.

This arrangement is obtained, as shown in the sketch (Fig. 2), by laying on the floor at right angles to the main drains, rows of brick, flat, each row separated from the other by the width of a brick; these are covered by dry brick laid in the opposite direction, as close as they can be laid. Over this cover the shingle is laid, and upon that the gravel and sand, the same as in the other filters.

These small brick drains deliver each by suitable openings into the main collecting drains, which again deliver into the collecting conduit.

The unfiltered water is delivered upon these last filter beds through an iron pipe having a vertical opening in the centre of the bed, apparently of 30 inches diameter.

When the water is drawn off the filter for cleansing, the refilling of it is begun from below, through the collecting drains, by which process any air can always be more surely expelled, and the refilling executed more rapidly and with less risk than where the filters are filled from above. But, in this case, the water used for refilling until the surface of the sand is covered, should be drawn from the filtered water. Where this is not done, the unfiltered water will deposit its objectionable qualities throughout the filtering materials.

The mode adopted for collecting the filtered water here is the most perfect of any that I have seen, but it is also, I should judge, the most expensive.

The water, after passing through the materials of the bed, has the shortest practicable space to travel to reach a collecting pipe or drain; there will, therefore, be little or no risk of its running in veins, or acquiring velocity enough to carry any fine sand with it, as may sometimes be the case where the clay pipe drains performing the same office are laid twelve feet and upwards apart.

The average amount of water passing in 24 hours through the filters was given me in 1866 as from 12 to 14 million gallons, and, judging from the working of the pumping-engines, it probably does not exceed this quantity in 1868.

But much the larger fraction of this amount passes through the filters during the day hours. The pumping-engines at work during my last visit (August

8, 1868) were delivering at the rate of 817,000 imperial gallons per hour. This, therefore, was the rate of filtration then.

There are six filter beds in service now, the seventh remaining at present void of the filtering material. These six filters have a joint area of 262,000 square feet, very nearly.

Assuming one of these filters to be undergoing the cleansing process, there remains say 218,000 square feet of filtering area in use, which, at the rate of 817,000 gallons per hour, is equal to 3.75 gallons per square foot per hour (90 gallons in 24 hours).

Before the last filter bed was added the rate of filtration during the day must have sometimes reached 4¼ gallons per square foot per hour. Judging by the pumping, it must vary now from an extreme of about 4 gallons per hour during the day, to 2 gallons per hour during the night.

The water is bright and clear after passing through the filters.

There are six rotary pumping-engines here, in three pairs, with a fly-wheel to each pair. The engines are all beam engines, and the pumps are all plunger and bucket pumps.

Four of these engines are double-cylinder engines, of like size ; the other two are single-cylinder engines.

The following are the general dimensions of the double-cylinder engines :

Small cylinder, 28 inches ; stroke, 5'6⅜".
Large cylinder, 46 inches ; stroke, 8'0.
Double beam, length c. c. 24 feet ; depth at centre, 5 feet.
One fly-wheel to the pair, 24 feet diameter.
Pump barrel and bucket, 27" diameter ; stroke, 6'11".
Plunger, 20" diameter.

The suction valves are four-beat valves, but not the Husband valve. The upper half moves independently of the lower half; the seats are of metal, and bevelled ; the delivery valves are flap valves, having each two hinged flaps.

The pump and crank rods of these engines are made up of wrought-iron plate and angle bars, very neatly rivetted together.

The delivery mains are of 20 inches diameter, but they are connected outside with a larger main. There is an air chamber upon the delivery main of each pump, 15 feet high and 5 feet diameter.

These mains are not connected with the stand-pipe.

The double-cylinder engines are used for the night service, and are rarely at work during the day, probably because their combined pumping capacity is below the requirements of the day service here.

They work into the Maiden Hill reservoir, which stands 115 feet above this station, making ordinarily 14 revolutions per minute.

There are two covered reservoirs at Maiden Lane, having a joint capacity of 14½ million gallons; they are distant 3½ miles from the Stoke Newington station.

The pair of single-cylinder engines have each the following dimensions:

Steam cylinder, 60-inch diameter; stroke, 8 feet.

Outer-pump barrel, 31½″ diameter; stroke 7 feet.

Outer-pump plunger, 22″.

Inner-pump barrel, 43″ diameter; stroke, 4′ 9″.

Inner-pump plunger, 30½″.

Double beam—length, c. c. 27 feet; depth, 6 feet.

One fly-wheel to the pair—diameter, 25 feet; weight, including shaft and crank, 60 tons; making 14 to 14½ revolutions per minute.

Suction valve, a large double-beat valve.

Delivery valve, a four-flap valve. ·

There is a stand-pipe here, into which the inner or larger pumps work.

The rising leg is of 48-inch diameter, the down leg, 42-inch. These legs have two connections, one at 87 feet from the water in the well, and the other at 130 feet.

The connection at the upper end is made by an iron tank; a 12-inch waste pipe is arranged to carry off the overflow from the tank.

These stand-pipes are of cast-iron, in 9 feet lengths, with socket joints caulked with lead in the usual way. They are protected by a brick tower, in which a light iron stair-case enables the workmen to reach any part of the pipes.

The lower connection only has been used thus far. The engines were pumping over this junction (87 feet), but the down leg was not full; on the contrary, the water at the time of my visit stood in it at 60 feet above the pump-well, or about 27 feet below the junction. I presume that it rises to the junction, or above it, when the day consumption is at its minimum.

From the down leg of the stand-pipe, a 36-inch main conveys the water to the district.

The small pumps of this pair of engines work through air chambers into a common main, which, passing round the outside of the stand-pipe tower, connects outside with the 36-inch main above mentioned.

These pumps at one time worked like the others, directly into the stand-pipe, but the arrangement has been changed to the advantage, it is said, of the machine.

The 36-inch main is connected with the Pentonville reservoir at Claremont Square, which stands 40 feet above this station, and has a capacity of 3½ million gallons. The main acts also intermediately as a distributing main ; its length was given me as 2½ miles.

This pair of engines pump every day of the week except Sunday, their large pumps working against the constant head of 87 feet, which the stand-pipe imposes, and their small pumps, against the varying head on the district, which, during the day, seems to average .60 feet, all delivering into the one main. To supply steam to the engines of this station, there are two batteries of nine boilers each, under one roof; the boilers are all connected, and the two batteries are also connected, so that the boilers of the one or the other, or as many of them as may be wanted, can be used at discretion.

At the time of my visit, 12 boilers were in use supplying steam to the pair of single-cylinder engines then at work.

The boilers have the following dimensions :

Shell, 6 feet diameter ; length, 31 feet ; single flue, 40 inches diameter.

About one-third of a mile north from the Stoke Newington Works, but under the same superintendence, and connected with the same filtered water, there are two reserve engines, used only in emergencies.

At Tottenham there is still another reserve engine, which, in an emergency, can be connected with the supply, taking its water in such case directly from the river Lea. This engine was described to me as a single-acting Boulton & Watt engine.

Steam cylinder, 60 inches in diameter ; 9 feet stroke.

Pump, 44 inches in diameter ; 9 feet stroke.

This is a direct-acting engine, having no beam. It is a bull engine, so called, except that the steam lifts water instead of lifting a plunger.

2. *The Hornsey Station.*

At this station there is a settling reservoir and three filter beds.

The settling reservoir has four acres of water area, with a depth of water from 15 to 20 feet. Not more than 7 feet of this water, however, can be drawn off upon the filter beds. The reservoir has been four years in use, and has not been cleansed out during that time. A sufficient quantity of the New River water is let into this reservoir to maintain it at about a uniform level. The water is received into the further end of the reservoir, and passes through it towards the filter beds. The amount of water used at this station does not reach probably more than 750,000 gallons daily ; the movement must, therefore, be very slow, and the opportunity for deposition considerable. The reservoir is bounded by slope-walls of stone paving, at 2 to 1.

From the settling reservoir the water is let at will upon either of the filter beds by appropriate sluices.

9

The sand area of each filter bed measures about 30,000 square feet. There are 90,000 square feet in the three filter beds. The sides are sloped at 1 to 1, and paved with brick.

At the time of my visit there was about 8 feet of water upon the filters, and all three were in use. One of them was evidently about choked, and ready for cleaning. The engine was pumping at that time at the rate of 45,000 gallons per hour. There is also a water-wheel at this station, delivering some water to the neighborhood. Making allowance for the action of this last, the rate of filtration with two of the filter beds in use did not exceed 20 gallons per square foot per diem. The filtering accommodation here is at present greatly in advance of the requirements of this section of the district, an anomaly in London practice, where the companies find it difficult to keep up with the rapidly increasing wants of the population. These filter beds are not usually cleansed out more than once in two or three months for each bed, at present.

The materials of the beds were stated to be as follows :

Sand originally,.............................	36 inches.
Fine screened gravel,........................	12 "
Coarse gravel screened,......................	12 "
	60 "

Small drains of brick, on edge, with perforated brick on top, are used for collecting the filtered water. The bottoms of the filter beds are paved with brick on edge, set in mortar, and resting on the natural bottom, which is clay.

At this station there is one Cornish beam-engine delivering the filtered water into Hornsey Lane reservoir, 313½ feet above Trinity, H. W.

The steam cylinder is 44 inches diameter ; stroke....	10 feet.
The pump plunger is 15 " " "	9 "

The engine was making 11 strokes per minute, and the gauge showed a pressure of 300 feet. It was said to be delivering 630,000 gallons per diem, working about 14 hours a day. (1866.)

At Hornsey Lane reservoir there is a small engine of 50-horse power, that pumps from that reservoir over a stand-pipe into the Hampstead reservoir, situated 415 feet above the Thames.

The two last-mentioned reservoirs are covered, and are stated to have a capacity jointly of about two million gallons.

Within the Hornsey ground, and on the line of the New River, a fall of four feet here is utilized by a breast-wheel working six small pumps. This wheel works 15 hours a day, delivering about 100,000 gallons daily. The water is passed over a stand-pipe, the head of which is 70 feet above the pumps.

3. *The Lower Station at New River Head.*

There is a small circular settling reservoir here surrounded by three filter beds.

The settling reservoir has a water area of one acre, which would be of little account were the water entering it turbid ; but its passage through the large reservoirs at Stoke Newington, together with its slow movement through the intervening canal, has deprived the water of most of its sediment before it reaches this point, and the chief duty of the filters consists in separating any remains of organic matters.

The three filter beds have a joint area of 2¼ acres (108,900 superficial feet). They were all covered at the time of my visit with from 3 to 4 feet of water, but one of them was ready for cleaning, and must have been filtering at a very slow rate, if any.

The materials of the filter beds are sand and gravel ; there are from 24 to 30 inches of fine sand, and 30 inches of screened gravel, the fine gravel being placed near the sand, and the coarse and large gravel at the bottom. Earthenware drain pipes collect the water into a central culvert, which again conveys it to a well, whence it is connected with the pumps.

The drain pipes are seven inches wide at bottom, and eight inches high. On the bottom they are flat, but on the top semicircular, as shown on the sketch. The holes or perforations are confined to the semicircle. One of the filters is cleansed ordinarily once in three weeks. The walls of the filters and of the settling reservoirs are of brick, and vertical.

There is no storing basin for filtered water at these works. At the time of my visit the pumps were judged to be delivering 244,000 gallons per hour. Supposing two-thirds of the filtering surface to be in action, this would give a rate of 80 gallons per square foot per diem.

With the entire filtering area in useful action, which can rarely happen, the rate would be 54 gallons per square foot per diem.

There are two Boulton and Watt engines here, which have been at work since 1812.

They are single-acting beam engines, of the same pattern, each working two lifting-pumps.

> Steam cylinder, 48 inches diameter ; stroke, 8 feet
> Pumps, one of 29 "   "   "   8 "
>   "   the other 18 "   "   "   6 "

One engine was in action making 14 strokes per minute. The other was at rest. The engines work three month shifts. The delivery was given as 294 gallons per stroke of the two pumps, but it did not probably exceed 275.

The pumps work into separate pipe mains over a stand-pipe with three legs, with a small cistern where the bend or connection would otherwise be. One leg takes the water up, another down, and a third leg is a waste-pipe. The water of the cistern stands 84 feet above the well. There is an air chamber on each pipe main.

At night the engine pumps into, and fills the Claremont Square reservoir, which stands 50 feet above the pump well.

This station (New River Head) has an elevation of 85 feet above the Thames, and the lowest portion of the district might be to some extent supplied from it by gravity. I could not learn whether this was the case.

From the capacity of the pumping engines alone, I judge that the whole delivery from this station may average (1866) 5½ million gallons per diem, or thereabout.

The whole delivery of the Works of the New River Company averaged nearly, in 1866, 23 million gallons daily, including the unfiltered water delivered into the city for watering the streets.

The delivery to consumers, with the exception after mentioned, is intermittent; and every house, therefore, has a cistern, or water butt, or in some other way holds in reserve water enough to meet the hours when the supply is interrupted. There are 1200 houses which receive from the mains what is called in London a constant supply, but the supply-pipe is throttled by a button, having in it a small hole of from $\frac{1}{16}$ to $\frac{1}{8}$ inch diameter, according to circumstances, rendering a cistern necessary in this case as much as in the other. This contrivance limits the amount of water delivered, and prevents waste; but it also neutralizes the advantages aimed at by a constant supply.

Mr. J. Muir is the Engineer to this Company.

EAST LONDON WATER WORKS.

The East London Water Works Company derives its supply of water from the lower section of the river Lea, by means of a canal or feeder constructed for that purpose, tapping the river Lea a short distance above Tottenham Mills, at a point 4½ miles above Old Ford.

The feeder conducts the water into large settling reservoirs at Waltham Stowe. The water, after passing through these, is conveyed by an open canal to filter beds situated at Lea Bridge. Here the water, after undergoing filtration, is conveyed by a 48-inch pipe main to the pumping engines at Old Ford.

The average delivery from these works was stated by the Engineer to be about 130 millions weekly to 89,000 tenements, or about 20 million gallons daily. There are no high service reservoirs connected with these works. The storage of water is large, but it is held in open reservoirs on the line and level of the feeder aforesaid, and outside of the parliamentary limits.

The Lea rises in Bedfordshire. The average daily flow of the river is given as equal to 90 million imperial gallons, but the minimum flow in very dry seasons, judging from the records of the East London Water Company, does not exceed 55 million gallons.

The New River Company is entitled to take 22½ million gallons daily, and the East London Water Company 22½ million gallons daily; the surplus is used by the River Lea Navigation Company, or runs to waste; but the two Water Companies are authorized to take and deliver as much more as can be obtained by the construction of storage reservoirs in the valley of the Lea, for the collection of its flood waters, so far as this can be done without impairing the rights of the Navigation Companies, or of the few mill privileges existing on this stream.

By means of such reservoirs the Engineers estimate that the supply of each Company from the Lea could be increased by eight to ten million gallons daily.

This system of storage reservoirs would be undertaken jointly by the two Companies.

In point of fact, the East London Company possesses now storage reservoirs at Waltham Stowe, constructed since 1864, and capable of adding at the rate of three million gallons daily, to its summer average, from the Lea ; but these reservoirs collect only a portion of the flood waters of the lower part of the Lea.

At this date, as elsewhere stated, the New River Company draws eighteen million gallons of its supply from the river Lea, the balance being obtained from wells and springs. The East London Water Company is dependent on the Lea for its entire supply, which at this date equals an average of 20, million gallons daily. But during the lowest stages of the river in the summers of 1863 and 1864, the daily flow for some weeks did not exceed 17½ million gallons, at the point where the East River Company taps the Lea, and during some days of 1864 it was as low as 15 millions. The Company was then requiring an average of 18 to 19 million gallons, to meet the current consumption. This condition of things led to the construction of the reservoirs referred to, as the most convenient as well as the most economical mode of increasing their supplies.

The water of the river, in its summer or low water stage, is but slightly discolored ; but after rains and in floods, its waters being gathered from a rich and well-settled agricultural country, it becomes turbid, and carries a good deal of sediment. For many years the waters were delivered to the Londoners, by the two Companies, in their natural state, no attempt being made to separate either the sedimentary or the organic impurities. Parliament at length interfered, in 1854, to protect the inhabitants, and required the filtration of all waters intended for domestic use. The means taken for this end are very simple, and have proved entirely efficient.

At Waltham Stowe station, there are now three settling reservoirs in use, and one under construction. The water area of the three amounts to 75 acres, and when the fourth is completed it will amount to 115 acres. The annexed sketch (Fig. 2, Plate XI.), which is not to scale, will explain their relative positions. They serve the purpose of storage as well as of settling reservoirs, and may be said to be about as important for the one purpose as the other.

Before these reservoirs were constructed, the feeder itself, some six miles in length, afforded the only opportunity between the river and the filter beds, for the deposition of that excess of sediment which occurs in times of flood ; the water must have reached the filter beds then, at times, in a very turbid state, causing the interruptions to be proportionally frequent for cleansing them, and largely increasing the cost of that process.

The reservoirs are so arranged as to admit of the water being retained in either pair at rest for a limited time, a course that might be necessary when the river was in flood and its water very turbid. Ordinarily, it is sufficient to pass the water through the reservoirs, causing it to divide and flow—one-half through No. 1 to No. 2, and one-half through No. 4 and No. 3 to No. 2.

In this way the water flows slowly through 1½ miles in length of reservoirs, where it deposits the larger portion of any matters held in suspension, and passes to the filters unusually well prepared, to be perfected economically by that process.

The reservoirs hold from 10 to 20 feet in depth of water, but not more than seven feet of this water can be drawn off, the remainder being below the level of the canal which conveys the water to the filter beds. The reservoirs are not expected to be cleaned out except at long intervals. They are all artficial. The bank slopes (3 to 1) are not paved, but covered with coarse shingle. In the centre of each bank there is a puddle wall of clay six feet thick at top. The Engineer gives the capacity of the three reservoirs as equal to 220 million gallons, which will be increased to 500 million gallons when the contemplated additions are completed.

There is an engine-house at this station, and a pumping engine of 100-horse power in it, which is not, however, in use.

The head of the canal which conveys the water from the reservoirs after settlement, is situated about 6 feet below the level of the feeder, which delivers the Lea water into the reservoirs. The length of this canal is about 1½ miles.

LEA BRIDGE.

The canal above mentioned terminates at the Lea Bridge Works.

At this station there are two sets of filter beds, one on the left bank of the river Lea and one on the right bank.

The accompanying sketch (Plate XI.) shows their forms and positions. On the right bank there are seven filter beds grouped round a central well, into which the filtered water is delivered ; these are marked p, p, p, p, p, p, and p, on the sketch.

On the left bank of the Lea there are six filter beds, grouped also round a central well ; they are marked q, q, q, q, q, q.

The filter beds were all covered, at the time of my visit, with from 4 to 5 feet of water, except one, which was bare, undergoing the process of cleansing.

The materials of the filters are sand and gravel 4½ feet deep ; the depth of fine sand varying from 18 to 30 inches, according to the time which has intervened since the last renewing. The gravel is screened and arranged with the largest size at the bottom. The bottom is of concrete, upon which are laid the drains and earthenware pipes, which collect the filtered water and carry it to the central well. I was not able to get the particular size and arrangement of these pipes in this case, but they are of the same general character as those used at the other works.

In the worst state of the river a filter bed is cleaned once a week, but usually it suffices to clean them once in three to four weeks. The Engineer informed me that the aggregate filtering area cleaned off during the year averaged 160 acres. This is equal to 3.08 acres cleaned off per week.

The entire sand areas of the filters amount to 12 acres, which would give an average of three filter beds cleaned each week, which would again give an average for each filter bed of a cleaning off every four weeks. About half an inch of sand is taken off in the process of cleansing. The foul sand is washed and used over again. The sand is not replaced upon each bed oftener than once in from 6 to 8 months.

These filter beds are not bounded by vertical walls, but by steep slope-walls, paved with brick. The air pipes come to the surface at the top of the slope.

In the filter bed, which was bare, there were three pipes visible at the foot of the slope-wall of one of the sides, for refilling and supplying it with water. Each of these pipes delivered its water into a small semicircular basin, the walls of which were flush with the surface of the sand. In commencing the refilling, the water overflows from these basins slowly upon the filter bed.

There being 12 acres of filtering area here, I will suppose 10 acres of it to be always available for service. The water supplied averages 20 millions per diem, but of this we may consider 15 millions as passing through the filters during the 12 hours of day, the filtered water reservoir at Old Ford not being large enough to equalize the rate of filtration through the 24 hours. This gives a rate during the day of about 70 gallons per square foot. With all the filter beds in service, the rate would be 57 gallons per square foot per diem.

The height of the water in the central well which receives the filtered water, as compared with its height or level on the filter beds, shows the head required to produce the flow through the filtering material. This head will vary with the rate of that flow, the extent of the filtering area in use, and the condition of the sand surface (whether it be recently cleaned or nearly closed).

The well belonging to the set of filters on the left bank of the Lea, stood at the time of my visit 3 feet 9 inches below the level of the water upon the corresponding filter beds.

Although the mode of filtration adopted on the London works was originally prepared with a view simply of depriving the river water of the sediment which discolors it after heavy rains, it is now conceded that the process of filtration is quite as desirable in summer, to deprive such water of the floating vegetable fibres and certain animalcules which it carries in suspension.

During certain of the summer months, this intercepted matter rapidly gums up the surface of the filter beds and induces vegetation there. At these seasons of the year the filter beds require to be cleaned off, in consequence of this coating of organic matters, about as frequently as when the river is in flood. In these filter beds, for instance (as related by Mr. Maine, one of the Company's Managers) during the month of July of every year, the slimy matter very rapidly deposits upon the sand, interrupting the filtration. In the month of August this slimy matter vegetates, producing green confervoid fibres, and spreading itself like a green carpet over the surface of the sand. Doubtless, the other London Companies could testify to the same kind of experience.

There is one Cornish beam engine (1866) at this station.

Steam cylinder, 100 inches diameter ; stroke 11 feet.
Plunger,   50   "   "   "   11   "

The engine was at work, making 7 to 8 strokes per minute, and delivering, I was told, 150 cubic feet per stroke. It works through a single-legged stand-pipe directly into the city main. There is also an air chamber on the main. It has a battery of eight boilers ; six at work, two at rest. Diameter of boiler 5 feet 9 inches each, by 30 feet in length. The flue 3 feet 6 inches diameter. Chimney 148 feet high. The engine has been working since 1854 day and night. During this period it has had no repairs other than such light work as could be done at the smithy on the premises.

Although this engine frequently makes 10,000 strokes in 24 hours, yet the ordinary week's work, I was informed by the Engineer, seldom exceeds 62 to 64 million imperial gallons for seven days. Its work, therefore, averages 9 million gallons per diem at present. The night service of the district is performed by this engine alone, the engines at Old Ford being then at rest. Since my visit to Lea Bridge in 1866, two new engines have been erected there, each with a steam cylinder of 84 inches ; the other particulars of these I am not able to give.

The 100-inch engine above mentioned seemed to be, on the whole, the most satisfactory specimen of the Cornish pumping engine to be seen in London.

The cost of such an engine now (1866), I was informed, would probably be about £15,000, complete in all respects.

There are two small water-wheels at this place whose pumps work into the local service pipes.

OLD FORD.

The 48-inch pipe main already mentioned, which conveys the filtered water from the filtering works to the Old Ford Works, is two miles in length.

10

At Old Ford, it delivers the water into a covered clear water basin. This basin, or low storage reservoir for filtered water, has an area of 2½ acres, with a depth of water when full of 12 feet. I calculate it to hold about seven million gallons of water. The filtered water is running into this basin night and day.

The pumping engines at Old Ford draw down this basin during the day hours when they are at work, and at night, when they are not at work, the uninterrupted flow from the filters fills it. The basin, however, is not large enough to make the rate of flow, and therefore of filtration, uniform during the day and night hours. From this basin the water has free access to the different pumping engines by a conduit with suitable sluices.

The 48-inch main has a lateral connection with the wells of the pumping engines, independent of the covered basin referred to, in order that, when that basin requires repairs or cleansing, the flow of filtered water to the pumps may not be interrupted. At this station there are also two open reservoirs, kept full of unfiltered water from the Company's canal. They are not, however, in use, although they have been permitted to remain, as a measure of precaution against unforeseen emergencies.

There are four single-acting beam engines here, of the Cornish variety. The general characteristics are as follows :

No. 1.—"*Hercules.*"

Steam cylinder, 85 inches diameter ; stroke, 10 feet, cutting off at one-third. 30lbs. steam shown by gauge in engine-room, making 8 to 9 strokes per minute. Double beam—length, 29 feet c. c.—depth at centre, 6 feet.

Plunger, 43-inch diameter ; stroke, 9 feet.

One stand-pipe to the four engines, with a single leg 135 feet in height and 5 feet diameter.

For suction valves, two double-beat valves.

Delivery valve, one double-beat valve.

The outer beat is 55 inches diameter ; the inner beat 43 inches. The beats are level, and metal to metal.

The engine works into the City main, not through the stand-pipe, but the main is connected with the stand-pipe.

The engine has a battery of 4 Cornish boilers, three of which were in use, the fourth in reserve.

Diameter of shell, 69 inches ; length, 30 feet.

Length of fire-place, 6 feet.

There is but one chimney here for the four batteries of the four engines, height 175 feet.

No. 2.—"*Cornish.*"

Steam cylinder, 80 inches; stroke, 10 feet, making eight strokes per minute.

Plunger, 41 inches diameter ; stroke, 9 feet.

This engine works directly into the stand-pipe. The gauge in the engine-room showed a pressure of 95 feet.

Suction valve, a double-beat valve.

Delivery valve, the same.

Four boilers, carrying 35 lbs. steam ; shell of boiler, 69 inches; length, 30 feet. Diameter of flue, 42 inches.

No. 3.—" *Ajax.*"

Steam cylinder, 72 inches ; stroke, 10 feet, making 8 to nine strokes per minute.

Double beam, cast-iron; length, 30 feet c. c. ; depth at centre, 6 feet. The flitches 8 inches apart.

Plunger, 36 inches diameter ; stroke, 10 feet.

The suction valve is a double-beat valve.

The delivery valve is one of Austin's patent cone valves, with horizontal india-rubber rings. This valve is considered good for delivery valves, but the other valve is preferred here for suction valves.

The delivery main is connected with the stand-pipe. The gauge in the engine-room showed a pressure of 85 feet.

Four Cornish boilers—shell, 69 inches ; length, 30 feet ; flue, 42 inches.

No. 4.—" *Wicksteed,*" 1847.

Steam cylinder, 90 inches ; stroke, 11 feet ; 30 lbs. steam in engine-room. Cutting off at one-fourth, 8½ strokes per minute.

Double beam, cast-iron ; length, 36 feet c. c.; depth at centre, 7 feet 6 inches ; weight, 35 tons ; gudgeon, 16-inch diameter.

Plunger, 44 inches diameter ; stroke, 11 feet ; 40-inch main from engine to stand-pipe.

Suction valve, double beat.

Delivery valve, double beat.

The pump was stated to be delivering at the rate of 5,700 imperial gallons per minute.

The gauge in the engine-room showed a varying pressure of 84 to 88 feet with each stroke.

This engine, like the other, has a battery of four Cornish boilers, of same dimensions each as those already given. The steam-pipe from the boilers was of 15 inches diameter, and cased. All of the four engines have steam jackets. In this engine and in the Hercules there is also a steam cover. The actual stroke made is usually from 2 to 4 inches below the lengths here given.

These four engines were all at work (1866). They are all kept at work during the day and all at rest during the night. I judged them, from their dimensions, to be delivering about 12 million gallons in 12 hours.

(On my visit to the works, on 4th August, 1868, there were but three engines at work, No. 3 being at rest ; but the river supply had been deficient that season, and the Company found it difficult to meet besides, the increased consumption produced by the great heat of the summer. On this day the water in the adjoining covered reservoirs stood 5 feet below its ordinary level.)

All the engines work directly into the mains, either through or connected with the single-legged stand-pipe, against not exceeding a hundred feet of head. Each engine is connected with an air chamber. Of the four boilers connected with each engine, three are in use in each case and one in reserve.

The engines were making 8 to 9 strokes per minute.

There are two small rotative beam engines at this station, serving generally a special high corner of the district.

The East Twin and the West Twin.

These engines are sixty years old. The East Twin working, the other at rest.

Steam cylinder, 36 inches ; stroke, 8 feet.

Crank and fly-wheel inside of the pump.

Crank, 2½ feet c. c.; fly-wheel, 13 feet diameter.

Two lifting-pumps. The outer pump, 18 inches diameter ; 8 feet stroke. The inner pump, 15 inches diameter ; 6 feet stroke. The outer pump was disconnected. The inner pump was working into the high service, against a pressure of from 140 to 150 feet head.

Each engine has an air chamber on the line of main, inside of the house. There were two Cornish boilers for these engines ; one only at work.

The liberal scale on which the settling reservoirs and filtering works of the East London Water Works are constructed must produce very satisfactory results, both as regards the sufficiency and the economy of the process. The pumping machinery here is more than usually uniform, and excellent of its class.

In 1849, the Company is reported to have delivered into its district a daily average of................................ 830,000 imperial gallons.
In 1855...................................... 1,600,000 " "
In 1866, the delivery averaged.................20,000,000 " "

Mr. Charles Graves is the Engineer of these works. They were at one time under the direction of Mr. Wicksteed, and it was here that what is now called the Cornish form of pumping-engine was first applied by Mr. W. to city water works.

LEICESTER WATER WORKS, June, 1866.

The city of Leicester is situated on the small river Soar, a tributary of the Prent. The city is supplied with water from Markfield brook, a small upland brook which runs into the Soar below Leicester. A reservoir has been constructed on the valley of this brook, near the village of Thornton, about 8 miles west from Leicester. The sources of the brook rise in a sandstone and shale district to the north of the reservoir. The water collected has about 9 degrees of hardness, by Clark's scale. Before the construction of these works the city was entirely supplied from wells, many of which are used now, although the well water is very much harder than the Thornton water.

The population of Leicester was stated to number about 75,000, of which 50,000 were supposed to be supplied by the Water Company.

The works consist of the reservoir above mentioned, four filter beds immediately below the reservoir embankment, and a reservoir near the city which receives and stores the water after filtration.

The reservoir has a water surface, when full, of 78 acres. It must have a capacity, I judge, of 100 days' supply, and yet, during two exceptionally dry years, its reserve of water had proved, as was stated to me, barely sufficient, and the Company have now under consideration the construction of a second reservoir.

The filter beds are situated immediately to the south of the reservoir embankment, low enough to command the entire water of the reservoir. From the reservoir there are two pipes to convey its water to the filter beds. One of these is a siphon pipe of 12 inches diameter. This is used until the water gets below the siphon mouth. The other is an 18-inch pipe, laid through the bottom of the embankment, which commands that portion of the water lying below the reach of the siphon.

The forms of the four filter beds are shown on the accompanying sketch (Plate XII.), where they are marked a^1, a^2, a^3, a^4. The central well (b), 66 feet in diameter, receives the filtered water from an overflow pipe in its centre. Each filter measures 100 feet by 66 feet, giving to each 6,600 square feet of sand surface. The walls of these filters are built of stone, and vertical. They are backed with clay puddle. The bottom is also puddled with clay, over which paving slabs are laid, and upon these a brick paving.

The materials of the filters are sand, gravel, and broken stone, to the depth of seven feet. The sand, originally 36 inches, is now reduced to 24 inches, it was stated, upon two of the filter beds ; on the other two it is 36 inches now, having been replaced, I presume, to that depth. The sand is coarser than any that I have seen used for this purpose. Deducting three feet of sand, there remains 4 feet of gravel and broken stone. A central brick drain, with clay pipes running from either side of it, collects the filtered water and delivers it into the clear water well (b). These pipes (6 inches in diameter) are not perforated. The water enters at the joints, which are kept apart about an inch, or as much as the size of the broken stone will admit.

A 10-inch iron pipe at the corner of each filter bed is connected with the reservoir pipe, and delivers the required amount of water upon the bed. The mouth of this pipe is surrounded with cobble stone, upon which the water over-flows slowly when the sand bed is bare and until there is a sufficient depth of water to protect the sand. There is a waste-pipe at another corner, standing 24 inches above the full water line, and the water in these filters is limited by the height of this pipe. To-day there were but 18 inches of water upon the beds. The filters are cleansed off from once in six days to once in three weeks, according to the character of the water. I was told that when the brooks were flooded and the reservoir at the same time rather low, the water became quite turbid. At the time of my visit the reservoir water was comparatively clear, but seen in a tumbler, there were numerous small animalcules visible, moving about briskly. The water after filtration was quite bright and entirely free from any appearance of this kind. These small living organisms occur, we presume, in all waters at certain seasons of the year. There they are visible twice a year for a short period. The only use of the filters for a large portion of the year is to intercept and remove all organic matters, vegetable or animal.

The sand removed in the cleansing process is washed and laid aside, to be replaced at intervals.

Two of the filters were in use at the time of my visit, the other two being dry and ready for use. When the reservoir is made turbid after heavy rains, three are used, and at the worst the whole four.

The average delivery of water by this Company to the city of Leicester is 1,200,000 imperial gallons (192,551 cubic feet), equal to 1,440,380 U. S. gallons per diem, as given me by the Superintending Engineer.

With two filter beds in use (sand area 6,600×2=13,200 square feet), the rate of filtration is about 109 U. S. gallons per square foot per diem. This was the rate at this time. When the water contains a perceptible portion of sediment, the rate with three filters averages 82 U. S. gallons, and with the four, 54½ U. S. gallons per square foot per diem.

An 18-inch pipe, whose mouth is covered by a grating, enters the clear water well b, and conveys the filtered water thence to the New Parks reservoir, situated about 2½ miles southwest of the city. The length of this pipe was stated to be about 7 miles. The clear water reservoir above mentioned stands 130 feet above the Hay Market, Leicester, and commands the entire city. This is a covered reservoir, with a capacity, Mr. Bevins stated, of two days' supply, that is, of about 2½ million gallons. This reservoir is sufficiently large to admit of (with some regulation) the rate of filtration being maintained uniform night and day.

These works were constructed after the designs of Mr. Hawksley. Mr. Bevins is the Superintending Engineer.

YORK WATER WORKS.

Yonk, 3rd *September*, 1866.

The city of York lies on the river Ouse, which delivers its waters into the estuary of the Humber.

The water for the supply of the city is derived from the Ouse at a point near Acombs' Landing, about two miles above the city.

The sources of the Ouse lie on the high lands dividing the North Riding of Yorkshire from Westmoreland.

The prevailing rocks there are the upper limestone shales and the millstone grit.

Whenever heavy rains occur, the water in the river is decidedly turbid at York. It was so at the date of my visit (September, 1866), though the river then was but four feet above its lowest stage. In extreme floods it rises ten to twelve feet, and spreads over a large extent of meadow lands.

The works of the "York New Water Works Company," situated at Acombs' Landing, consist of an engine-house and two pumping-engines, two settling basins, three filter beds, and a reservoir for the filtered water placed upon sufficiently high ground to command the city.

The two pumping-engines are in all respects alike. They are of the Cornish form of single-acting beam engines.

Each engine has two plunger pumps, one of which is used for lifting the river water into the settling basins ; and the other for lifting the filtered water into the high reservoirs, whence it passes to the city.

The two pumps are not worked at the same time, one of them being thrown out of gear when the other is in use. There was but one engine at work at the time of my visit, pumping into the high reservoir. In practice one engine pumps the filtered water through the 24 hours, except 10 to 15 minutes ; and the other pumps the river water for 9 to 10 hours daily, the greater size of the low-service pump enabling it to do its work in so much less time. The engines alternate under this arrangement from month to month.

The general dimensions are :

Steam cylinder,	36 inches diameter ;		8 ft. 4 inches stroke.		
River pump,	30 "	"	9 "	"	"
Clear-water pump,	20 "	"	6 " 4	"	"

11

The engine was making 12¼ strokes per minute, the service requiring that rate, but 10½ strokes is considered its best working rate.

The delivery per diem was stated to average 1,500,000 gallons into the high reservoir. For the last week of August, on record, it was 10,800,000 imperial gallons, which was equal to 1,542,855 gallons per diem.

The water in the high reservoir stands 110 feet above the clear-water pump well. The river-water pump has a lift ordinarily of 24 feet, varying with the stage of the river. The walking beam of each engine carries two sliding blocks of cast-iron, whose position is adjusted according as the low or high service pump is in use. The river water is carried to the engines by a 21-inch pipe, and is delivered to the settling basins through a 21-inch pipe.

The pipe, or rising main, which delivers the filtered water from the small pump to the high reservoir, is 12 inches diameter, and about 2,500 feet in length. A second rising main of 21 inches diameter was being laid.

The accompanying sketch will show the arrangement of the settling basins and filter beds. (Plate 13.)

The two settling basins are intended to hold 2,500,000 gallons each when full. After being filled the water stands usually 14 hours in each settling basin before being drawn off upon the filter beds ; but this advantage is in part lost by the mode of drawing off, which is from the bottom. The original arrangement had in view the drawing off the water from the surface, where it is always clearest ; but some defects in its working led the attendants to use the other method. The settling basins are each cleared out once a year.

A 12-inch pipe carries the water from the settling basins along the head of the filter beds. From this pipe a 9-inch branch, with a stopcock, communicates with each bed—the water being delivered from the 9-inch pipe upon each bed by four smaller pipes of 4-inch diameter each. At the terminus of each small pipe a wooden trough, perforated with holes, receives the water and delivers it upon the sand. The box is intended to break the flow from the pipe, and defend the sand-bed from being rutted.

The sides of the filters are pitched with a rough pitching of 9-inch stone, sloped at 2 to 1, resting on 4 inches of concrete and grouted. The bottom is puddled, and there is a puddle wall in each dividing bank, and around the outer boundaries.

The materials of each filter are as follows :

Sand...................................... 30 inches.
Fine gravel............................... 6   "
Broken stone or large shingle, screened........ 24   "
                                          ——
                                          60 inches.

A layer of 4 inches of concrete intervenes between the puddle and the shingle, and forms the base of the filter bed. Upon this surface of concrete a central dry-stone drain runs lengthwise of each bed, into which 6-inch clay pipes, laid on either side of this centre, deliver the filtered water. This drain is carried into a well-hole, from which a 15-inch pipe carries the water to the clear-water pump. At each of these well-holes a sluice enables the attendant to regulate the action of each filter bed.

These filter beds are overworked at present, and the company is about constructing a fourth filter to be circular, and 160 feet in diameter. This new filter, if the side walls are built vertical, as was stated, will possess a capacity of filtration about equal to the other three. When a filter is clean, 12 inches of head will readily pass the proper amount of water ; but as they become clogged with sediment, 3 feet of head is frequently necessary. In these filters the three feet, as I gathered, is sometimes exceeded, showing that the filter beds are allowed to become very foul before being cleaned off. In these filters the additional head is given by adding to the depth of water over the filter bed.

One of the filter beds was being cleansed at the time of my visit ; the other two were covered with water—the one having four feet of water upon it, and the other five feet.

A filter is cleaned off once a month, and the Superintendent informed me that the cleansing was as necessary when the river was low, and comparatively clear, as when it was high and turbid. When low the fine vegetable threads and particles carried by the water then, being intercepted by the sand, form a compact and close coating, like velvet, as he described it. But this would not be so sensibly felt if the filter beds were cleaned off oftener. When the filter is cleansed off, the sand, which has always packed considerably, is loosened by delving it with spades and afterwards smoothly raking it over before the water is let on. I was informed that the sand became discolored for 9 inches below the surface here—a proof apparently of the undue pressure under which the water is passed through it, according as the filter gets foul ; in other words, of the proper time for cleansing it off having been usually passed. The sand was fine and of good quality, but containing many black particles of slate or shale.

Each of the filter beds has a sand area of 60 feet by 120 feet, or 7,200 square feet. The three filters have a joint sand area of 21,600 square feet. The amount of water used daily being 1,500,000 gallons, the rate of filtration with the three filters in use is about 69¼ imperial gallons per square foot per diem, and with but two in use it is at the rate of 104 gallons per square foot.

The clear-water reservoir is situated upon a piece of high ground within half a mile of the works above described. It is open, and consists of one apartment, holding 12 feet of water, and having a capacity of about three million gallons. It stands 110 feet above the filter beds. A 15-inch pipe main, a little over two miles in length, carries the filtered water from this reservoir to the city.

To meet the wants of a small district of the city too high to be commanded by this reservoir, a stand-pipe has been erected on the reservoir ground, whose bend is 18 feet above the full water of the reservoir. For a certain number of hours every night the engine pumps over this stand-pipe. During these hours the 15-inch pipe main is disconnected from the reservoir, and also from the lower part of the city, and the houses on the high ground referred to are enabled to fill their cisterns. The service upon the city is constant for twelve hours. To meet the wants of the other twelve the houses have cisterns, butts, or vessels of some kind for the necessary reserve of water.

In 1851, the population of York was 36,303 ; in 1861, 40,377 ; and in 1866, it is supposed to be 43,000. The Water Company, however, supplies certain suburbs outside of the census population, raising the population supplied by its waters to at least 45,000. This gives a rate of delivery per head of upwards of 33 gallons. This rate includes, as usual, the water applied to all other purposes. It is more than generally obtains in England, and is an unusually liberal supply for a provincial city.

Mr. John Watson, the Secretary of the Company, furnished me very politely with the requisite facilities and information to understand the works, as did Mr. Edward Hastler, the Superintendent.

LIVERPOOL WATER WORKS.

LIVERPOOL, *August*, 1866.

The city of Liverpool, lying upon tide-water on the right bank of the Mersey, is, commercially speaking, the most important city of Great Britain. The tonnage of this port exceeds that of London.

In 1861, the population, by the census, was 437,740 ; at this date it is supposed to amount to 500,000.

Up to 1857, all the water of Liverpool was obtained from wells sunk in the new red sandstone strata which overlie the coal beds of Lancashire.

The water supplied to the city at this date is derived in part from these wells and in part from the new works at Rivington. The portion derived from wells was stated by Mr. Duncan, the Engineer, in 1863, to average 6.63 million gallons per diem, from seven wells. At present the amount received is 5.61 million, from six wells ; but when the improvements now in progress at two of the well stations are completed, the amount is expected to be increased to 7.61 millions per diem.

The increase has not been gained by sinking new wells, but by deepening two of the old ones, and by adding to the pumping power there.

The water from the wells is very clear and exceedingly palatable. It is delivered into the same pipes and reservoirs as the Rivington water, which is derived from surface collections.

There are seven wells or pumping stations, and 12 pumping engines. The wells are from 130 to 250 feet in depth. The practicability of increasing the well supply is at present being tested by boring 250 feet below the present bottom of one of the wells, into a lower series of sandstone.

The pumping engines are, some of them, single-acting Cornish engines, and some of them rotary engines. The working expense of the first have been found, by Mr. Duncan, to equal 17 shillings per million imperial gallons, per 100 feet of lift, and the average expenses of all the engines to be equal to 39 shillings per million imperial gallons, per 100 feet of lift.

The rotary engines, however, are mostly old engines. We know that there is but little difference in the fuel economy of the one engine over the other, when the rotary engine is equally perfect in its workmanship, in its ability to use steam expansively, and in its boilers, and when it is equally faithfully tended.

The delivery of water by the Corporation Works, at this date (August, 1866), was stated to average 13,000,000 gallons imperial per diem. The amount received from the new works is therefore (13,561) 7.39 million gallons per diem, at present.

The population of the city of Liverpool, at this date, has already been given as 500,000, but the Corporation Water Works supply as well the town of Prescott, and the outskirts between Prescott and Liverpool, comprising on the whole a population of about 600,000. The rate per head, therefore, averages but little above 20 gallons per diem, a rate which does not satisfy the growing wants of the population.

This port which, as regards tonnage, is the largest and most important in Great Britain, requires for its shipping alone, and for the purposes of its docks, stores, and wharves, a large amount of water. The supply at present is not constant through the 24 hours, but it is constant for 12 hours of each day. With a more abundant supply this system would be changed to that of constant service through the 24 hours. All the water received from the Rivington Works is filtered. The water from the wells does not require filtration.

The water of the Rivington Works is collected from the high grounds lying between Blackburn and Bolton, in Lancashire. A part of this water-shed consists of cultivated ground, though the larger portion of it is in pasture. The rock formation belongs to the sandstones and shales of the coal measures, and to the millstone grit. There are six collecting reservoirs, five of which serve as well for compensation reservoirs, delivering a fixed daily quantum of water to the mill properties below, in compensation for the water taken for city use. The reservoirs are as follows :

NAME OF RESERVOIR.	Water Area.	Capacity in Millions of gallons.	Height above Tide.	Greatest Depth Full.
	Acres.		Feet.	Feet.
1. Upper Roddlesworth,	38.	180.	620.	61.
2. Lower Roddlesworth,	16.4	99.	550.	78.
3. Rake Brooke,.......	13.8	79.6	550.	78.
4. Anglezark,..........	191.6	1019.6	470.	35.
5. Chorley,...........	10.2	48.3	430.	39.
6. Rivington in 2 divisions	275.	1841.	428.	40.
	545.	3267.5		

The filter beds, which stand 382 feet above tide, are situated in the valley of the Douglass brook, immediately below the embankment of the lower Rivington reservoir. These reservoirs are not all situated in the valley of the same stream. The higher ones are upon brooks which are tributaries of the Derwent river, and the lower ones upon tributaries of the Douglass river, both rivers delivering into the Rebble. The water of each reservoir, however, is carried by an open cutting into the reservoir below it, with the exception of what is measured off to the millers, and of any portion that may run to waste at the overflows. The whole of the available water of all the reservoirs becomes thus concentrated upon the lower division of the Rivington reservoir. These works were designed by Mr. Hawksley, and constructed from his plans. The drainage area, or water-shed of all these reservoirs comprehends 10,000 acres. The water due to the millers, under all circumstances, and delivered into the several streams for their use, amounts in all to 8,300,000 imperial gallons per diem.

In designing the works, the mean rain fall of the district (in defect of precise information) was taken at 48 inches, and of this the amount collectable was assumed to be 36 inches (75 per cent.), of which 12 inches was intended to be given to the millers for compensation. This estimate of the amount available has not been verified.

In 1861, 1862, and 1863, a considerable portion of water was wasted over the waste weirs of the several reservoirs. The rain falls of these years were respectively, 46.4, 48.5, and 51 inches.

In 1864, 1865, and 1866, to date, no water has been lost over the waste weirs. The whole of the water has been utilized, and had not the year 1865 derived some assistance from the collections of 1864, as 1864 did from 1863, the city would have been put to serious inconvenience for want of water. The rain fall in 1864 was 39 inches; in 1865, 34.8 inches; and for the first five months of 1866, 15.1 inches. The whole amount collected in 1865 equalled 23.35 inches, being 67 per cent. of the rain fall of that year. Of this 13½ inches (8.3 million gallons per day) was delivered to the millers, and there remained but 10 inches available for city use, equal to an average of 6,176,865 gallons per diem.

Except in such low years of rain fall as 1864, 1865, and 1866, the amount available from Rivington for city use frequently reaches an average of 9 and 10 millions of gallons per diem, and when the water overflows from the reservoirs 12 million gallons per diem could occasionally for a few weeks be drawn from that source.

The amount delivered to the city being about a fixed quantity per diem while the amount available from Rivington Works is (according to the wet or dry season) a very variable quantity, the result is made uniform by varying the deliveries from the wells, lessening the latter according as the Rivington water exceeds its low water or minimum rate. In other words, the more of the Rivington water there is received, the less pumping power is requisite at the wells, and if the Rivington water yielded thirteen million gallons per diem, which is the present rate of delivery to the city, the entire pumping apparatus could, for the time being, be relieved from duty. At present the city is trained throughout the year to the low water rate of consumption due to low seasons of rain fall on the Rivington district, to avoid the dissatisfaction and discomfort which would ensue from a serious reduction of the supply after the habits of the people had accommodated themselves to the larger and freer use of water, which the unrestricted supply of a wet season would permit.

The accompanying sketch shows the arrangement of the filters. (Plate 14.)

There are six filter beds, and two clear-water basins for receiving the filtered water. These basins have a joint capacity of 12 million gallons.

Through the reservoir embankment, immediately above them, there are two tunnels, with four slide-gates or sluices in each. The one tunnel passes off the compensation water to the millers ; this tunnel draws its water from the bottom of the reservoir. The other tunnel passes off the portion of water to be filtered and sent to the city ; this tunnel takes its water from a point 14 feet above the bottom of the reservoir.

The water for the filters flows into an open canal or race, as shown on the accompanying sketch, from whence it is drawn at will upon each filter bed. The sand surface of each filter measures 300 by 100 feet. The sides are sloped at 2 to 1, and paved very neatly with dimension-stone, laid dry. To prevent the water passing through the joints of this paving, the slopes to the surface of the water are covered with sand.

The materials of the filter beds consist of sand, gravel, and broken stone, in the following proportions :

Fine sand .... 30 inches.
Fine gravel 6   "
Half-inch gravel 6   "
Three-quarter-inch gravel 6   "
One-inch gravel 6   "
Two-inch cubes 9   "
Broken stone, four-inch cubes .... 24 "
                                                    ----
                                                    87 inches.

Two dry rubble-drains, situated as shown in the accompanying section, run through the 24-inch course of cobble-stones, and collecting the filtered water there, carry it to the clear-water basins, as shown on the sketch-plan. Four air-pipes rise from each of these drains to above the surface of the water. The bottom of the filter bed is puddled, as are the sides under the coursed paving. The depth of water on the filters is limited to two feet. The ice here, the Superintendent informed me, had not exceeded one inch in thickness on the filter beds. although it has been five inches thick upon the reservoirs.

At the time of my visit (August, 1866), the water of the reservoir was 19 feet below its full water line.   It was of a brownish color when seen. in mass, but apparently held little or no sediment in suspension.   The Superintendent informed me that it carried, however, sufficient organic matter, apparently vegetable and very minute, to gum up the surface of the filter beds, so that they required to be cleaned off at present (the whole series) once a fortnight.   When, in addition to this, the water is turbid from floods, the beds have occasionally to be cleaned once a week, but the average for the year is about once a fortnight. The fine vegetable matter referred to is most troublesome in midsummer.

The depth of sand pared off during the year by these repetitions of the process of cleansing amounts to 15 to 18 inches from each bed.   This sand is washed and laid aside, to be replaced once a year.   The apparatus for cleansing the sand is very complete.   The sand is moved from its box of deposit by a screen into the wash trough, is moved along the wash trough and well stirred in water there in the same way, and after being washed, is drawn out of the water and delivered into carts by a similar arrangement.

The cost of filtering, as stated by Mr. Duncan, the Engineer, averages very nearly £100 per annum for every million gallons filtered daily—say, $500 in gold. This is at the rate of $1.37 (gold) per million gallons per diem.   Each filter bed has a sand area of 30,000 square feet.   The six filter beds have a sand area of 180,000 square feet.   As the beds are cleaned one by one, there are always five of them in use ; the minimum sand area in use, therefore, is 150,000 square feet. When filtering five million gallons per diem, the rate for five filters is 53½ imp. gallons per square foot per diem.   This may be considered the average rate at the time of my visit, for even when the six filter beds are covered, as they were then, one may be assumed to be nearly ready for cleansing.   When the five filters are passing ten million gallons, the rate is 66⅔ gallons per square foot, and with twelve millions it would be 80 gallons per square foot per diem.   The last-mentioned rate Mr. Duncan considered to be in excess of the proportion most favorable to economy in the process, as well as to entire limpidity and regularity under all states of the water, and as the reservoir facilities in this region will have to be increased to meet the growing demands of the city, it is contemplated to construct two additional filter beds at this place.

Mr. Duncan is of opinion that an average of one-half cubic foot of water per square foot of sand surface per hour should never be exceeded, and that a better rule would be to limit it to one-third cubic foot of water per hour.   The first is equivalent to 75 imperial gallons per square foot of surface per diem, and the second to 50 imperial gallons.

From the two clear water basins (c, c, on the sketch) a 44-inch pipe, 23½ miles in length, carries the filtered water to the Kensington reservoir in Liverpool.

This reservoir stands 225 feet above tide, or 157 feet below the clear-water basins at Rivington. The pipe is relieved in its course by three "balancing reservoirs," so called ; small basins where the water delivers into air, and the aggregate pressure due to the difference of level of the extreme points is thus divided. The distances of these relieving basins from the Rivington basins, and their heights above tide, are as follows :—

	DISTANCE.	HEIGHT ABOVE TIDE.
Aspell Moor	3 miles.	375 feet.
Mountrey House.....................	11 "	328 "
Prescott	17 "	280 "

From the Prescott basin the town of Prescott is supplied with water. A supplementary main of 24 inches diameter is also carried from this basin to Liverpool.

The Kensington reservoir is a covered reservoir with a capacity of 17 million gallons. There are besides four other covered reservoirs at different points of the city, deriving their waters from the 44-inch main, or from the Kensington reservoir. These have a joint storage capacity of 9 millions, so that, with the Kensington reservoir the reserve in store in the immediate neighborhood of the city may be said to be equal to two days' supply at the present rate of consumption. At the Audly street reservoir there is a pumping engine delivering water into an iron tank there, situated 80 feet above the level of the Kensington reservoir. This tank has a capacity of 250,000 gallons, and commands certain pieces of high ground which are not controlled by the other reservoirs.

This great city is very inadequately supplied with water at present, and looking to its rapid growth, the means hitherto depended on hardly admit of such an extension as will satisfy its future wants. The city will probably be driven to seek a sufficient supply in the mountains of North Wales, as suggested by Mr. Duncan and other engineers ; but until the proper sources of supply can be determined on, and until it can be made available, considerable additions will have to be made to the present works to meet the current requirements of the place.

I am indebted to Mr. Thomas Duncan, the Engineer of the Liverpool Water Works, for the information which I have sketched above, and for the facilities afforded me to understand and examine the works.

EDINBURGH WATER WORKS.

EDINBURGH, *July and August*, 1866.

The water for the supply of the City of Edinburgh is derived from the northern slopes of the Pentland Hills, a mountain range lying to the south and south-west of the city. The Water Company supplies from the same sources the adjoining suburban towns of Leith, Newhaven, and Portobello.

The greater part of the water is derived from springs, but a certain portion of it is obtained from the small mountain brooks of the same district. This last portion is withdrawn from storage reservoirs, constructed in the valleys of these brooks to collect that portion of the flood waters which would otherwise run to waste. A determined quantity of the flood water thus stored up is measured out to the brooks day by day throughout the year, as compensation to the mill owners below for the springs and that fraction of the brook water which is applied to city use; hence they have been called compensation reservoirs, although, with three exceptions, they serve at the same time as storage and settling reservoirs for that portion of the brook water made use of for the city.

The three exceptional reservoirs alluded to are strictly " compensation reservoirs," so called because waters stored in them are applied solely to the use of the mill owners, no portion of it being drawn off for city use ; their names will be given further on.

The mill owners are thus in reality benefited by what at first sight would appear to be their loss. In other words, the Water Company furnishes the capital necessary to store up their surplus mechanical power and render it available in low stages of the water, and the mill owners in return pay the Company in kind, that is with a certain measure of water, whether from springs or otherwise ; in the last three cases, solely from the springs of the district in which these reservoirs are situated.

The history of the Edinburgh Works, which are the growth of four separate stages of construction, is very interesting. It will be found detailed in a pamphlet by Mr. Alexander Ramsay, the Manager, printed in 1865. I give here only the leading features as of interest in connection with the filtering works, and to some extent explanatory of their origin and necessity.

The first stage of the works of the present Water Company, and the most interesting, as standing first in perfection of design and character in Great Britain, at the time of its conception, was completed in 1822, when the city became thus for a time abundantly supplied with pure mountain water.

The water was obtained from that portion of the valley of Glencorse brook which lies within the Pentland range. The valley is narrow here, and bounded with steep mountain slopes.

A very copious spring, called the Crawley Spring, occurs at the mouth of the valley. This spring, which discharges very regularly an average of at least 60 cubic feet per minute, delivered its water into the Glencorse brook, and rendered the flow of that brook, to that extent at least, very reliable and valuable to the owners of mill property down the stream. The Water Company obtained the right to take this spring, and, in order to compensate the mill owners for its loss, they constructed the Glencorse compensation reservoir, placed about half a mile above the outlet of the spring.

A fountain-house at the outlet of the spring receives its water and serves as a cistern, with which the pipe which conveys the water to Edinburgh is connected, and from which it is supplied. Into the same fountain-house a certain portion of the hill or Glencorse water, from the reservoir above, is now delivered after filtration. Since the first opening of the works in 1822, the embankment of the Glencorse reservoir has been twice raised, and the storage capacity of the reservoir largely increased. The right to use a portion of the reservoir water for the city followed these enlargements.

From this point an underground drain was run up the valley a short distance, crossing and keeping close to the channel of the brook. The object of this drain was to secure the water of another spring, as well as to gather a portion of the brook water filtered through the gravel which intervened between the brook channel and the tunnel. The tunnel, however, when the brook was small did not deliver enough, and when it was in flood did not deliver the water clear. To correct the last-mentioned difficulty, the channel of the brook has been since diverted away from the line of the underground tunnel, which still, however, collects as well the waters of the small springs referred to.

The pipe which conveys the water to Edinburgh is 8 miles in length (42,240 feet), and varies from 20 to 15 inches in diameter. It delivers its water directly into the distributing pipes of the city, its governing pressure, however, being limited by the altitude of a cistern on the Castle Hill of Edinburgh, with which it is connected, and into which its surplus water overflows. At present the Crawley water does not rise to the level of this cistern during the day, but during the night hours, when the consumption of the city is at its minimum, it overflows into this cistern, and with the pipe mains from other quarters of the Pentland range, restores to the cistern what has been drawn off from it during the day. The other pipes communicating in the same way with this cistern are the Comiston, the Swanston, and the Colington pipes. The cistern holds 27 feet of water when full. Its capacity is about 1,542,000 imperial gallons. The Castle Hill cistern (a small covered reservoir) is situated 225 feet below the fountainhead at Glencorse, and 320 feet above tide. The Engineer calculated that the pipe would deliver 253½ cubic feet per minute. The delivery now is given as equal to 253 cubic feet per minute.

At the opening of the Works, in 1822, this quantity was not needed in Edinburgh, but when it became necessary it was ascertained that during certain exceptional seasons of rain fall (more especially 1842) it could not be obtained. The Glencorse reservoir was found then insufficient to supply at the same time, the amount of water deliverable to the millers (130 cubic feet per minute at that time), and the wants of the city. Indeed, for a short period, the millers were entirely deprived of their portion, and the city supply reduced to 80 cubic feet per minute.

The reservoir at that time had a capacity, when full, of about 30,000,000 cubic feet. The drainage area, applicable to Glencorse reservoir, amounts to 3,694 acres.

To remedy the defects above mentioned, the dam of this reservoir was further increased in height, and its capacity increased, and a new storage reservoir was constructed further up the valley, called Loganlea reservoir. The drainage area was not modified by this process, but the ability to store up the flood waters was largely increased. The present capacities of these reservoirs are as follows :

> The Glencorse reservoir,................55,000,000 cubic feet.
> The Loganlea reservoir,................19,000,000   "   "
>
> Total,..............74,000,000 cubic feet.

The Crawley spring must be in part derived from the same drainage area.

In ordinary years of rain fall the whole of the flood water is not collected by these reservoirs. On the contrary, a very large portion still runs to waste ; but even this portion of the flood water is rendered more valuable to the millers by the existence of the reservoirs, inasmuch as these lakes modify importantly the time of its delivery, distributing their surplus flood waters over days instead of hours.

In 1863, when the rain fall was 39.3 inches, the amount wasted over Glencorse waste weir, as ascertained by daily gaugings, was 254 millions cubic feet, being 45 per cent. of the rain fall of that year. On the other hand, I have been informed, that during at least one year of very low rain fall, the Glencorse reservoir has not been quite filled, showing that during that year the whole of the flood water was utilized.

Mr. Ramsay, in his paper on the rain fall of the Glencorse district, gives the amounts delivered to the city and to the millers, from the reservoir, as equal to the following inches of rain fall :

1. Appropriated to town supply,.............. 8.150 inches.
2. In supply to mills,........................ 7.071 "

Total utilized by the reservoir,........... 15.22 inches.

The surplus of any rain fall over these figures is one part lost by evaporation and absorption, and the residue, if any, passed over the waste weir into the Glencorse burn. The amount passed over the waste weir, in 1863, Mr. Ramsay makes equivalent to 18.964 inches of rain, and the portion lost by absorption and evaporation as 5.115 inches, stating that the ground was maintained very moist throughout that year, in which, consequently, the loss represented by the 5.1 inches would be due mainly to evaporation.

The waste weir of the reservoir is sixty feet wide. The water passing over it after very heavy rains, the reservoir being full, occasionally reaches to 12 inches in depth. On one occasion of unusually severe rain fall, when some bridges were carried away on other streams, the depth flowing over the waste weir rose to 24 inches.

The pipe from the Crawley fountain-head delivers now its full complement of water, consisting of :

From Crawley spring,............. 60 cubic feet per minute.
From Glencorse brook, through its
    reservoir, ...: 193   "   "

Total to the city,............. 253   "   "

The water delivered to the millers
    since the construction of the Logan-
    lea reservoir amounts to a uniform
    rate of....................... 220   "   "

Total,.................... 473 cubic feet per minute.

The reservoirs are responsible for the delivery of this quantity, estimated by Mr. Ramsay as equivalent to 15.22 inches of the yearly rain fall. That portion of the water drawn from the reservoir for city use is filtered.

When the Glencorse reservoir is full, the water for the city is drawn off by means of a pipe whose mouth is situated 20 feet below high water of the reservoir, while the portion of water deliverable to the millers is drawn off lower down, at a point 53 feet below full water of the reservoir. With the reservoir full, the water within control of the city pipe is clear and could be used without filtration, except as filtration benefits river water, under any circumstances, by depriving it of the floating organisms before referred to. When, however, the reservoir water has fallen below the mouth of the pipe alluded to, the portion required for the city is drawn from the same low point, as that delivered to the millers, and that point being near the bottom, the water is liable to pass off there more or less turbid. Under this condition of things the filters become specially necessary to remove the sedimentary discoloration.

There are three filter beds in the bottom of the valley, situated a short distance below the reservoir embankment. Through the kindness of the Engineer, Mr. Leslie, I am enabled to give the details of construction of these filter beds, and I refer to the accompanying sketch as explanatory of these. (Plate XV.)

When a filter bed is bare the water is let on from six pipes, each controlled by a stopcock. The surface of the sand is waved, so that the water rises upon the bed without producing any sensible current on the sand. When the water has to be drawn off for cleansing the filter bed, the waste pipe enables the attendant to draw off directly the lower and most turbid portion of the water.

The reservoir has not been so low for some years as to deliver turbid water; the filter beds are not cleansed (according to the attendant), except at long intervals, at present not oftener than once in six months. The attendants assume that from the apparent purity of the water there is little or nothing to intercept, but in this I believe them to be mistaken. The difference in level between the water on the filter beds and the water in the clear-water well, said to be four feet at the time of my visit, showed that the surface of the sand was more or less choked, since with clean sand a head of twelve inches would have passed the water through the filters. The fact that the water had at several times broken through the filtering materials into the drains below was evidence in the same direction. The sand of the filter beds was all but choked on its surface, and an unusual head became necessary to force the water through, which would tend to break into well-holes at the weakest spots.

The materials of the beds are as follows :—

Fine sand.............................	18 inches.
Coarse sand...........................	6 "
Shells................................	6 "
Fine gravel...........................	6 "
Coarse gravel.........................	18 to 24 inches.

This is the depth of material over the collecting drain, which is 18 inches deep by 24 wide, and surrounded by coarse gravel. From the collecting drain six clay pipes of 6 inches diameter each extend on either side to the foot of the slope. The collecting drain carries the water to a measuring well, where the proper amount passes off to the Crawley fountain-house for the city supply. The usual depth of water over the filter beds is four feet. It was from 4½ to 5 feet at the time of my visit.

The sand surface of each of these filter beds measures 90 × 90 feet, equal to

8,100 superficial feet. There are, therefore, 24,300 square feet in three filters. The amount deliverable by the Edinburgh pipe is limited to 253 cubic feet per minute, but of this amount, 173 to 193 cubic feet only is receivable from the reservoir, equal to at most 2,078,974 U. S. gallons per diem ; the remaining 60 to 80 c. feet of spring water is received below the position of the filter beds. The maximum rate of filtration, then, with the three filters in use, would be 85½ U. S. gallons per square foot per diem. With but two filters in use during the time that the third is being cleansed, the rate of filtration would reach 128 U. S. gallons per square foot per diem.

The portion of the Edinburgh supply derived from the Glencorse valley consists thus of one part of spring water and three parts of filtered brook water. The actual supply to Edinburgh now from all sources, as well as its progressive increase, will be understood from the following table obtained from Mr. Ramsay's paper and descriptions.

	Population supplied.	Imperial Gallons per head.	Delivery, cubic feet per Minute.
1842	166,878	13.41	249.5
1848	185,806	22.21	460.06
1852	195,984	23.74	518.68
1856	199,782	25.17	560.40
1862	207,381	30.38	702.30
1863	208,647	31.20	731.80
1869	220,000	40.	992.00

The additional works under construction in 1866, and completed in 1868, have increased the supply to 992 cubic feet per minute ; this is equal to 8,900,894 imperial gallons, or 10,685,770 U. S. gallons per diem.

The cost of the works was given by Mr. Ramsay, in 1866, at £500,000, equal to two and a half million of dollars in specie.

The amounts of population given above include Leith, Portobello, and the village of Newhaven. The returns of 1861 give their respective populations as follows :

Edinburgh	163,121
Leith	33,628
Portobello	4,366
Newhaven, not given, probably	2,000
	203,115

Without attempting to trace the separate constructions in their order, which have produced the progressive increase in the supply, I will here give the names of all the springs and reservoirs belonging to this Water Company.

SPRINGS.

NAME OF SPRING.	Average Yield in cubic feet per Minute.	Brought in Year.
1. Crawley Spring..:..............	60 to 80	1822
2. Bavelaw Springs...............		
3. Liston Shiels Springs...........	150	1847
4. Black Springs.................		
5. Colycum Springs...............	200	1858
6. Crosswood Springs.............	70	1868

RESERVOIRS.

NAME.	Capacity, cubic feet.	Rate of Delivery to Mill Owners, cubic feet per Minute.	Applied to City use.
1. Glencorse...........	55,000,000	220	193
4. Logan Lea.........	19,000,000		
2. Threepmuir........	33,000,000	All.	
3. Harlaw............	26,000,000	All.	.
5. Bonaly	8,000,000	.	Overplus.
6. Chubbiedean.......	10,000,000	60	Overplus.
7. Torduff...........	19,000,000		Overplus.
8.	85,000,000	All.	
9. Crosswood.........	25,000,000	All.	

The covered cistern on the Castle Hill receives all these waters, and commands by its height all the dwellings within the city, with the exception of the castle and a few houses in its vicinity. It is capable, when full, of holding about one million and a half imperial gallons.

To meet the wants of the houses at the head of the High street, and the dwellings within the Castle limits, an iron cistern has been placed upon the highest ground of the Castle rock, capable of holding 100,000 imperial gallons.

13

This cistern is in two divisions; the one applicable to the Castle buildings, the other to the highest buildings outside of the Castle. This cistern is filled by the Swanston pipe.

At Torduff there are three filter beds, designed to filter the brook water collected on that side of the Pentland slopes. It is but rarely, however, that there is occasion to use them, the water drawn off from the reservoirs in that vicinity being very rarely discolored by sedimentary or other foreign matters.

The relation of these new reservoirs to their respective drainage areas, and the percentage of rain fall which can be gathered and depended on will, it is hoped, be communicated to the public at some future time.

The original works, then confined to the Glencorse valley, as well as their first enlargement, were designed by Mr. James Jardone, a man whom all engineers agree to honor, and constructed under his immediate superintendence. The subsequent enlargements have been made under the immediate directions of Mr. James Leslie; Messrs. Rendall and Beardmore having in one case been joined with him as Parliamentary Engineers. Mr. Leslie is at present the Engineer of the Company.

DUBLIN WATER WORKS.

DUBLIN, *August*, 1866.

The city of Dublin receives its supply of water at present from two canals, which terminate on tide water here, and from the river Dodler, by an open conduit. The river Liffey runs through the centre of the city, and at present receives its sewerage, but does not contribute to its water supply. The north side of the city is supplied from the Royal Canal, and the south side from the Grand Canal and from the Dodler water lead. All these sources of supply are said to be exposed to a variety of polltiuons; they will be entirely dispensed with when the works now under construction are completed.*

The population to be supplied by the new water works is estimated at 304,000. The consumption of water at present is said not to exceed six million gallons daily.

The new works have been under construction during the last four years, and are expected to be sufficiently completed this season to admit of the introduction of the new water. This supply is to be drawn from the upper branches of the river Vartry, a clear mountain stream, whose sources are found on the southern slopes of the great Sugar Loaf mountain, and the eastern slopes of the Djouce mountain. The rocks of this region are granite, mica-schist, and a very hard clay slate, and the water is stated to be very soft in character. The ground was selected by Mr. Hawkshaw, and the scheme is founded upon his general plans. The works are being constructed under the directions of Mr. Parke Neville, the Engineer to the Corporation of Dublin.

These new works consist of a large collecting reservoir in the valley of the Vartry, a system of filter beds near to this reservoir, two distributing reservoirs within five miles of Dublin, and the pipe mains connecting the collecting reservoir with the distributing reservoirs and with the city.

The collecting reservoir, named the Roundwood reservoir, is distant 25 miles from the city of Dublin. An embankment has been formed across the valley of the Vartry here, 66 feet in depth at the deepest point, and about 2,000 feet in length. The embankment is 28 feet wide at the top, with a slope of 3 to 1 on the inside, and of 2½ to 1 on the outside of the bank. The inside is pitched with dry

---

* April, 1869, they are now completed and in use.

stone, 18 inches thick at top, and 12 inches at the foot of the slope. The pitching rests upon a bed of small stone, 12 inches thick. An arched tunnel (14x14) founded on the solid rock passes through the bank. A stone screen or piece of solid masonry, 20 feet thick, built within and across the tunnel, separates the water end of this tunnel from the land end. Two pipe mains pass through this screen; one of 33-inch diameter, and one of 48-inch. The 33-inch main is connected with a water tower situated inside the reservoir, having three pipe connections through the tower, at the heights of 10, 20, and 30 feet from its high water. The 48-inch pipe commands the lowest point of the reservoir and forms a waste pipe to admit of the water being drawn off to bottom if required. In any emergency requiring a rapid discharge of the water, the 33-inch pipe, by a branch, can be used in the same way.

Although the 33-inch pipe is the one intended for the service of the filter beds, the 48-inch pipe has a connection with it, by which the water from the lower portion of the reservoir can as well be delivered to the filter beds, when necessary.

At the lower end of the tunnel there are two valves on the 33-inch pipe, and one valve on the 48-inch pipe. The 33-inch valve is divided into two slides or plates, the 48-inch valve into three slides. Each of these slides works independent of the other. The force required to move them is thus very much reduced, and they are more under command and more easily kept in good condition than the ordinary single disk valves. The greatest depth of water in the reservoir when full will be sixty feet. The water area of the reservoir is 409 acres. It is calculated to hold 2,400 million imperial gallons of water. A waste weir of 300 feet in length carries off any surplus water, delivering it by means of a by-wash into the Vartry valley below, over a rock slope and entirely clear of the works.

The drainage area commanded by this reservoir measures 13,992 acres, or 22 square miles nearly. No observations had been made of the rain fall within this region previous to the construction of the works. Observations made since their commencement give the following averages over this area:

1861	60.87 inches.
1862	60.48 "
1863	44.85 "
1864	48.39 "
1865	"

In the narrow valley immediately below the embankment the filter beds are placed. The 33-inch main from the reservoir is carried into a circular basin 88 feet in diameter. Whatever the height of the water in the reservoir, the water in this basin can always be maintained at a uniform height by adjusting the tunnel valve accordingly. From this circular basin the water is carried by two open drains to the filter beds, connecting with each by a pipe and stopcock. There are seven filter beds, the positions and arrangement of which will be understood by reference to the accompanying sketch (Plate 16). At the time of my visit (August, 1866) one of the filter beds was completed ; on another the filtering materials were being deposited and arranged, the others were in various stages of construction, but not quite so far advanced. There are two open basins for the reception of the water after filtration. The two basins when full will hold 2,730,000 gallons. Three of the filter beds lie on the south side of these basins, and four on the north side.

Each of the filter beds communicates with the one or the other of these basins by a passage which can be sluiced off at discretion. The bottom of each filter bed, when not solid rock, is puddled with a layer of clay puddle two feet thick. The sides are sloped at 1 to 1, with 9-inch dry pitching. The materials of the filters are as follows :

Sand	30	inches.
Fine gravel, pea size	6	"
Coarse gravel, nut size	6	"
Broken stone, 3-inch ring	6	"
Clean quarry spauls, 5 to 8 inch	30	"
	78	inches.

The quarry spauls rest on the puddle. Resting on the puddle and imbedded in the layer of large stones last mentioned, are two dry stone drains (30x24 each) to collect the filtered water. These are united at one end, as shown in the sketch.

Each filter bed measures 213x115 feet at top of its slopes. At the surface of the sand it measures 203x105. The sand area of each is therefore 21,315 square feet. The depth of water over the filter bed is limited to 24 inches. Six of these filters are supposed to be always serviceable, the seventh undergoing the process of cleansing.

Although the amount of water used in the city now does not exceed six million gallons, the character of the Vartry water is so superior to that of the canal water in use now, that the consumption will in all probability reach nine millions shortly after the completion of the works.

With six of the filter beds in use (127,890 square feet), and a consumption of nine million gallons per diem, the rate of filtration would be 70 gallons per square foot of sand surface per diem. With a consumption of twelve millions the rate would be 93 gallons per square foot per diem.

The ample receiving reservoirs at Stillorgan will enable the filter beds to be operated continuously night and day. The large size of the collecting reservoir will insure great freedom from sediment at its lower end, for probably the first 30 feet of its water. From that level downwards the water may be expected to be rendered more or less turbid by floods. The filter beds are intended to be used during all stages of the water; but when the reservoir is full their duty will be mainly confined to the separation of floating organic matters, vegetable or animal. All vegetable fibre, seeds, small fish, and the water insects upon which they feed, are intercepted by the filters, and this forms a very important part of their duty during the summer stages of all rivers. When the reservoir gets low and the water becomes turbid from floods, the filter beds will be more severely taxed.

The city pipe main which conveys the water to the tunnel below (hereafter mentioned) has an independent connection with each of the pure water basins, marked C C on the sketch. It has also a connection with the reservoir pipe, to admit of the water, if needful, being passed on directly to the city without filtration.

The height of the full water of the reservoir is 692 feet above ordnance datum (which assumed base is the level of low water of a 12-foot tide in Dublin harbor). The height of the water in the pure water basins will be about 620 feet above the same datum, and 518 feet above the highest street in Dublin. From the pure water basin a 42-inch pipe, 2,100 feet in length, conducts the water to a tunnel 4,367 yards in length, which passes through a mountain spur here of hard gneiss rock. At the lower end of the tunnel there is a relieving basin and measuring weir, where the water for the supply of the city can be gauged daily. This basin or tank is 606 feet above ordnance datum.

From the tank a 33-inch main conveys the water to the distributing reservoirs at Stillorgan.

The length of this main is 16¾ miles, and the height of the first of the two distributing reservoirs above datum is 274 feet.

From the tunnel tank to the distributing reservoir there is, therefore, a fall of 332 feet.

The 33-inch pipe follows the irregularities of the intervening ground. To relieve it, however, from the great pressure to which it would otherwise be subject, it opens to the air at three intermediate points on its length, situated respectively 473, 414, and 341 feet above the ordnance datum. At each of these points there is a small open basin, into which the pipe delivers. From the opposite side of the basin a mouth-piece, with stopcock and self-acting valve attached, delivers the water into the next section of the pipe. Under this arrangement, each section of the pipe is subjected only to the pressure which prevails between two of these small tanks or basins.

The 33-inch pipes are cast in lengths of 12 feet 5 inches, and are of eight different weights, the least corresponding with a thickness of $\frac{7}{8}$ inch, and the heaviest with a thickness of $1\frac{1}{4}$ inch, the intermediates varying by sixteenths, viz. :

Inch.	cwt.	qrs.	lbs.	lbs.
$\frac{7}{8}$	34	2	0	3,864
$\frac{15}{16}$	36	3	0	4,116
1	39	0	16	4,384
$1\frac{1}{16}$	41	2	0	4,640
$1\frac{1}{8}$	44	0	0	4,928
$1\frac{3}{16}$	46	2	0	5,208
$1\frac{1}{4}$	48	3	8	5,468
$1\frac{5}{16}$	51	1	0	5,740

At Stillorgan there are two distributing reservoirs; the one situated 274 feet, and the other 271 feet above the common datum. The water of the lower reservoir stands 191 feet above the highest ground in the city. The two reservoirs have a water area of 18 acres, and a capacity, when full, of about 110 million imperial gallons.

Two pipe mains, of 27 inches diameter each, convey the water over a distance of $4\frac{3}{4}$ miles to Dublin.

The works, when finished, are estimated to cost about £460,000 (equal to about $2,280,000 in gold). The supply which they can control in the present state will not exceed, so far as I can judge, a rate of from 12 to 14 million gallons per diem.

I am indebted to a descriptive pamphlet by Mr. Neville, and to the Resident Engineer, Mr. Pallas (who accompanied me over the works), for much of the information given above.

PERTH WATER WORKS.

NATURAL FILTER.

The city of Perth lies on the right bank of the river Tay, a large and rapid stream, whose sources are widely spread on the mountain slopes dividing Perthshire from the counties of Argyle and Inverness. The lochs or lakes Erracht, Rannoch, Tummel, and Tay, gather a portion of its head waters, and act as storage reservoirs to the river, whose channel, in the driest months of summer, must on this account be more than usually well supplied with fine water.

The mountain slopes referred to are mostly composed of gneiss granite, and mica slate, and the waters shed from them are soft and pure accordingly.

Near the lower boundary of the city the upper end of a long island in the river, composed entirely of gravel, has been taken advantage of to construct what is called a natural filter. The island referred to leans towards the left bank of the Tay, leaving, as the accompanying sketch shows, but a small channel between it and the main land on that side. The main channel of the river passes between the island and the city.

On the island above mentioned an underground tunnel has been constructed, situated parallel with the river shore and about 100 feet from it.

The bottom of this tunnel, as near as I could learn, is about 30 inches below the low summer water of the Tay. The length is 300 feet. For 250 feet of this length the tunnel is 4 feet in width inside, and 8 feet in height. The bottom is not paved, but open to the coarse gravel of which the island is composed.

The side walls are of stone, laid dry. The top is covered with paving stone. This forms the tunnel as originally built. It was afterwards extended 50 feet at its upper end, but the extension was described to me as being only of half the dimensions of the main tunnel. About midway of the tunnel a circular well, 8 feet in diameter, comes to the surface, and forms a man-hole of descent for examination and repairs. From the bottom of this well two lines of 12-inch pipes, each 550 feet in length, proceed, and are laid across the bed of the river to the engine-house well, situated as shown on the sketch. The upper pipe is the only one now in use; the lower one, which had been rendered useless by the construction of the railroad bridge, is now being repaired and made serviceable, the delivery of but one pipe having been found, at certain stages of the river, insufficient to supply adequately the pump well.

At the time of my visit, July, 1866, it was low water of the river, and the stream was within 3 inches of its lowest stage. There was at this time, as near as I could judge, 24 inches of water in the tunnel ;.the draft upon it appeared moderate and the water clear and limpid. The water in the river was not turbid at the time, but it was brownish in color. The water which filters through the island of gravel into the tunnel was stated to be always clear, whatever might be the condition of the river. The Superintendent thought that the draft from it might be doubled without impairing its quality. The difference in level between the surface water of the river and the surface water in the tunnel was stated not to exceed from three to six inches. The gravel and sand, through which the water passes to reach the tunnel, must, therefore, be very free.

The depth of water in the tunnel varies with the level of the water in the river. The city of Perth lies at the head of tide water of the Tay, and the rise of the tide at this place is from 4 to 6 feet, the depth of water in the tunnel corresponding. The water, however, is not brackish here at any stage of the tide, the long and tortuous channel between the sea and this point preventing the salt water from being felt at Perth.

The population of Perth numbers 27,000. The daily supply of water to the city now was stated by the Superintendent to average 200,000 gallons, a very low rate of supply for the population, showing that wells must still be used by many. All of this amount is derived from the filtering tunnel.

If we take the open bottom of this tunnel as the measure of its rate of filtration, which is the usual practice, it gives ($\frac{2,0,0,0,0,0}{1,1,0,0}$) 182 gallons per square foot of bottom per diem ; but the dry stone side walls must increase the effective bottom, say to 6 feet in width instead of 4, giving a rate of 121 per square foot per diem.

We should fear that any great increase of this rate would draw with it sand into the tunnel. The tunnel, however, admits of being lengthened both up stream and down stream, and the supply can consequently be largely increased at discretion.

The filtering tunnel, it will have been understood, is on the left side of the main channel. The engine-house is situated on the right bank of the river, and the connection between the two is made by the 12-inch pipe already mentioned. There are two pumping engines here, and a well to each engine, supplied by the pipe from the filter gallery. This well has not been laid low enough to secure a sufficiently rapid supply to the pumps when the river is low ; the head, then, or the difference of level between the mouth of the pipes in the filter gallery and the bottom of the well, is insufficient. This defect is expected to be remedied by the

14

second pipe. In the engine-house there are two beam engines, with a small fly-wheel to each. These engines have been 35 years in use.

The two engines are of the same pattern. Steam cylinder 24 inches diameter, stroke 36 inches ; pump barrel 10 inches diameter, stroke 36 inches. The pumps are double-acting pumps, with solid pistons, taking water at top and bottom. One of the engines was at work, the other at rest. The engine was making 20 revolutions per minute ; when well supplied with water it makes 26 revolutions. The two engines cannot work together, except at about high water, when the increased flow into the pump well admits of it. Each engine is provided with an air chamber.

A 12-inch pipe main, 5,000 feet in length, proceeds from the pumps to a storage reservoir, the bottom of which is 72 feet above the pump well. The pipe main to the reservoir serves as well for a supply main to the city. During the day, therefore, the engine may be said to be pumping into the city, the reservoir aiding it then, in this respect. During the night hours, the engine pumps into the reservoir, replacing what had been drawn off during the day, and refilling it. The reservoir when full holds 500,000 gallons, equal to two and a half days' supply. Mr. A. Bates is the Superintendent of the Perth Works.

BERLIN WATER WORKS.

PRUSSIA, *May* 17, 1866.

The supply of water for the city of Berlin is derived at present mainly from the river Spree, a tributary of the Elbe, which flows through the centre of the city. The Spree has its sources on the slopes of the northern and western spurs of the Iser Riessen hills, where numerous small lakes store up the surface waters, and must to some extent regulate the flow of the river. The works for the transmission of the waters from the Spree are situated above the city, just outside of the walls, on the right bank of the river. They were executed in 1854–5 by a private company, and the delivery of the water to the city from this source commenced in 1856. The place was previously supplied principally from numerous wells scattered all over the city. Many of these are still in use. The new works, however, which give a constant supply under pressure all over the city, admitting of the water being delivered into the highest stories of the houses, have already largely displaced the old mode of supply.

The city possesses as yet no general system of sewerage, and from the numerous cesspools which at present exist, more or less leakage must escape and contaminate the waters of the wells. At present there are no public fountains (other than the well pumps) whence the poor, as in most continental cities, can obtain water free.

The works referred to consist of 8 pumping engines, a system of filtering works, and a small storage reservoir, situated on a hillock to the north-west, about $3\frac{1}{2}$ miles from the pumping station, and about one mile outside of the city wall. The pumping engines are in pairs, each pair being connected with a fly-wheel. They are double-acting beam engines, each engine working two pumps. In the four pumping engines first constructed the two pumps referred to are of unequal diameter and of unequal stroke, the diameter of the pump barrels being respectively 38 and $21\frac{1}{2}$ inches, the stroke 32 and 36 inches. The large barrel is used for the delivery of the river water to the filter beds, and their connecting basin, under a pressure not exceeding 20 feet; the small barrel was used for the delivery of the filtered water into the city under a varying pressure of 90 to 120 feet, averaging during the day by the gauge 110 feet.

In the four pumping engines last constructed, the two pumps to each engine are of equal diameter and equal stroke, viz., $24\frac{1}{2}$ inches diameter and 36 inches stroke. These last engines are at present used solely for the high service, the first engines being now confined to the low service and worked with the small or high service pump disconnected. They are in a condition, however, to be used as before, if required. The pumps are all double-acting plunger and bucket pumps. The boiler-house contains twelve boilers of the Cornish pattern. The length of each boiler is 30 feet, the diameter of the shell 58 inches, and the diameter of the flue 30 inches.

The amount of water delivered from these works into the city was stated to average 750,000 cubic feet per diem, equal to 5,610,400 U. S. gallons.

The population of Berlin was given in 1863 as 455,000. It is supposed to exceed 500,000 now. If we take but 300,000 as deriving their supply of water directly or indirectly from these works, it gives a rate per head per diem of about 19 U. S. gallons, a very low rate for a city of this character. It was stated to me, however, at the office of the Water Works, that for that portion of the population actually paying for the water, the rate per head averaged 22 imperial gallons throughout the year, much exceeding this rate in the hottest summer months.

The want of a system of sewerage must discourage the free use of the water, and the floating baths in the river must to some extent take the place of house baths.

The pumping engines work directly into the city mains, but the small reservoir already mentioned, and the stand-pipe alongside of it, operate to control and regulate the pressure upon the city. The stand-pipe is double-legged, and the legs are connected at four points, each connection, except the highest, being controlled by a stopcock. The highest connection is 200 feet above the pump well of the engine-house, the lowest about 115, and the others intermediate. The water of the small reservoir, when full, stands at about 110 feet above the pump well. The highest connection does not seem to be used. The water, and therefore the pressure, cannot rise above the connection which happens to be open, as the overflow escapes thus by the down leg into the reservoir. When that is full the pumps are stopped, and the reservoir is left to supply the city. (See sketch of stand-pipe on Plate XVIII.)

The capacity of the reservoir does not exceed one-third of the daily supply ; it is, under the ordinary working of the engine, filled every day, and meets four to five hours of the night consumption, allowing the pumping engines this extent of intermission from constant work.

The surface of this great city is remarkably regular in plane, the difference in the level of any one point from another, as we were informed by the Engineer, not exceeding 15 feet.

The filter works, as originally arranged, comprised one settling basin, four filter beds, and one open basin for the reception of the filtered water. As now applied, the settling basin A on the accompanying sketch is not considered necessary as such ; it is nevertheless kept full, and forms a reserve of river water, permitting the filter beds (to the extent of the capacity of the clear-water basins) to operate and deliver when the pumps are at rest.

There are now six filter beds, the original clear-water basin having been formed into two filter beds. These are marked B 1, B 2, B 3, B 4, B 5, and B 6. A new and small clear-water basin, arched over, has been built between the filter beds and the pump-house (C), forming the clear-water well of the high service engines. This small basin has a capacity, I judge, of about one million U. S. gallons.

The entire area of the filter beds, by my calculation, comprises 211,600 square feet, but as there are but four in operation at once, the area in use does not exceed 145,400 square feet.

All the water delivered to the city passes through the filter beds ; at the rate of delivery given above, of 750,000 cubic feet in 24 hours, the flow through the filter beds is equal to 39 U. S. gallons nearly per square foot of their surface per diem. As the clear-water basin is not large enough to secure a continuous flow when the pumps are not at work, its capacity not being equal to one-third of the capacity of the reserve basin A, the actual movement through the filter beds during the day hours probably reaches 75 gallons, and in the hot summer months must exceed 100. New filter beds are about being constructed, and I understood the Engineer to say that the existing ones were sometimes taxed to a rate of more than ½ cubic foot per square foot per hour (equal to 89¾ U. S. gallons per square foot per 24 hours), a limit which, in his opinion, should never be exceeded.

Of the two filter beds which I have considered as in disuse (except in winter), the one was being cleansed, and the other was being drained of its water preparatory to undergoing the cleansing process ; this process consists in the removal of a thin layer of the surface sand, which, after being thoroughly washed, is replaced and used over again.

The refilling of an empty filter bed with water, which in all cases is an operation of some delicacy, is effected here by filling it from below. An air pipe, connected with each central drain, helps to relieve it from air. The filling from below is the safest for the filter bed, if filtered water is used for this purpose. The filtering materials here consist of sand, gravel, and small boulder stones. These small stones, which lie on the bottom of the filter bed, serve the purpose of permitting the water to reach a small culvert placed along the centre line of the filter bed, which collects and conveys the filtered water to the proper pipe outside, by which it is carried to the clear-water basin. There are no perforated pipes in the bottom of these filters to perform this duty. A layer of coarse gravel lies over the stones, and prevents the sand from reaching and filling up

their interstices. The sand is 3 feet in thickness, consisting of a layer of coarse
sand, 6 inches thick, over the gravel ; a layer of less coarse sand, 12 inches
thick, over this last, and the surface layer of fine sand, 18 inches thick. I was
unable to ascertain the separate thicknesses of the gravel and small stones, but
the entire filtering material is stated to be 58 inches in depth. The depth of
water over the filter beds is from 4½ to 5 feet. During certain months of summer the entire filtering surface is cleansed once a week, the separate beds being
taken in rotation, day by day.

When the low service pumps are in action, the river water is pumped
directly upon the filter beds, without any previous process of settlement. The
water does not carry, it is said, sufficient sediment to render such a process
necessary in this locality. The stream is very sluggish in its velocity, being
held back by locks for the purpose of navigation.

There are, besides, certain small lakes on its course, not far above the
works, through which its waters flow before reaching the city. For these causes
the stream, for miles above the city, becomes an effective settling reservoir,
where everything like palpable sediment subsides, except in extreme cases,
before reaching the locality of the pumping works. The shallow ponds and
lakes referred to communicate to the water a dark vegetable tinge. The water
of the river opposite to the filter beds is clearer than the Mississippi water of
midsummer, after it has undergone 36 hours settlement. The filtering process
clarifies the water from the faint sedimentary tinge, which still remains, and
also separates from it considerable vegetable impurity, which in summer is
carried along with it.

The long and severe winters here made especial care and precaution necessary in the use of filters during the months of severe frost. The filter beds cannot be laid bare in midwinter, for the frost would in that case penetrate the
body of the filter and render it useless. All the filters are, in consequence,
during the winter months, kept constantly covered with their maximum depth
of water, four feet. Luckily the river water during the winter months is in its
best state as regards freedom from turbidity, and also as regards freedom from
vegetable discoloration or impurity. The filters, therefore, have, comparatively
little to intercept, and, the river water is flowed continuously upon them, and
passes through them without very sensibly impairing their efficiency. To make
provision, however, for an unusually long winter, or for an exceptional condition of the river then, which may occasionally occur, it is evident that a larger
filtering surface is desirable than would be necessary in a milder climate.

The ice forms upon the filter beds 15 inches thick, and sometimes,
though rarely, 24 inches thick. To protect the enclosing walls of each filter
from damage, the ice is kept separated from the walls, 6 to 12 inches, by
attendants appointed to that duty, and so long as the cake of ice is kept float-

ing in this way, the masonry is safe from any damage by its thrust. That this service has been well performed is demonstrated by the condition of the walls which are in the best of order, and no where out of line, or abraded, that I could perceive.

The containing walls are nearly vertical on their faces, and it is evident that for such a climate vertical walls must be more convenient as regards ice, than the slope walls which usually have place in such works. The protection of the filter beds from the severe frosts of a northern climate seems in this case to have been very efficiently managed.

Cast-iron pipes deliver the water upon the filters, one branch to each filter, controlled by a stopcock.

The present Engineer and Manager of the works is Mr. Henry Gill, to whom I am indebted for access to the works, and for much courtesy in affording me such information as I sought to obtain. As a commercial enterprise the works have proved very successful.

HAMBURG WATER WORKS.

HAMBURG, *May,* 1866.

SETTLING RESERVOIRS—NO FILTRATION.

The water supply of Hamburg is derived from the river Elbe.. The city is situated on the right bank of the river, about 50 miles from the sea. The population was given me as 200,000. In 1860 the population of the city proper was 134,022, and of its faubourgs, 44,661, or for both, 178,683.

The sources of the Elbe lie principally on the northern slopes of the Bohmer Wald hills, but the southern slopes of the Erz hills and of the Iser Riessen hills also shed their waters into the Elbe.

These groups enclose the basin in the centre of which lies the city of Prague. ' From this upland region the river flows towards the sea through an immense alluvial plain, richly cultivated. At Hamburg the river is but slightly turbid, except when it comes down in flood. It is, however, as seen in mass, dark and cloudy, even when not in flood, and passing, as it does, for the larger part of its course, through the rich agricultural region of country alluded to, it gathers besides a certain amount of vegetable impurity, which becomes palpable in the settling basins, and prejudices the character of the water.

The works for the supply of Hamburg with water are situated on the bank of the Elbe, about two miles above the city. At this place there are three set-·tling basins, with a fourth just about completed. These basins are filled at discretion from the river. They are each connected with the river by a pipe or conduit, having the necessary stopcocks or sluices to shut off or let on, and they are each connected by a separate pipe with the pump well of the pumping engines.

While one of these basins is in communication with the pump well and being drawn off, one of the other two is full and at rest, and the third one is being filled, or also at rest, as the filling process may happen or not to be completed.

When these works were finished, in 1848, it was supposed that the capacities of the basins would admit of the water in each remaining at rest 7 to 8 days before being drawn off, and that during this time it would become clarified, by subsidence, of all the impurities held in suspension. The clarification may have been comparatively satisfactory under the early circumstances upon which the works were predicated. It is not so now, however.

The consumption of water in the city has increased rapidly, while the capacities of the settling basins have not been increased in the same proportion. The basins hold each now from 2 to 2½ days' supply, according to the season of the year, and this was acknowledged to be insufficient to clarify the water when the river came down in flood. When I visited the works, in May, 1866, the river stood three feet above its low water zero ; the water was not in flood, and, though discolored, it carried but a slight amount of sediment in suspension.

The water was improved by the time allowed it for settlement in the settling basins, but it was not rendered limpid, and a considerable amount of vegetable growth was visible in the bottoms of the basins, and the vegetable froth of the river was gathered in knots on the surface.

The Engineer of the works informed me that they would probably convert part of their space into filtering basins by and by, instead of enlarging the capacities of these basins, to render the process of subsidence alone efficient. The Engineer who designed these works had in view their availability for such a contingency, as the growth of the city and further experience might indicate its advisability.

The depth of water in these basins averages 12 feet. Their arrangement will be understood by an inspection of the accompanying sketch. (Plate XIX.)

The superficies of each basin was given me as equal to 220,000 square feet. My own measurements agree with this statement. The capacity of each, according to my calculations, is about 2,400,000 cubic feet.

The basins are of very cheap construction. It was not, indeed, necessary, in this connection, that they should be strictly water-tight. Their water lines are not provided with walls, as at Berlin and Altona, but rest on flat slopes of 2 to 1, defended from the action of the water by loose stones. The water of the Elbe being comparatively clear in midwinter, the basins are probably kept full then, without being drawn down alternately, as in summer. The ice would. otherwise prove very troublesome on these flat slopes. These basins are cleaned out twice a year.

The consumption of the city in 1864 was 396,552,680 cubic feet—equal to 1,086,445 cubic feet Hamburg per diem, which is equivalent to 905,371 cubic feet English, equal to 6,772,667 U. S. gallons per diem. If the population is taken at 200,000, this would give a delivery of 34 U. S. gallons nearly per head per diem.

The pipe distribution of the city is divided into a high and a low service. The low service is constant, and includes the mass of the city. The high service is intermittent, the water being delivered for that service between the hours of 12 P. M. (midnight), and 5 A. M. only. The buildings which receive this

15

high service are, therefore, provided with cisterns, which are filled during the hours mentioned.

There are three Cornish pumping engines at the works. The engine-house is marked *a* on the sketch.

The engines are beam engines, and have each two plunger pumps.

The two engines first built have each the same dimensions. The steam cylinder has an interior diameter of 48 inches, with 8 feet stroke.

The pump nearest the beam centre is of 20 inches diameter, and 5 feet 6 inches stroke; the other 16½ inches diameter, and 8 feet stroke.

The third engine has a steam cylinder of 70 inches diameter and 10 feet stroke; the near pump is 28 inches diameter and 7 feet 6 inches stroke; the other of 24 inches diameter and 10 feet stroke.

A fourth engine is now being built, the engine-house for which is being constructed at *b* on the sketch. In this engine the steam cylinder will have 85 inches diameter, with 11 feet stroke, the near pump to have 28 inches diameter and 8 feet stroke, and the other pump 34 inches diameter and 11 feet stroke.

The three engines now in use works into a stand-pipe, as will the last-mentioned when finished. The stand-pipe has two legs and two connections of these legs at different altitudes. The position of the lower connection is 120 feet above the pump well, that of the upper connection 212 feet. The brick tower which protects and sustains the stand-pipes is 240 feet in height, and 35 feet diameter at the base. A brick chimney, of 5 feet interior diameter, occupies the centre of the tower, and is connected with the boiler-house. The stand-pipes rise on either side of the chimney, and are of 30 inches diameter up to the connection for the lower service, and 20 inches diameter above that point.

During all but the few hours beyond midnight, the lower connection is open, and the engines work each both of their pumps against that head, satisfying then the lower service of the city.

During the hours from midnight to 5 A. M., the lower connection in the stand pipe is closed, and the engines work each one pump against the high service head of 212 feet. The other pump is then working in air, and not thrown out of gear. This arrangement meets the requirements of the two heads very satisfactorily. The engines were in excellent order and evidently well cared for. They were stated to work each 23 hours daily, all the three being required to meet the demands of the city.

There are other two engines belonging to the city, situated upon the river bank, within the city limits. These belonged originally to some other works. They are now held in reserve to meet the contingencies of the excessive consumption of water which occasionally occurs in midsummer, as well as the contingencies of any extraordinary repairs being required upon either of the engines above mentioned. These reserve engines have no settling basins connected with them, and when in use pump the water into the city mains directly from the river.

To meet the requirements of the low service for the city during the five hours when the engines are pumping for the high service, there are three small reservoirs provided, situated at different points within the city, and each at about 100 feet in height above the pump well. These are each arched over, and covered with earth, and contain respectively—

100,000 cubic feet.
100,000   "   "
400,000   "   "
_____
600,000 cubic feet.

The whole when full containing 600,000 cubic feet, or about two-thirds of a day's supply.

These reservoirs are filled daily during the working hours of the pumps for the low service.

The Hamburg Works were constructed after the designs and under the direction of Mr. J. Lindley, Civil Engineer. They commenced the delivery of water in 1849, and have been in successful operation since that date.

I desire to express my obligations to Mon. A. Lienau, the Engineer in charge, for the facilities and information afforded me.

ALTONA WATER WORKS.

ALTONA, *May*, 1866.

The smaller city of Altona lies immediately below the city of Hamburg, and on the same bank of the river Elbe. The population in 1866 was given me as numbering 52,000, in 1860 it was 45,000. It is a thriving and prosperous city, evidently growing rapidly.

Before the construction of the works which now supply the city with water, the inhabitants depended mainly upon wells within the city, many of which are still used by them.

The new works were constructed by a private company, which still retains the management and control of them. The plans were prepared by Mr. T. Hawksley, Civil Engineer, of London. They were completed in 1860, and have proved very satisfactory to the inhabitants, and, as I was informed, remunerative to the Company.

The works comprise as follows : An engine-house and two pumping engines, situated on the river bank, about eight miles below the city ; a system of settling basins and filter basins, situated on the high grounds to the north of the engine-house ; a small reservoir within the city of Altona ; and the pipe mains which connect these with each other and with the city.

There are two engines in the engine-house, each of the same plan and dimensions. The engines are double-cylinder engines, each with crank and fly-wheel attached, and each working a plunger and bucket pump. They are not arranged to work in connection. The steam cylinders are respectively of 35 inches diameter, with 7 feet stroke, and of 20 inches diameter, with 5 feet 3 inches stroke. The engines work very uniformly an average of $16\frac{1}{2}$ strokes per minute. The pump is a plunger and bucket pump, the barrel 21 inches diameter, and the plunger 15 inches diameter, the stroke 3 feet 6 inches.

The altitude of the full water of the settling basins above the pump well, at low water above the Elbe, is 280 feet. The rising main connecting the pump with these basins is 18 inches diameter, and about 2,250 feet in length.

The work of one engine is more than sufficient to supply the city at present, so that there is always one in reserve to meet accidents or repairs. The engines work alternately, week and week. The work of one engine 12 hours a day for four days in the week is competent to the present consumption of the city

The water in the settling basins and upon the filter beds forms the real reserve to meet the consumption of the remaining two days, the small reservoir in the city being of little account in this respect; during the winter months, as the water upon the filter beds cannot then be drawn down, the reserve is reduced to the water of the settling basins.

The engine-house and engines were in excellent order, everything being neat and clean, and well cared for. The settling basins and filter beds, as already mentioned, stand on high ground, 280 feet above the pump well.

The water of the Elbe does not seem to carry enough of sediment in suspension to damage the pump valves rapidly, and under such circumstances, and the ground being exceedingly convenient for the purpose, the works are simplified by having but one lift for the pumps instead of two, as would have been the case had the clearing works been placed contiguous to the river, and a separate reservoir constructed on the high ground. The settling basins are two in number; between them there is a smaller basin and two strainers, so called. An examination of the accompanying sketch (Plate XX.) will show their positions The pipe main from the engine-house discharges into the small basin a; thence. the water overflows into the strainers b b', and from the strainers finds its way into the settling basins c c', through holes left for that purpose in the intervening wall. The strainers were originally filled with small stones and gravel, but the difficulty experienced in cleansing and keeping open this mixture has led to its removal, and the strainers are now only filled in part with stones, without admixture of gravel.

The settling basins are cleaned out twice a year, which of itself shows that the amount of sediment carried down by the river, although sufficient to discolor the water, is small in body except during heavy floods. I could not learn that the depth of mud in the settling basins, when cleaned out, exceeded 15 inches, but in the small basin (a) the mud accumulates much more rapidly than in the settling basins. The settling basins are each 138 feet long by 66 feet wide, and they contain 11 feet in depth of water, though not more than 10 feet of that water is ever drawn off. The side walls are of brick, and nearly vertical. The contents of each of these basins at 10 feet of water is about 91,000 cubic feet, or for both, 182,000 cubic feet. The average consumption of the city being at present 80,000 cubic feet per diem, this is equal to 2¼ days' reserve. If we add to this the water upon the filter beds and in the clear-water reservoir at present, it would reach to five days' supply.

There are four filter beds (d^1, d^2, d^3, d^4) each 136 feet long by 66 feet wide. The depth of water upon the filters is four feet; their surface waters, when full, are on a level with the bottom of the settling basins.

The filtering materials are principally sand and gravel, arranged as follows :

	FT.	IN.
Fine screened sharp sand	3	0
Fine gravel	0	6
Gravel of size of hazel nut	0	3
Gravel of size of walnut	0	6
Large pebble stones 3 to 4 inches diameter	0	9
	5	0
Small gathering drains and large stones	1	0
Total	6	0

At my visit (May, 1866) three of the filters were covered with water and one was being cleansed. The cleansing of one filter in three weeks is sufficient at this season of the year. When heavy floods prevail, one filter cleansed per week is still sufficient. Here, as in Berlin, the filter beds are quite as useful for separating from the water all vegetable impurities as for its clarification, and they intercept as well fish of every description.

The superficial area of the four filters amounts to 36,432 square feet. Assuming three of the above filter beds to be constantly serviceable, this would give a filtering capacity of 27,324 cubic feet, equal to 2,869,105 U. S. gallons per diem.

The average daily consumption of water now, being 80,000 cubic feet, or 598,440 U. S. gallons, the filter surface is sufficient to meet four times the present rate of supply. A considerable portion of the population, however, still draws from the old wells; but as the number using the new works is rapidly augmenting, and the city growing rapidly, the anomaly of an over-abundant provision will not long continue.

The present rate of filtration, with three filters in use, averages but 19 imperial gallons (23¼ U. S. gallons) per square foot per diem.

The filters discharge into a clear-water basin (C), which is arched over and covered with earth. This last has a capacity of 109,500 cubic feet, equal to 819,116 U. S. gallons.

The amount of sand removed from the surface of a filter bed in cleansing, the attendant described to me as about half an inch in thickness, or as thin a layer as can practically be removed.

This sand is not cleansed and used over again here, but it is replaced by a thin layer of fresh sand.

Upon the settling basins and filter basins, the ice in winter forms to the depth of 15 to 20 inches. The walls in all these basins are vertical. The ice is not allowed to form close up to the walls, but a space of from 18 inches to 24 inches is kept clear all round in all the basins. In this way they find it easy to protect the walling from any damage by ice. The walls were all in line and in good order. During the winter months, the filter beds are all kept covered with water, and are not then laid bare for the purpose of cleansing. Luckily, the river water then is usually in its best state, and the filters do not get choked during the long interval. It is evident, however, that for such climates a larger filtering space should be provided than in situations where the formation of ice does not take place.

From the clear-water basin to the city the pipe main is about 7 miles in length, and of 16 and 15 inches in diameter.

Two large villages on the route are supplied with the same water. It was stated to me that the population supplied at this date did not probably exceed 30,000, which would give a rate of 20 U. S. gallons per head nearly.

The small reservoir alluded to as situated within the city was built, in some measure, to meet the contingency of a break in the pipe main between the works and Altona, to provide water during the time of its repair. It is situated on the highest ground of the city, and raised some 30 feet above the street. It has a capacity of 16,000 cubic feet, which is equal to about 120,000 U. S. gallons.

For much of the information obtained during my visit to these works I am indebted to the Engineer in charge of the works, Mons. H. Salzcuburg.

TOURS, ON THE LOIRE RIVER.

April, 1866.

The city of Tours lies on the river Loire, but its supply of water, with the exception of a small quantity got from artesian wells, is derived from the river Cher, a tributary of the Loire. The Cher enters the Loire about six miles below the city, which lies on the ground intervening between the rivers Loire and Cher, resting, however, directly upon the Loire. The Cher river has its sources in the granite slopes of the Auvergne and Limousin mountains, in the departments of Creuse and Altier. The river at Tours, by its passage through the rich plains above, has acquired a muddy hue, and it is only during its very low summer stages that the water becomes comparatively clear. Although deeply discolored when seen in mass, as in the river, the amount of sediment held in suspension, in April, 1866, was very small. The population of the city is stated at 42,000.

The works (Rochepinard usine hydraulique) on the river Cher, for the supply of the city, consist of an artificial filter in two divisions, a canal from the river passing over this double filter, and acting also as a mill-race to two turbine wheels; an engine-house, containing eight pumps, worked by the two turbines, and two extra pumps worked by an auxiliary steam-engine; a tail-race thence to the river. These works, which lie on the banks of the stream, within its dyke, are distant about 2½ miles from the city proper.

The river Cher has been long used for what is called slack water navigation, and there existed a dam and lock on the river at this point (the Rochepinarde dam), before the construction of the water works was contemplated. Advantage was taken of this dam to obtain water power for operating the pumps. The relative positions of the canal, the pump-house, and the tail-race, are shown on the accompanying sketch (Plate XXI.)

The water drawn from the river to operate the two turbine wheels passes over the filter beds. The cross section of these filters will show that the surface of the filter beds and the bottom of the canal correspond. The central wall, shown on the sketch, which divided the canal into two mill-races, separates the one filter bed from the other. The two divisions of the canal, or the separate mill-races for the two turbines, form as well the two separate filter beds.

These filters are entirely artificial, as contradistinguished from what are called natural filters. They are composed of 4 feet 6 inches in depth of fine sand and gravel, resting on a layer of dry brick, which again rests on a bed of beton. The beton lies here upon a calcareous rock. A small conduit, about 20 inches square, as shown on the cross section, collects the filtered water and conveys it to the pump well. The filtered water finds its way into the conduit by small holes arranged in the bricks of its side walls for this purpose.

The depth of water lying on these filter beds is regulated by the sluice gates above. There were about 4½ feet of water over them on the 19th of April, and this depth was, we presume, necessary then, to work the turbine wheels. The head of water on these filter beds would depend on the height of the water in the pump well. Upon this head, however it may be regulated, depends the velocity of the water through the filtering material, an important element in the process of filtering.

The two filter beds have a joint area of 9,688 square feet. This area, at 90 U. S. gallons per square foot, would filter efficiently 871,920 U. S. gallons in 24 hours ; or, if we suppose but one filter in operation, the other undergoing the process of cleansing, 435,960 U. S. gallons in 24 hours. But the consumption of water in the city averages about 924,700 U. S. gallons in 24 hours.

The filters are therefore too small to furnish under all circumstances the requisite supply, although in 1856, when these works were opened, and the population was not so large, they would have been ample, and doubtless satisfactory, had the system been in other respects perfect. But there were no settling reservoirs provided to rid the river water of the heavier portions of its sediment and prepare it for the successful action of such filter beds. It is well understood now, that no artificial filter beds will operate regularly and satisfactorily if the river water, as it comes down in heavy floods, is thrown directly upon them, and all the sediment *then* in suspension permitted to deposit itself upon the filter bed. The surface sand, under these circumstances, becomes speedily clogged and inoperative.

The works were opened in 1856, and these filters, as we are informed by the Engineer in charge, have been inefficient from the first season ; the supply now is drawn directly from the river.

These filters are not arranged, or intended to be cleansed as in the ordinary English practice, by laying them bare at short intervals, and removing the thin layer of sand upon which the intercepted sediment has accumulated. The mode of cleansing designed here, was by reversing the flow of the water through the filter, and forcing it upwards through the filtering material under such a head as would carry with it the sediment deposited by the turbid water on the surface of the filter bed.

To effect this the river sluice gates of the filter bed to be cleansed were

16

closed. This would cause the water over the filter to sink to about the level of the tail-race. The small conduit of this filter was then put in communication with the water of the other filter bed, the difference of level varying with the stage of the river. Under the head thus produced the water rose upwards through the filter to be cleaned, in process of time carrying more or less of the surface sediment with it.

The Engineer states that the head of water at command was not sufficient to make the process efficient, and that between the averred difficulty and the deficiency in area of the filter beds, or other reasons, they never, from the beginning, have operated satisfactorily, and are unserviceable now.

The turbine wheels work, each, four single-acting pumps ; the pumps are each (0.32 m.) 12½ inches diameter, and (0.50 m.) 19½ inches stroke. Their united delivery at a velocity of 16 strokes per minute, which may be taken as their maximum, was stated to us to be equal to 100 litres (3.53 cubic feet) per second=8640 cubic metres, or 2,282,515 U. S. gallons per diem, but their ordinary work, or the average delivery of water into the city, does not evidently exceed (3500 cubic metres) 924,700 U. S. gallons per diem.

This amount, for the population of 42,000, is equal to 22 U. S.gallons per head. At the time of my last visit (21st of April, 1866), one of the turbines was working three pumps at 10 strokes per minute, and the other one two pumps at 11 strokes per minute. The river was in flood, and the head upon the turbines about 0m. 35 (13¾ inches).

The water in the river at its very lowest stage leaves the surface of the filter beds (the bottom of the canal or mill race) so nearly bare as to render the turbine wheels inoperative. At the highest stage of the river the turbine wheels become equally incompetent to the work required of them. In high floods the dam is drowned, and the available fall of the wheels is at times reduced to 4 inches. To meet these difficulties, as well as to admit of the more convenient maintenance and repair of the other machines, a steam-engine is provided, working two pumps of 0m. 33 (13 inches) diameter each, and 0m. 40 (15¾ inches) stroke. The delivery of the steam pumps reaches 30 litres per second (2592 m. c.) 684,807 U. S. gallons per diem (16.3 galls. per head of the population).

The water in the river, 19th April, 1866, was 1.60 metres (5¼ feet) above (l'etiage) its lowest stage. The river was then in flood, and although the dam here has a height of (1.5 metres) about 5 feet, and would give that amount of available fall in moderate stages of the river, the fall available at the turbines at this time was but 12 inches. The highest flood on record, 4th June, 1856, rose to (5.90 metres) 19 feet above extreme low water.

There is but one pipe main of 11.8 inches diameter into the city, but a second is to be laid shortly. There is no receiving reservoir of sufficient capacity to relieve the pumps from constant service. One of the machines requires to be constantly in operation. A small reservoir, holding about 58,000 gallons, has been placed in the Charlemagne tower, and would be of service in a case of fire, or some very short interruption of the supply ; but as it can hold but about 1½ hours consumption, it is too small to relieve the pumps from constant service. The water in the reservoir stands, when full (22 metres), 72 feet above the floor of the pump-house, or about 82 feet above the water there at this date. The city stands low and level, and this head permits the water to be delivered into the first and second stories of such houses as desire it. The inhabitants, however, draw the most of their water, as is usual in French cities, from the public fountains, which are numerous over the city.

The reservoir, which is an iron tank 8 metres deep, was empty when I visited it (23d April, 1866), the head of water on the turbines at this time not being sufficient to lift the water as high as the tank. Under such circumstances the supply is limited to the fountains and the lowest floors of buildings. So far as I can learn, there have been 13 borings made in the city to obtain water by artesian wells, seven of which deliver water now ; the others are not in use. The largest of these belongs to a brewery, which uses the water for brewing and cleansing casks. The larger portion of it, however, was running to waste. Such of the neighbors as fancied the water, supplied themselves from it. The water was described by the brewer as slightly sulphurous and ferruginous in its character, and that this mineral taint was characteristic of all the artesian wells here. The depth of this bore was 160 metres, about 500 feet, and they all ranged from 350 to 500 feet. This well was stated to deliver 1,000 litres per minute, and so far as I could learn, the flow of all was about 2,000 litres (528 U. S. gallons) per minute. The flow from these wells has varied very much, and lessened very much, since they were first sunk. Mr. Darcy describes them in his work on the fountains of Dijon, 1856. Most of these wells seem to have been sunk for private use, and much of their water is allowed to run to waste.

Mr. Chavran, the Architect and Director of the Tours Works, was very courteous and obliging in giving information and permitting me to copy the plan of the filter basins. I am also greatly indebted to Mr. Claude T. Roussel, the mechanician at the works, for the facilities and assistance afforded me towards understanding them.

ANGERS WATER WORKS.

Avgust, 1866.

NATURAL FILTRATION.

The city of Angers lies on the river Maine, a tributary of the Loire. The river Loire flows within three miles of the city, and it is from an island in the Loire, at the Ponts de Fe, that the city is supplied with water. The Loire has its sources in the mountains of Lazere, Vivarais, and Auvergne ; but its many tributaries from calcareous regions change the character of its original streams, and render the water at Angers and Nantes turbid and somewhat hard. The population in 1863, was 51,797, it may now be taken at 53,000 ; but the portion supplied with water from these works does not exceed 50,000. The works are under the immediate control of the city authorities. Upon the island referred to, the engine-house is placed. It contains two steam pumps with the requisite boilers. The well of the pumps is connected with and receives its water from fiftering galleries, situated as shown in the accompanying sketch. (Plate XXII.)

The works have been in operation ten years (since 1856). Until 1861, the only filtering galleries were those marked A and B, each of about the same length and size. In low stages of the river the supply from these galleries was not sufficient to keep the one pumping engine at work uninterruptedly ; but by working intermittently, that is, by stopping the engine every 2 or 3 hours, and allowing the galleries to fill up, the supply to the city was generally maintained. During the very low season, however, of 1858, the river fell so low as to render the supply insufficient, even when gathered intermittently in this way. For upwards of 30 days the amount thus obtained per diem ranged from 1,000 to 800 cubic metres, amounts much below what the city required then. The necessity for extending the filtering galleries was thus brought home to all, and the third gallery, C, was projected and built in 1861.

With this gallery, the Engineer informed me that they could rely on a delivery of (3,000 metres cubic) 792,600 U. S. gallons at the lowest stage of the river. The average consumption now is (2,156 metres cubic) 569,700 U. S. gallons, which, for the population of 50,000, gives a rate per head of about 11½ U. S. gallons.

The materials of the island in which the filtering galleries are placed, consist of earth, sand and gravel, resting on a bed of argillaceous marl, which is impervious to water. The sand predominates. The bottom of the first galleries, A and B, are carried down to this clayey substratum, but the new gallery is not carried so low.

The clayey basis (Talle) is found at (8 metres) about 25 feet below the general surface of the island. The island is covered with water in high floods.

The bottom of the wide portion of the first galleries (see the cross sections) is (2.90 metres) 9½ feet below (l'etiage) the lowest water of the Loire, the bottom of the wings (2.30 and 2.40 metres) 7½ and 7¾ feet below the same line, and the bottom of the new gallery (1.68 metres) 5½ feet below it.

The total length of the first galleries, with the two short branches, is (88 metres) 288 feet. If we take the extreme low water per diem of this gallery, as given by the Engineer (800 m. c.), 211,360 U. S. gallons—and this, where there are no storage reservoirs to collect surplus water, is the only safe measure for the city—we have, in this case, a delivery of 739 U. S. gallons per lineal foot of gallery at low water.

The total length of the new gallery is (300 metres) 984 feet. If we take the low water capacity of the new gallery from the same data (3,000=808= 2,200 m. c.) at 581,240 U. S. gallons, we have a rate per lineal foot of 590 U. S. gallons. The new gallery stretches towards the main channel of the Loire. The islands here divide the river into three channels. The first galleries are placed near the smallest channel, which is all but dry in very low stages of the river.

The first galleries, as will be seen by the sketch, are open at the side ; the usual mode of referring their capacity of delivery to the square feet in the bottom is therefore hardly applicable here. I will, however, give the indications by this mode.

The first galleries have the following bottom widths and areas :

26 metres in length by 1.66 wide at 10.76 sq.
    feet per sq. metre=.................... 464 sq. feet.
62 m. length and 1 m. wide=.............. 667   "

                     1131 sq. feet.

This is equal to 187 U. S. gallons per square foot of bottom.

The length of the new gallery is 300 metres by 0.60 metres width of bottom=1,937 square feet.

This gives a rate of 300 U. S. gallons per square foot of its bottom.

The entire lengths of the galleries (1,272 feet) give 623 U. S. gallons per lineal foot.

The size and form of the galleries will be seen on the accompanying sketch. The old galleries rest upon a construction of timber and cobble stone, the whole depending upon the permanence and solidity of the timber. The body of the wide part of the old galleries is 10 feet in width, the rest of it 6½ feet, but the bottom widths are but 5½ and 3¼ feet respectively. The new gallery has a width of 2 feet.

When I visited the galleries (April 27th, 1866), the river stood 6½ feet above low water, and the water in the filtering gallery at noon, 0.85 metres above the same low water, or (1.15 m.) 3¾ feet below the river as it flowed then. The water of the new gallery was not then in communication, being cut off by a tight sluice prepared for that purpose. ·

The old galleries supply an abundance of water at the present stage of the river. The new gallery is not needed at this stage ; when the river is in flood, as now, its water is discolored, and for that reason cut off. When the river is not in flood, the new gallery is kept open, and when it is very low, the aid of the new gallery is indispensable ; the river water being comparatively clear when low, the water from the new gallery is then clear and unobjectionable.

I was disappointed in the water of the old galleries. Although clear, it was not so perfectly so as the water of the same character of galleries at Genoa, Toulouse, and Lyons. Here the water was not entirely limpid. This would show that the galleries are on too small a scale for the material in which they are situated, and that the draft into them has a velocity sufficient to carry some portion of sediment with it.

It may be mentioned here that, during the great flood of 1856, the water rose (6.76) 22 feet above its lowest record. When the river is so high as to cover the island, the filtering galleries do not produce clear water.

The water accumulates in these galleries during the night, when the pumping engine is not at work ; and when the engine begins work at 5 A. M., the water stands in the gallery at nearly the same level as the water in the river. The water is lowered by the pumping process about 3½ feet. During the last two or three hours of the working of the pumps, the water ceases to lower, showing that the flow into the gallery then equals the quantity withdrawn by the pumps.

By reference to the cross-section of the new gallery, it will be seen that no provision is apparent there for the entrance into it of the filtered water. The bottom is composed of a thin layer of beton, and the side walls and arch are of masonry ; the stones bedded in part in hydraulic cement mortar.

The Engineer informed me that the walls were thin, and the water found its way sufficiently through the joints of the slaty stones of which it is built, rendering special openings of any kind unnecessary. The backing of stones behind the walls prevents the sand from reaching the masonry and filling up these crevices.

The delivery of a gallery of this description cannot fairly be compared with galleries of an entirely different character, as regards the provisions for the entry of the water.

There are two steam pumping engines at the work.

The oldest, which has been in use since 1856, has a vertical steam cylinder, with fly-wheel attached. The pump is directly under the cylinder. The pump is a plunger and bucket pump, the plunger 0.40 diameter (15¾ inches), and the bucket or pump cylinder 0.50 metres diameter (19¾ inches) ; the stroke is (1.25 metres) four feet, and the engine was making 18 strokes per minute.

This engine has worked during the month of April very regularly an average of 11 hours per day, delivering in that time 2,156 cubic metres, against a head of water at this time of 50 metres (164 feet), increasing or decreasing with the variations in the water of the Loire, which again affect the position of the water in the galleries.

The second machine, which has been built within the last five years, was under repairs, and is not used except in the hot months of summer, when the city consumption is much increased, or when the other machine is under repair. It has a horizontal steam cylinder, connected, like the other, with a fly-wheel. The pump is vertical ; it is a plunger and bucket pump, of the same diameter as the other, but with a stroke of only (6.50 metres) 1 foot 8 inches. This engine, we are informed, made 28 revolutions per minute.

A pipe main, of (0.35 metre) 13¾ inches diameter, delivers the water into the city, where a net-work of smaller pipes distributes it through the streets.

Connected with this pipe main, there are two cisterns or tanks in the Rue de Madeline of 300 cubic metres each (79,354 U. S. gallons), the water of which stands when full 52 metres (170 feet) above the pump well ; and one larger cistern, near the Champ de Mars, of 2,500 cubic metres (660,450 U. S. gallons) capacity, the water of which stands about 33 metres (108 feet) above the pump well. The lower cistern is connected with the lower part of the city, and the action of the upper ones is confined to the pipes of the higher grounds. The overflow of the high cisterns supplies the lower one with water by two special pipe mains for that duty, and the lower cistern has no other connection with the pumping engines. The pump, therefore, is working always under the head of water which prevails in the high cisterns, which are soon filled.

The three cisterns have a joint capacity of 819,000 U. S. gallons, and supposing them to be but little over two-thirds full, they have thus a reserve of one day's supply, a reserve that is sufficient to relieve the pumping engine from continuous work, and to admit, therefore, of its being easily kept in ordinary repair.

During extraordinary repairs, requiring some days or weeks of intermission, the second engine is in reserve to meet the required supply. .

The head of water available is sufficient to reach the different stories of all the houses except those situated on the highest grounds, where it can only reach the first story.

The public fountains are kept open 7 hours a day—from 6 to 9 A. M., and from 3 to 7 P. M.

The Engineer in charge of the works very obligingly furnished me with a sketch of the ground, and with the details which accompany it, of the filtering galleries.

NANTES WATER WORKS.

NANTES, *April* 25, 1866.

The city of Nantes is situated on the right bank of the river Loire, just above tidal influence. The population at this date is estimated at 112,000.

The water for the supply of the city is obtained from the Loire, whence it is pumped into three small reservoirs, situated (40 metres) 131 feet above ordinary water of the river. The pumping station is placed at the upper end of the city, within its suburbs, and just above its sewerage influence.

The works were constructed by the "Compagnie General des Eaux," and are under the charge and direction now of the officers of that Company.

The pumping-house lies within 200 feet of the river. Two steam engines work, each, two single-acting lifting pumps. The engines are each double cylinder engines, with a walking-beam, to which the pump rods are attached, connected by a crank with a large fly-wheel. The two pumps of the one engine have each an interior diameter of (0.38 metres) 15 inches, with (1 metre) 3 feet 3 inches stroke. The two pumps of the other engine, (0.44 metres) 17 inches diameter, and the same stroke.

The engines are said to average 18 revolutions per minute, and they work an average of 12 to 14 hours a day. The smaller engine was making 18 strokes at the time of my visit, and the larger 14 to 15 strokes. They have been in operation since 1855—11 years—and have performed, says the Engineer, very satisfactorily.

There is a rising main from each engine to the reservoirs or basins already mentioned. These pipe mains are each (0.29 metres) 11½ inches diameter, and about (2 kilometres) 6,560 feet in length.

The record kept at the office of the Company of the daily work of the pumping engines gave an average daily delivery to the city, during March, 1866, of 5,770 metres cubic, equal to 1,524,434 U. S. gallons. This, for the population given, is at the rate of about 13.6 gallons per head.

There are two sytems of pipes in the streets of the city—one for the delivery of filtered water to such as desire it, and one for the delivery of the river water in its natural state. Water is taken into the houses from either system, according to the choice of the proprietor, but the public fountains are only sup-

15

plied with the unfiltered water. There are no fountains supplied with the filtered water.

The filtered water supplied in March was calculated to average (400 metres cubic) 105,680 U. S. gallons per diem. A large portion of the unfiltered water delivered was consumed by the public buildings, hospitals and fountains, the city having a claim on the Water Company for a daily delivery to the extent of 4,000 cubic metres if necessary.

The public fountains are only supplied for four hours each day, from noon to 4 P. M. Within these hours such of the inhabitants as have not pipes within their dwellings must lay in their store of water for 24 hours. The usual liberality and waste which obtains in other French cities is reduced to a minimum here. This will to some extent account for the low rate of consumption per head. A small portion of clarified water from the Loire, is supplied by another Company, and sold about the streets in casks; but as the amount from this source does not exceed 50,000 gallons per day, its effect on the general rate per head is very small.

The reservoirs or basins aforementioned as situated 130 feet above the pump well are three in number. They are open basins grouped around a central covered basin or tank which receives the filtered water. The accompanying sketch (Plate XXIII.) shows the arrangement.

The basins A and B are used for settling basins, and the river water is at rest alternately in the one or the other from 12 to 18 hours before being passed through the filtering materials. One basin can be filled by the pumping engines in much less time than is occupied in passing the other through the filter, for the amount of filtered water consumed in the city is comparatively small. The fountains do not receive it, and the extra price, but more especially the incompleteness of the process, probably prevents its more general use by householders.

The amount of filtered water, it has been seen, does not much exceed one-fifteenth of the total supply; but the amount used at the public fountains, during the four hours of their service, was stated to exceed one-half of the whole supply. These statements are vague, but are indicative of the system, if nothing more. I give them as received.

The filters occupy a narrow space on that side of each settling basin which is proximate to the covered basin. By reference to the accompanying sketch it will be seen that they are arranged along the side wall referred to in groups of six; two groups or 12 small filters to each settling basin. Each separate filter is (1 metre) 3¼ feet square, and contains about 3 feet in depth of filtering materials.

The river water, after having been allowed a certain time to settle or deposit its heavier sediment, passes through these filters into the covered tank, whence it passes by pipes to the city.

Each of these settling basins holds (1,800 cubic metres) 475,000 U. S. gallons, or, allowing for the water near the bottom which is not passed to the city, each basin has a capacity equal to one-third of the city consumption.

The filtering materials as described to me were composed of broken stone, pebbles, sand, and sponge. The entire materials were taken out once a month, cleansed, and replaced.

The materials rest in each case upon a perforated cast-iron plate, through which the water passes into the shallow drain below, which communicates with all the six boxes of the group, and has a connection with the filtered water basin.

Instead of sponge, a preparation of wool is often used, obtained from the workings of the woollen factories, and this is more thorough in its operation on the water than sponge. They are never used mixed. The sponge or wool which forms the surface layer of the filter, is covered with a perforated plate, and compressed by means of a screw. The top of the box or compartment is then covered by a water-tight plate, and the water of the settling basin reaches the filter through a short tube in the centre of this plate. An india-rubber tube is attached to the central hole, and carried to the surface of the water, where it is held in suspension by an india-rubber ball. By this means the water for the filter is always drawn from the surface water of the settling basin.

The filters seemed to be on too small a scale, and the clarification effected at this station arose mainly, at the time of my visit, from the process of settlement in the settling basins; I compared the water of the settling basin which was then being drawn through the filter, with the same water after it had passed through the filter, and could distinguish no difference. The settlement had not entirely clarified the water, though it had improved it; and the passage through these small filters had produced no perceptible change. The filtered water was not limpid, but retained the slight milky hue which appeared in the basin. The river water at this time was but slightly turbid.

The settling basins are cleansed at short intervals, by flushing off about 2 feet of the bottom water, and making it carry the accumulated sediment with it, the sediment being stirred up and brushed off the bottom by men using sweeps and brooms.

The third basin, C, shown on the sketch, is not in any way connected with the filtering apparatus now, but forms a reserve of river water, holding, when full, (2,400 cubic metres) 63,400 U. S. gallons, or half a day's supply. It was about half full at the time of my visit. At midday, when the public fountains are open, it is always drawn down, the pumping engines not being competent then to meet the full draft on the city pipes.

Each of the pipe mains from the engines to the reservoirs connects, in its passage through the city, with the pipe distribution.

We were informed by the officials that the want of a large reservoir in connection with the works was much felt, and that it was in contemplation to construct one. The Engineer who planned and constructed these works, and who is still in charge of them, very obligingly showed me the original plan of the works, and, together with the machinist, communicated frankly the necessary explanations. Although the filtered water, at the time of my visit, was not sufficiently limpid to be satisfactory, I was informed that its usual condition was unobjectionable.

THE FILTERING GALLERIES AND BASINS AT LYONS.

NATURAL FILTERS.

The population in 1866 was variously stated to be 300,000 to 315,000. The water supplied to the city of Lyons is derived mainly from the river Rhone. A slight difference in the character of the river water and that of the filtering galleries, as stated by the chemists, shows that some water from springs or sources containing a larger proportion of the salts of lime than the river water mixes with the underground flow from which the filter basins and galleries are supplied. The difference is stated by Mr. A. Dumont, the Engineer, to be 2½ degrees of the hydrometer of MM. Boudron and Boudet. The increase in hardness in this case is so slight as to be of little practical importance.

The head waters of the Rhone are found in the granite regions of the Swiss Alps, whence they pass into and through the Lake of Geneva. Between Geneva and Lyons the river acquires the turbid hue which marks it at the latter place, and from the calcareous formations through which it passes after leaving the Alps it probably acquires the hardness which characterizes it at Lyons. The velocity of the stream in its ordinary stages does not exceed three miles an hour at Lyons, since small steamers ply on it there freely. The works for the supply of the city are situated in the narrow gravel plain of Petit Broteau, situated on the right bank of the Rhone, above the city proper, in the small suburb of the Croix Rousse.

The works there consist of. two filter galleries and two filter basins, with one engine-house for the low-service engines, one engine-house for the high-service engines, and an engine-house for a small auxiliary engine now used to supply a small reservoir in the Jardin des Plantes with the river water occasionally, when, as during very low stages of the river, the filtered water becomes deficient in quantity. The relative positions of the separate works are shown on the accompanying sketch. (Plate XXIV.)

The low-service engines deliver their water into a low-service reservoir of 10,000 cubic metres capacity=2,641,800 U. S. gallons, situated (its bottom) 45.70 metres, or 150 feet, above extreme low water (l'etiage) of the Rhone. The high-service engines deliver their water into a high-service reservoir of 6,000 cubic metres (1,585,080 U. S. gallons) capacity, situated 94 metres, or 308 feet, above low water.

To supply the small district of Fourvieres, situated above the last-mentioned reservoir, a small pumping engine, placed near the high-service reservoir, pumps the water for this highest service into a tower 55 metres, 180 feet high, containing the necessary stand-pipe to that end. In the low-service engine-house there are three engines of the Cornish type, each of the same power (170 horse). In the original arrangement, one of these engines was adapted to the high-service duty, one to the low-service, and one held as a reserve, and made applicable to either. They are all three applied now to the low-service duty.

The pumps are plunger pumps, of 1 metre (39½ inches) diameter, and 2.50 metres (98 inches) stroke, each, the engines making ordinarily 7 strokes per minute. The actual delivery of the pump is given by the Engineer as 1.80 cubic metres (63½ c. feet) per stroke. The supply of the city at present requires about 20 hours' work per diem, two engines being occupied, and one always in reserve.

There have been added, within the last two years, two engines for the high-service duty. They are duplicates in plan, and not of the Cornish type. Each engine is connected with a fly-wheel. The pump is placed directly under the steam cylinder, and is a plunger and bucket pump ; the stroke 1.25 metres (49 inches) ; the diameter of the pump barrel, 0.57 metres (22½ inches). The engines made 15 to 16 revolutions per minute. One of these engines, working about eight hours daily, maintains, we were informed, the supply for the high-service, the other engine being in reserve.

The daily consumption of the city now for all purposes, I infer from the work of the pumping engines to be about 25,000 cubic metres (882,925 cubic feet), or about 22 U. S. gallons per head daily. At the lowest stage of the river the delivery of the filtering works does not exceed, as stated to me, 22,000 cubic metres per diem, or 5,812,400 U. S. gallons. This gives a rate per head of the population of but 19 gallons daily. The larger quantity of 22 gallons per head is felt to be insufficient. In comparing this with American and English rates of consumption, it is to be remembered that the proportion of water to be expended on public fountains in Lyons, and in all continental cities which I have visited, very much exceeds the quantity used for like purposes in American or English cities. The rate per head applicable here to domestic purposes would hence appear to be unusually low.

The supply of water from the present works commenced in 1856, and has been since continued without interruption. The water delivered into the city is perfectly clear, and it is obtained in this state here, as in Toulouse, by taking advantage of what is called the natural filter.

The narrow plain on which the works are situated consists of coarse gravel and sand, very pervious to any waters in its vicinity, whether they percolate into it from the river or from the bluffs to the north of it, or from the plain above, of which it forms but a small part. In this gravelly deposit the water stands, when not interfered with, at about the same level as the river, but divested of the turbid character of surface streams, and clear and colorless. This body of water is tapped by the filtering works to be described, and can always be depended on within certain limits for the invariability of its results as respects freshness and limpidity.

The water from the river might have been made as clear by an artificial filter, but the temperature would not have been so uniform nor so satisfactory, and the daily expenses attending the manipulations of the filtering works would, to all appearance, have been greater. Whether the first cost would have been more, remains yet to be seen, for the present filtering works here are acknowledged to be insufficient for the wants of the city, and the last-built gallery will evidently have to be extended.

These galleries are technically called filtering galleries, but in reality they are mere receptacles and conduits for gathering the water already filtered by a natural process. They serve nothing towards the filtration of the water, but only towards the collection of a portion of it, and its transmission to the pumping machines.

The first gallery constructed is marked No. 1 on the accompanying sketch. It has a length of 120 metres (394 feet) and a width of 5 metres (16.4 feet). There are no openings in the sides for the collection of the water; but only on the bottom, which is entirely open—the coarse gravel being all along visible. With the pumping engines at work the water in this gallery stood 3 to 4 feet deep, and its surface stood 6½ feet, as we were informed, (2.0 metres) below the surface water of the Rhone, situated within 80 feet of the gallery.

At a few points the water boiled up in small springs conveying some fine sand with it. The form of the gallery is shown on the accompanying sketch. The arch is covered with 3 to 4 feet of earth, but the gallery is well ventilated and well lighted by a number of uncovered man-holes.

This I understand to have been the only gallery constructed when the works were opened for use in 1856.

The water obtained from this gallery having proved insufficient in quantity; a square basin was excavated alongside of it, marked No. 2 on the sketch. The bottom of this basin was carried lower than the bottom of the gallery No 1 by from 2 to 3 feet. Its waters, however, deliver into No. 1, and are carried by it to the pump well. The basin is vaulted over and covered with earth ; a number of man-holes give it light and ventilation.

The consumption of the city requiring more water than these openings produced, a second basin was constructed somewhat larger than the first; it is marked No. 3 on the sketch. This basin is vaulted and arranged like No. 2. Its waters deliver also into the gallery No. 1. It was completed in 1859.

But the construction of these three works did not sufficiently meet the wants of the city, the consumption of water by the inhabitants having probably much exceeded since 1856 the consumption which had prevailed previously.

A new gallery was consequently determined on, of larger dimensions than the first, and placed up stream along the bank of the river, breaking into new ground, as it were, and collecting from the same gravel plain and underflow of water, but away from the existing works. A portion of this new gallery was constructed and opened in 1863. Where the Geneva Railway crosses it, its dimensions are reduced from 10 metres (33 feet) in width to 2½ metres (8 feet). The portion completed is therefore in two pieces, as shown on the sketch, and is in all 100 metres (328 feet) in length. Its continuation, it was stated, is required now, and probably will soon be determined on. The form and size of this new gallery are shown on the accompanying sketch.

At the lowest stage of the Rhone (l'etiage) its surface water opposite the works stood at 165 metres (541 feet) above the sea. At the highest flood on record (1862) the water rose to 169.51 (556 feet), a difference of 15 feet between extreme low and extreme high water; but the river rarely rises within 5 feet of the above mark.

The water in the galleries stood during our visit, according to the scale attached to the first gallery, at 0.85 metres (2¾ feet) below its zero (l'etiage), or 164.15 metres (538½ feet) above the sea, and in the river, by our information, it stood at 166.15 metres (545 feet) at the same time, the difference in level being 6½ feet.

According to the book of Mon. Dumont, the Constructing Engineer, the bottom or filtering areas of the three first works are as follows. The sketch to which I have referred is founded on the one given in his book, the position of the new engine-house and the new filtering gallery being added by me. Its basins do not correspond in size by scale with the figures given by Mr. Dumont, but I accept these figures in preference to dimensions obtained from the sketch. The basins being full of water rendered it impossible for me to verify their sizes.

	Metres, Square.	Sq. Feet.
No. 1 on the sketch. The first gallery constructed, opened in 1856. Area of its open gravel bottom..........	600	6,454
No. 2. The first filtering basin built to increase the supply. Area of open bottom.....	1,600	17,200
No. 3. Second filtering basin, completed 1859. Area of its open bottom..............................	2,168	23,306
	4,368	46,956
No. 4. The new filtering gallery, built in 1863. 328 feet long (100 metres) and 33 feet wide (10 metres). Area of gravel bottom.................................	1,000	10,750
Total filtering area at this date............................	5,368	57,706

This extent of area for 22,000 cubic metres which is the filtering capacity at low water of the river, is equivalent to 100.7 U. S. gallons per diem per square foot of open bottom. But as the shape which the filtering excavations have taken here is probably not the best for a maximum delivery, it will be better to take the new gallery by itself as a fairer measure of the amount of pure water obtainable from this particular deposit by underground galleries. An experiment made to test the water capability of the new gallery gave, we were informed, a result of 6,000 cubic metres in 24 hours. The bottom area being 1,000 metres square, this is equivalent to 147 U. S. gallons per square foot of bottom.

This rate of delivery is very much less than that of the new filtering gallery at Toulouse. The velocity of the stream at Toulouse, held back by the dam below, did not exceed from one to $1\frac{1}{4}$ miles an hour, while here it appears to be from $2\frac{1}{2}$ to 3 miles an hour. This would not sufficiently account for the difference, which must be influenced by some difference in the character of the filtering material, and in the extent and volume of the underground flow.

For the measures of the water capacities of such works, I am necessarily dependent on the officials in charge, and although the data have undoubtedly been communicated with much frankness and good faith, it is not in the nature of such things that the experiments on which they are founded, hurriedly as these must often have been made, should always be correct.

The delivery per lineal foot of this gallery is by the same experiment 4,833 U. S. gallons in 24 hours. This contrasts less disadvantageously with the result of the new Toulouse gallery. At the lowest stage of the river the water in the filtering galleries and basins is reduced 2 feet below its present level, and it becomes troublesome then to work the pumping engines, except by intermitting their action and allowing the water to accumulate in the basins and rise to a convenient height in the pump wells.

Mr. Dumont states in his book that, of the two elements required in certain proportions for a free delivery of water in a filtering gallery, area and depth, the last is very much the most important. But by the last he meant, more particularly, head, or difference of level between the surface water of the underflow in its natural state and that water when drawn down in basins, or otherwise, by artificial means. This will be readily admitted ; but it is at the same time conceded that the velocity upwards or sideways through the gravel deposit must not be so great as to carry with it sand into the basin, or, if near a river, it must not be so great as to draw water from that river in a turbid condition. The velocity into the filter basin must be very moderate to insure safety to the works, and an unvaried purity of supply.

With the view of increasing the supply here without extending the filter basins, and of testing, too, the effect of drawing down the water in the filter basins below the level necessary for the action of the original pumps, a small

18

engine was built at the suggestion of the Engineer, and the original pump wells being cut off from the filter works, these wells were temporarily supplied by this new engine. By this action the water in the filter beds was reduced below its ordinary level, the head of the inflow was correspondingly increased, and the rate of delivery sensibly augmented. But this increase in velocity of the inflow through the gravel proved in this case to be in excess of what the circumstances admitted of. The water concentrated itself in springs, and brought with it sand in sufficient quantity to risk the undermining of the vault foundations. The maximum for the situation had been overreached. The use of the new machine was therefore stopped, and the works restored to their old regime. The engine is now used as an auxiliary to furnish water directly from the river to the reservoir in the Jardin des Plantes, at such very low stages of the river as inconveniently reduce the supply from the filters. The frank statement of this result, which I have gathered from Mr. Dumont's report, is very honorable to the Engineer, and very valuable to the profession.

THE FILTERING GALLERIES AT TOULOUSE.

NATURAL FILTERS.

The population of Toulouse is stated to amount to 100,000 souls at this date (March, 1866).

The water is derived from the Garonne, indirectly, by means of subterranean galleries situated in a bank of gravel on the left bank of the river.

The sources of the Garonne are found on the slopes of the Pyrenees chain of mountains, in the department of Ariege. The velocity of the river at Toulouse was stated to me to average ordinarily 1 metre per second, or about 2¼ miles an hour. Immediately opposite the filtering ground the velocity does not exceed 2 miles an hour, the dam erected a short distance below having modified importantly the current there.

The bank of gravel and sand in which the galleries have been constructed lies within the city limits, but in what may be called the suburbs; the dense portion of the city lies below this point as regards the river, and upon its opposite bank.

The annexed sketch (Plate XXV.) will show the position of the filtering galleries, and of the pump-house (Chateau d'Eau), upon which the galleries all concentrate.

It is important to understand the relation of this gravel bank to the lowest stage of the Garonne, and to its flood waters. The surface water of the Garonne at its lowest stage is recorded to have stood 433 feet (132.09 metres) above the level of the sea. The surface of the gravel bank referred to is on an average (136 metres) 446 feet above the same level, or about 13 feet above the lowest stage of the river. The river floods rarely cover this bank; in long intervals, however, extreme floods set over it, and the one of 1832 rose to 451½ feet (137.69) above the sea, covering this gravel meadow, therefore, with some 5½ feet of water.

The rise of the river in ordinary floods may be taken at 8 to 10 feet. In the highest flood on record referred to it rose to 18 feet above the lowest water of the river opposite to the present pumping engines.

In the pump-house there are two breast wheels (10½ feet diameter each, exclusive of the buckets, and 5 feet wide each). Each wheel works four plunger pumps of 10½ inches (0.27) diameter each, and 3.80 feet stroke. All the pumps were at work both days that I visited the pump-house, and according to their velocity at that time they would deliver into the city about 4,500 cubic metres per 24 hours. The delivery was stated to me to average 5,000 cubic metres per diem (176,585 cubic feet), equivalent to 13½ U. S. gallons per head of the population. Each set of four pumps delivers its water into a vertical pipe of 10 inches diameter, which is carried up the pump-house tower to a height of 66 feet above ordinary water of the river. At this height the waters of the two rising mains are delivered into two city mains of the same diameter, and the head thus acquired enables the numerous fountains to be well supplied, and admits of the lower stories or ground floors of many of the houses receiving the water into the house. In this last respect, Toulouse is at present very imperfectly accommodated. There is no reservoir connected with the pumps, which are, therefore, necessarily kept perpetually at work, except as one wheel must be occasionally intermitted for repairs.

These pumps have been in use since 1839. The new pump-house and engines now under construction, and nearly completed, are upon a scale to admit of a delivery of water into the city equivalent to a rate of 50 U. S. gallons per head. The old pumping machines will be altered and made auxiliary to the new.

The new works include a sufficient reservoir to defend the city against accidents to the works, and to admit of their more leisurely repair and examination. They are so arranged as to admit of the water being received into the highest stories of all the buildings. These new works are being constructed in all respects most substantially and thoroughly, and we looked over their details with much interest and satisfaction.

The form and size of the gravel bed in which the filtering galleries are situated will be best understood by reference to the annexed sketch. In this sketch the filtering ground is colored brown to enable the reader to understand its extent, but upon the surface it is covered with grass. The deposit consists of gravel and sand of different degrees of fineness—its surface, however, covered with a thick bed of rich soil. The whole rests upon a compact tufa or marl, and as will be seen by an examination of the sketch, the depth at which any filtering galleries can be laid is limited by this impervious base. The surface of the marl is situated here about 12 feet below the low water of the river.

The river water at the time of my visit did not carry much weight of sediment, but it carried sufficient to give the stream a dirty, muddy color.

The body of sand and gravel referred to above, so much of it as lies below the level of the water in the river, it is superfluous to say, is saturated with water, and this water, although evidently derived from the river and its affluents, has passed through such a width or depth of material at a very slow velocity, on the wide plains above, as to have deprived it entirely of the matter which gives the muddy hue to the stream. In the filtering galleries, therefore, it is found colorless and limpid. Immediately under the bed of the stream, or in too close proximity to it, this result would not probably have place. The first filter gallery or drain (C D on the sketch) was laid at a distance of about 60 metres (197 feet) from the bank. The bottom is situated only about 4 feet below the lowest water of the river. The form is square, the interior width 1 foot 8 inches, the height 3 feet. The side walls were of brick laid dry, with a flagging stone for the cover, and with no paving on the bottom. The bricks were laid dry and the bottom left uncovered, that the water might have free access to the culvert. The inside of this culvert was filled up with small stones, probably to prevent the side walls, which were not in mortar, from being pressed inwards. The trench in which the culvert was laid was filled up again with the materials taken from it. A coarse gravel was found at the bottom of the trench mixed with flints. The gravel became finer as the depth lessened from the surface, and ended in a fine river sand, covered at present with from 2 to 3 feet of soil.

The length of this first filtering culvert is 656 feet ; it is said to have delivered at all times clear water ; but the quantity was soon found to be insufficient for the demands of the city. To increase the supply, a second filtering arrangement was projected and built, differing somewhat in character from the first. In this second case eleven wells were sunk along the margin of the river, covering a distance of 300 feet (g h on the plan). They were carried to the same depth as the culvert, and steined up with dry brick. The wells were connected together by iron pipes, and from their lower terminus a connection was made with the pump well of the pump-house. The water from this second filter turned out bad, and it has consequently been for some time in disuse.

A third filtering culvert was constructed on the same plan as the first, but larger. In the lower part of its course it is situated farther from the river than the first culvert, and in the upper part nearer to the river (c e f on the sketch) ; the length was given me as 1,476 feet (450 metres). Like the first, it has always produced good and clear water.

The total length of these old filtering galleries (excluding the wells in disuse) is 2,132 feet. The growing wants of the city and the increase of its population rendered necessary a further and more liberal supply of water, and a new filtering gallery has been constructed within the last two years in the same bank of gravel.

It will be convenient to note here the water capacity of the old galleries so far as I am able correctly to understand it. This capacity has been given me as equal to 5,000 cubic metres per diem, and I judge this from other circumstances to be its maximum. $\frac{5000}{2132}$ gives a rate per foot per diem of (2.345 metres cubic) 620

U. S. gallons, or 82.82 cubic feet. The new filtering gallery is of larger dimensions than the others, and it is laid lower in the bed of gravel, and, consequently, has a greater capacity of drainage from the underground reservoir of the neighboring plain, of which the particular gravel bank of these works may be said to form a part.

It differs in other respects importantly from the old filtering conduits. Its contour is of mortared masonry (in this case beton) of sufficient strength to defend it from the outer thrust of the material in which it is imbedded, and its interior is not filled with stones, but void—forming thus in itself a considerable reservoir of water. The water finds its way into the conduit from the gravel deposit in which it lies, in part by small earthenware tubes placed on both sides of the gallery, but mainly through the bottom, which is left (six-sevenths) unpaved for that purpose, and where the clear water rises, therefore, from the coarse gravel which has place there.

At every seventh metre a buttress is thrown across of one metre in width, and to this extent (1-7) the bottom is impermeable. The surfaces of these buttresses, which are intended to defend the side walls against movement from the back thrust, do not rise above the prescribed level of the bottom of the conduit.

The interior height of the new conduit is 8 feet 8 inches (2.65 metres), the width 7 feet 6 inches (2.30 metres). Its form and position is shown on the annexed sketches. The bottom is placed at 129.45 metres (424.6 feet) above the sea, or 8 feet 7 inches below the lowest stage of the river. It is therefore 4½ feet below the bottom level of the old galleries. The present length of the new gallery is 1,180 feet (360 metres); but the intention is to extend it gradually to double this length, or more, according as the requirements of the city may demand it. An experiment made by the Engineer of the new works, Mons. Hepp, indicated, as I am informed, its capacity of delivery at the low water of the river to equal (10.000 cubic metres) 2,642,000. U. S. gallons per diem. Its extension will, it is supposed, double this rate of delivery. The capacity of this new gallery at low water is therefore equal to ($\frac{2,642,000}{1073}$) 2,462. U. S. gallons per foot of its length, while that of the small conduits was but 620 gallons per foot, an improvement due to its position and mode of construction combined.

It will be observed that the new gallery is not based on the marl or tufa upon which the gravel bed rests, but is kept from 2 to 3 feet above it. This has been done to permit the water to percolate easily into the gallery from the bottom, where it is expected that the mass of the water will enter it, rather than from the side tubes.

With the present rate of delivery into the city (5,000 cubic metres per diem), 1,320,900 U. S. gallons, the water stands now in the new gallery (131.60 metres) 2½ feet below the ordinary river water. During the experiment referred to, when the draft from the gallery was at the rate of 10,000 cubic metres,

2,641,180. U. S. gallons, it stood in this gallery, according to my notes, at (128.15 metres) 4 feet below the lowest stage of the river water. When the new pumps are completed and the city is supplied with a better head of water, the capacity of the new gallery will be more thoroughly tested.

I have given above the experimental rate of delivery of the new gallery per lineal foot. It would be preferable to give its rate per square foot of the open bottom; but in this case the proportional effect of the side pipes is difficult to appreciate. If we take the whole width and length of the gallery, as including a sufficient allowance for the side pipes, and to that add the bottom area of the small auxiliary galleries, we shall have a rate of delivery at low water of 228 U. S. gallons per square foot of open bottom. The delivery is elsewhere given in a pamphlet published at Marseilles, as equal to 27.6 metres cubic per metre courant, or 2,223. U. S. gallons per lineal foot.

The dam in the river below the present pump-house, produces comparatively still water opposite to the filter ground, and must encourage that kind of sedimentary deposit there, which the natural current of these rapid mountain streams does not admit of, except in eddies, and then only until the scouring operation of a heavy flood clears the channel of such accumulations. But when the underground material of the plain, for some distance above, consists of an equally open gravel, it can be of little consequence that the river bottom, within the influence of the dam, should become comparatively water-tight. The water will, in any case, reach the filter galleries from above, and from a somewhat greater distance, and the only effect would be to reduce the rate of delivery somewhat, and perhaps render a greater length of gallery necessary.

MARSEILLES WATER WORKS.

MARCH, 1866.

The supply of water to the city of Marseilles is especially noted for its abundance, the amount at present passed through the city reaching frequently, as I was informed by the Engineer, a rate of (550 litres) 145 U. S. gallons per head per diem ; but a large portion of this water, as he stated, is flushed into the harbor to carry off the sediment which would otherwise accumulate in and choke the pipes. The water passes at present into the city in its natural state, and without filtration. The reasons for this state of affairs will appear hereafter.

The population of Marseilles is given as 250,000 in 1864 ; Mr. Pascales, the Engineer, stated it at 300,000 at this date, 1866, and I find it elsewhere stated at the same figures.

The water is derived from the river Durance, and the boldness of the project will be admitted when it is stated that the point of derivation is distant 62 miles from Marseilles. The river Durance in its upper reaches is a rapid mountain stream, flowing over a stony, gravelly bed.

The sources of the river are widely spread upon the eastern slopes of the lower Alps.

The canal of supply commences on the Durance near the bridge of Pertuis.

In the construction of the canal the city had two purposes in view—the supply of the city with water, and the improvement of the lands in the vicinity of Marseilles by irrigation. The amount of water which can be drawn from the river Durance at the lowest stage of its water is limited to 5.75 cubic metres (203 cubic feet) per second; but the ordinary flow into the canal reaches 7 metres per second (159¾ millions U. S. gallons in 24 hours). Of this amount 1½ cubic metres per second (34,240,320. U. S. gallons) is considered as applicable to the city, although that amount is not used there at present. The rest is available for irrigation and water power, and in this respect has been a source of great benefit to the intermediate country.

The Engineer estimates one-seventh of the water to be lost by evaporation and filtration.

The canal has a fall of 6 inches to the mile, very nearly (0.30 metre per kilometre), and its dimensions are adapted to the required flow mentioned above.

There is no navigation upon it. It is open throughout, except at the tunnels, which are numerous. The main canal is carried to the sea below Marseilles, delivering its surplus waters there.

The city is supplied by a branch 3¼ miles in length. The distance from the Durance river to the Marseilles branch is 58½ miles, and to the filtering works at Longchamps, as already stated, 62 miles. The waste water from the fountains, which are numerous, and from the flushing of the pipes, passes into the harbor through the sewers, which are thus effectually scoured. The health of the city is said to be very much improved since the introduction of this supply.

The Durance river is represented as carrying an unusual amount of sediment, and as presenting in this respect greater difficulties, as regards filtration, than any other river in France. The average amount of sediment is given as equal to $\frac{1}{76}$ of its volume, but this is probably an exaggeration; Mons. Bernard, Engineer at Arles, gives $\frac{1}{1000}$ as the result of his experiments for one year.

In all arrangements for filtering turbid river water by artificial means, that portion of the sediment which will settle in comparatively still water within 24 hours is always supposed to be got rid off before placing the water upon the artificial filter.

The means provided upon this canal for clarifying the very turbid waters of the Durance were as follows :

A filter bed was constructed at Longchamps, in the upper part of the city, the surface of which is (72 metres) 236 feet above tide in the harbor.

This filter bed is of very costly construction, as will be seen by examination of the accompanying plan and section. (Plates XXVI. and XXVII.) The filtering materials rest on arches, a vaulted chamber of like dimensions with the filter bed being constructed below it for the reception of the filtered water. This chamber or reservoir will hold about 540,000. U. S. gallons.

The filter proper is composed of sand, gravel, and stones, in about the following proportions, as shown on the accompanying sketch :

1. A layer of small stones over the arches, about
   8 inches thick at the top of the arch . . . .   8 inches.
2. Broken stone   3   "
3. Small gravel   4   "
4. Coarse sand from river   8   "
5. Ordinary sand of "Goudet"   3   "
6. Fine sand of "Montredon" 12   "

Total . . . . 38 inches.

19

In other words, the filter is composed of two feet of sand, resting on gravel and broken stone.

This filter is said to have operated well and satisfactorily while the water that was passed upon it had been prepared for filtration; when this ceased to be the case, it became rapidly unserviceable. When I saw it there was from 3 to 4 inches of compact mud over the surface of the sand, and it had not been used, except as a reservoir for water, for two years.

It is vaulted over throughout, and therefore not very conveniently accessible for cleansing or renewal. The filter bed is in two divisions, which can be used together or separately, as may be desired. The areas are as follows, excluding the pillars upon which the arches rest :

Division No. 1	47,613 square feet.
" " 2	44,753 " "
Total	92,366 square feet.

Filtering at the rate of 90 U. S. gallons (72 gallons imperial) to the square foot, these filters would be competent to clarify 8,312,940 U. S. gallons in 24 hours, or half this quantity with but one in use. The population supplied from them did not probably exceed 230,000 when they were in use, which would give a rate of 36 U. S. gallons per head with both filters in operation, or of 18 with but one. I have been informed that this filter will be used again when the means proposed to be provided for the preparatory removal of the grosser parts of the sediment by settlement shall be completed; but it is obvious that for a population of 300,000, increasing from year to year, more extended arrangements somewhat in unison with the general project would be required.

When these filter beds were in use they were cleansed at intervals by reversing the movement of the water and forcing it upwards through the filtering material. While this upward movement was in progress the surface sand of the filter was raked and disturbed by laborers with suitable tools, to facilitate the removal of the sedimentary deposit. The turbid water thus produced was run off into a sewer. The water used for this purpose must have been the clear water of the reservoir below. When water is in such abundance as in this case, the amount used in this way may be of little moment. If it had all to be raised by steam power, it would make this mode of cleansing the filters a very costly one.

To get rid of the mass of the sediment of the river by settlement, and sufficiently prepare the water for filtration, five reservoirs or settling basins were constructed on the line of the canal, in certain of the small valleys which it crossed, where their application was convenient and economical. Dams were constructed across the valleys indicated, sufficiently high to bring the water up to the canal level, and through these dams, pipes and sluices were provided for flushing off the sedimentary deposits.

The water of the canal was made to flow into one end of each of these reservoirs, and passing slowly through it, the reservoirs being deep, it parted with a portion of its sediment and left the reservoir at the other end in a less turbid state, returning to the main channel there. These reservoirs, or settling basins, for such was their use and intention, were:

1. The Ponseret reservoir.
2. The Garenne   "
3. The Vallonbiere "
4. The Realtort   "
5. The St. Marthe   "

With the five in use, a superficial area of 220 acres of water was available for settlement, which, including the effect of the canal itself, must have been abundantly sufficient to prepare the water for the filter beds at that time.

But from some defect in the construction of the Realtort dam, this reservoir, much the largest (185 acres), does not appear to have been long in use. Of the others, the Ponseret basin (No. 1) is the only one now serviceable, and this has a surface area of but 2½ acres. The other three, for reasons growing out of the difficulty of, or neglect in, withdrawing the sediment, have been allowed to fill up, and are now entirely unserviceable. A considerable quantity of sediment is deposited in the canal itself, which is cleansed out twice a year; but the velocity of the water in the canal maintains that water in a very turbid state, and it consequently reaches the filter beds now in a condition which makes their application impracticable. The water passes into the pipes of the city, at present in its dirty, muddy state, to the great dissatisfaction of the inhabitants.

Should the large reservoir of the Realtort be brought into use again, with the means of scouring it proposed by the Engineer, Mr. Pascales, the water may again be rendered fit for filtration. Many of the citizens advocate the application of the natural filter, by the construction of subaqueous galleries, on the banks of the Durance, and it remains still somewhat uncertain what process will be adopted to render the water tolerable. Under any circumstances, its condition, in summer, after being exposed for 62 miles to the sun, cannot be very palatable.

GENOA WATER WORKS.

Genoa, *March*, 1866.

NATURAL FILTER.

The city of Genoa is supplied with water from two separate quarters, the oldest supply being derived from the south side of the maritime Alps; the modern works, from the north side. The first is still in charge of the city authorities; the second was constructed by, and is operated by, the Nicolay Water Company, under a special concession or charter.

The construction of the old works was completed in 1729. The water in this case is derived from the river Bisagno, at Stigliera, by damming the main stream there and two of its branches; at low summer water the amount available does not exceed from 80 to 100 litres (say 3 cubic feet) per second. The water is conducted to the city in a small masonry conduit, 22 kilometres in length (13.6 miles). The width of the conduit is 0.80 metres ($2\frac{1}{2}$ feet); its depth varies. About half of it is stated to be covered, the rest uncovered. The water is used at one place outside of the city for mill-power, and a portion of it in the same way inside of the city. It passes through the city as a covered conduit, delivering its water on either side, but not under pressure. There are no filtering arrangements connected with this branch of the water supply.

The population of Genoa is variously stated at from 150,000 to 165,000.

The new works of the Nicolay Company derive their water from the valley of the river Scrivia, near Busallo, at a point distant (26 kilometres) 16 miles from Genoa.

The river Scrivia has its source in the northern slopes of the maritime Alps. It is a rapid mountain stream, the channel at Busallo evidencing, by the coarseness of the gravel or shingle composing it, the rapidity of the current. The water is gathered from underground galleries in the valley of the Scrivia, is conveyed thence by cast-iron pipes to Genoa without exposure anywhere, and is introduced into the city under pressure by a net-work of pipes, whence it can be carried into the highest stories of all the city buildings. In all respects the scheme is more complete in its parts, and more liberal in its dimensions and preparation for the growth of this thriving seaport, than usually obtains in continental cities.

The Engineer of the project was Guilio Sardi ; the Constructing Engineer, Aleso. Moschini, and the President of the Company, Paulo An. Nicolay, to whom I am under great obligations for the facilities which he afforded me toward obtaining access to the galleries.

The accompanying sketch will explain the position of these galleries with reference to the river. (Plate XXVIII.)

The wide bottom of gravel over which the river flows here is, as well as I could learn, 40 to 50 feet in depth, except in the immediate channel of the river, where the depth does not exceed 30 feet. It rests upon an irregular bed of compact rock, and the underground flow of filtered water is held up by this rock. This underground flow is doubtless moving down the valley, which has a considerable fall here, but at a very slow velocity as compared with the river, its movement being impeded by the body of sand and gravel through which it percolates.

The side walls of the galleries, which tap this underground flow, are carried down to the rock above mentioned, as will be seen by the cross-sections given in the accompanying sketch. The underground flow cannot, therefore, pass under the gallery. Referring particularly to that portion of the gallery which underlies the bed of the river at right angles to its course, the underground flow is dammed to a certain extent by the position of this gallery, and must rise over the top of its arch in its course down stream. The galleries are built of hydraulic masonry, and the water enters them by pipes built in the side walls of the up-stream side. There are no pipes on the heavy side walls of the down-stream side of the galleries. The effect of this damming process must be to increase the head of the underground flow at this point, and to that extent to increase the volume of water delivering through the side pipes into the galleries.

At the points m, n, and q on the sketch, there are large man-holes, with stairs for descending into the galleries. These man-holes had houses over them. When I descended, in March, 1866, the galleries were full, and the water stood some feet above the soffit of the gallery arch. It was perfectly clear and limpid, and reached the city through the pipes in the same state. At the point n there are sluices established in the gallery, by which that part of it from n to r can be separated and its waters cut off from the portion south of n. In high stages of the river these sluices are closed, the water from the portion of the gallery south of n (580 feet in length) being then sufficient for the city supply. The shutting of the sluices at such times is said to relieve the lower southern part of the gallery, situated alongside of the railroad tunnel there, from the superfluous pressure of the flood waters, and from any risk of leakage into that tunnel.

The galleries are five feet in width, by seven to eight feet in height, in

English measures. The amount of water derivable from these galleries much exceeds the amount required by the city of Genoa now, and the works are, therefore, in a condition to meet liberally the growth of the city for some time to come.

The water consumption of Genoa from the Nicolay Works was stated by Mr. Nicolay to average 500 ounces daily, the ounce being equivalent to 800 litres (28.25 cubic feet) per hour. This gives a rate per diem of about 10,000 metres, strictly 9,600, which is equal to 2,536,128. U. S. gallons.

If we take the population at 160,000, and allow three-fourths of it to be supplied from the Nicolay Works, it will be found equal to 15.8 U. S. gallons per head of the population supplied. An experiment made during a very low stage of the river in 1865, to ascertain the minimum capacity of the filtering galleries, gave a delivery then of 500 litres per second (1,765. c. feet), which is equal to 11,413,440. U. S. gallons in 24 hours. This minimum rate will admit of a delivery to the city of over four times its present consumption.

But the ordinary delivering capacities of these galleries must approach to double its minimum rate, and when it shall become necessary, the minimum rate can be largely supplemented by providing storage reservoirs for accumulating the surplus water of the more abundant months.

The galleries being 1,780 feet in length, the minimum capacity is equal to $(\frac{11413440}{1780})$=6,412. U. S. gallons per lineal foot of this length. This is a greater rate of delivery than the Toulouse or the Lyons galleries indicated, and may be referred, in part at least, to the peculiar mode of construction across the channel of the stream. Two cast-iron pipes, of $17\frac{3}{4}$ inches (45 centimetres) diameter each, convey the water from the south terminus of the filtering gallery, along the line of the Turin Railway to Genoa. The altitude of the Scrivia at Busallo is (360 metres) 1,181 feet above the Mediterranean, but this is reduced within a mile of the Scrivia by a safety-valve to (280 metres) 918 feet. At Genoa the pipe distribution is divided into a high-service and a low-service. The pressure at the terminus of the main at Genoa, used for the high-service, indicated 320 feet, and at the terminus of the low-service main 203 feet. Both pipes reached Genoa under the same pressure, but for the low-service a safety-valve, wasting a certain amount of water, reduced the pressure as indicated. The vault in which these gauges were situated was estimated to be about 30 feet above the sea. There are, doubtless, contrivances along the line for relieving the pipes of their superabundant head, and reducing it to the manageable pressure which we find existing, as above stated, at their entrance to the city. The length of these pipe conduits has been already stated to be each (26 kilometres) 16.15 miles. A small fraction of the water delivered by these pipes is applied in the city to milling purposes; but this is understood to be in addition to the city consumption proper, as given above.

LEGHORN WATER WORKS.

LEGHORN, *March*, 1866.

FILTERING CISTERNS.

Leghorn is supplied with water from a number of springs on the slopes of the low mountain range of Maggiore and Corbolone, where the head waters of a branch of the river Tora take their rise.

The springs are brought together and conducted to the filter-house or cistern of " Pian di Rota " by a small covered conduit of masonry. The length of this conduit was given us as (14.05 kilometres) 8.73 miles. The water space in the conduit is but 12 inches in width and 17 inches deep (see Plate XXIX). It is conducted over the valleys upon neat bridges of masonry, and through some ridges by roomy tunnels. The amount of water flowing through the aqueduct (10th March, 1866), as measured that day in one of the tunnels, was 568,760. U. S. gallons in 24 hours. In low summer water, according to the Superintending Engineer, it has been reduced (June, 1864) to 276,000. U. S. gallons per diem.

The population in 1848 was 72,400; it is stated at 80,000 in 1861, and may be safely taken at 82,000 now. This, for the amount of water delivered by the aqueduct at this date, which was considered an average of the spring months, is equal to but about 7 U. S. gallons per head. During the hot summer months the supply is very inadequate to the requirements of the population, and its increase is under consideration.

Leghorn is a seaport, and there is very little irregularity in the level of the streets, which are generally from 10 to 15 feet above the water of the Mediterranean.

The altitude of the springs above the sea is (256 metres) 840 feet.

The altitude of the filtering-house or cistern mentioned above is (48 metres) 157 feet above the sea. From this filter-house the water is conveyed by a 9-inch pipe main to a larger cistern-house within the city, which had also apparently a process of filtering in contemplation, and is curiously divided up towards that end ; no filtration, however, is attempted there now.

Both of these cistern-houses are tasteful and monumental, as specimens of architecture, but costly for the engineering duties required of them.

The length of the pipe main, or the distance of the two cisterns apart, is (3,309 metres) 10,856 feet. The water in the city cistern stands ordinarily about 28 feet above the sea. The pipe mains deliver the water freely into the city cistern, unchecked or throttled by a stopcock, so that the pressure due to the altitude of the outside or country filter-house is not applied to the city, the small amount of water at present available probably making such an application impracticable.

From the city cistern, water is distributed by pipes to the numerous fountains, and it is to these fountains that the inhabitants go or send for water.

A supplementary covered cistern in another part of the city acts as an aid to the city cistern above alluded to, in increasing the small provision made for the storage of the water flowing on through the aqueduct and pipe main during the night hours.

We have, then, as a summary of the works, the pipes and fountains excepted :

1st. The cluster of springs situated (17.36 kilometres) 10.78 miles north-easterly from the city.

2d. The aqueduct from the springs to the water filter-house.

3d. The principal filter-house or cistern, situated (3,309 metres) 2.05 miles from the city.   (Plate XXIX.)

4th. The large cistern or covered reservoir within the city (Plate XXX.), auxiliary to which is the smaller cistern in the city, increasing simply the reserve of water in store.

The Leghorn Water Works have been spoken of as possessing very simple and efficient arrangements for the filtration and purification of the water, and it was therefore that I was desired to visit them. I will endeavor to describe what these arrangements are.

The principal filter-house (Pian di Rota), which is outside of the city, may be called the outer filter-house. The water chamber of this house (see the accompanying Plate) is divided into seven divisions.

The bottom of the first five divisions is covered with a filtering material composed of gravel and charcoal in the following proportions :

1. A layer of coarse gravel..................	8 inches.
2. A layer of wood charcoal.................	12 "
3. A layer of coarse gravel	8 "
4. A layer of fine gravel	12 "
Total thickness	40 inches.

No sand is used, and the charcoal is not laid in the shape of powder, but, as described to me, is broken to about the size of very large gravel and so laid; much of it, however, must get broken up smaller during the manipulation of laying and covering it.

In the sixth chamber, the material is simply gravel, without charcoal. In the seventh chamber, which forms the receptacle for the water after passing through the others, there is no filtering material on the bottom.

The first division, marked a in the Figure, receives the water from the aqueduct. The water cannot pass from a into the second division b, except by the small holes provided for that purpose at the bottom of the division wall, and to reach those holes it must pass downwards through more or less of the filtering material in a, and after passing through the holes it must pass upwards through more or less of the filtering material in b, to fill the division b.

Thence the water can only reach to fill the division c by flowing over the top of the wall dividing b from c, there being no holes in that wall. Having got thus into c, the same process is repeated between c and d, the water after passing through holes at the bottom of the wall dividing c from d, flowing thereafter over the top of the wall dividing d from e. Thence it finds its way through the bottom of the wall dividing e from f, and after filling the division f, overflows into the final division g.

At the time of my visit the water from the aqueduct flowed into the first division, perfectly clear. There were fourteen feet in depth of water in all the divisions, and we could see the gravel bottom of the first six, and the paved bottom of the seventh, quite distinctly. Two American Engineers accompanied me in my visit to these works, Mr. W. H. Talcott and Mr. L. B. Ward, and they assisted me in my examination of the water, and the measurement already referred to of the flow. A tumbler of water taken from the aqueduct where it flows into the first division a, was compared with a tumbler of water from the last division g, and we could not distinguish any difference. The water entered the filter-house clear, and there was consequently no duty thrown on the filter beds. We were informed by the attendant in charge, that the filtering material was cleansed or changed once in two or three years; the last cleansing was after an interval of two years. This account was corroborated by the Engineer in charge. We were further informed, that when the aqueduct water came down turbid, which was very rare, it was wasted, by means shown us, into the neighboring valley, and not passed through the filter-house. There were means provided, besides, for connecting it with the city main, without passing it through the filter-house.

As two and a-half feet of open gravel could evidently be of no use in rendering turbid water clear, the material relied on for that purpose must have been the charcoal, the gravel being used only to keep the charcoal in place.

20

How far the charcoal would have answered the purpose had the water been turbid, and how frequently it would have required, in that case, to be uncovered, and more or less renewed, cannot be gathered from the experience of these works, for we were informed that turbid water was not allowed to be passed into the filter-house, and that indeed the aqueduct water, coming from a collection of springs, and not from the channel of a stream, was rarely otherwise than clear. The works were not considered, by those in charge, as valuable, or as necessary for filtration, but simply as monumental cisterns, admitting of the storage of a certain amount of water.

The area or superficies of the filtering material in the six divisions referred to is about 7,450 square feet.

The city cistern or reservoir (Plate XXX.) is in plan divided into four spaces. Into two of these, m and n, the main pipe from the country reservoir delivers its water. The floors of divisions m and n are covered with about 12 inches of gravel, as is the bottom of the small square division p. From m and n the water reaches p by holes along the bottoms of the respective division walls, passing through the gravel to reach these holes, and to fill the division p. From p the water overflows into the large space q, and thence communicates with the city fountains by a system of cast-iron pipes.

There is no charcoal used with the gravel in this house, and although the divisions indicate a provision for filtration in case it should have been necessary, no operation of this kind is necessary now, and no adequate materials for that purpose are therefore provided. The house, therefore, is only of use as a storage cistern.

The Engineer in charge, Mons. A. Della Valle, and his aid, Mons. Francesco Pelligrini, very obligingly gave us access to the works, and permitted us to copy the drawings of the reservoir houses. The Engineer of the project, Mons. Paschal Poccianti, of Florence, who enjoyed a high reputation as an architect, has been some time dead.

WAKEFIELD WATER WORKS.

MR. THOMAS SPENCER'S PROCESS.

I visited Wakefield in August, 1868, for the purpose of seeing in operation the process of Mr. Thomas Spencer, of London, for the purification of objectionable water. Although this special application of Mr. Spencer is not requisite upon any of our Western rivers now, a report on filtration would be incomplete without some allusion to it. The population of Wakefield was given me at 25,000. The supply of water is in the hands of a Water Company. It is a constant supply, and not intermittent. The water is taken from the river Calder, at a point about a mile below the city. This river rises in the high moor lands, west of Halifax, which divide Yorkshire from Lancashire. In its course it receives the sewerage of Halifax and many small places, and it has received the sewerage of Wakefield before reaching the point whence the water is taken by the Water Company; it is also contaminated by the refuse waters of various dyeing establishments and other factories situated on the river. On the other hand, the river receives at Wakefield the lockage water of a canal which has not been subject to the same extent of pollution. At this date (13th August, 1868) the long season of drought and the low state of the stream made the water unusually objectionable. A tumblerful taken from the river at the connection of the Company's conduit was of a dark, inky hue, and slightly offensive to the smell. When the Company established its works here some twenty-three years back, the river water was comparatively pure; but the increase of the population resident on the river since that time, and the growth of factories, has rendered it entirely unfit for domestic use in its natural state. This condition of things induced the Company four years ago to try the application of Mr. Thos. Spencer's mode of filtering and purifying such waters, and the result has been wonderfully satisfactory.

As my only object is to give an idea of the materials and arrangement of this filter, I will refer very briefly to the general arrangement of the works: On the left bank of the river, at a point about a mile below Wakefield, there are two settling reservoirs, having a water surface of six acres. The water is pumped into one of these, and passes thence through openings in the division

wall into the other, whence it is drawn by a conduit to the pumps, which lift it
to the high grounds at Fieldhead where the filter beds are situated. The water,
in its course through these two settling reservoirs, has deposited the greater
portion of any sedimentary-matter held in suspension. There are two pumping
engines for this service, each of them operating both a low-service and high-service pump at the same time.

The high land at Fieldhead, on which the filter beds and storage reservoirs
are placed, commands by at least fifty feet the highest ground in the city. It is
situated, as given me, 150 feet above the pumps already mentioned. From the
pumping engines two mains, of 10 and 15 inches diameter respectively, convey
the water to the filters.

There are four filter beds at Fieldhead, and two small storage reservoirs.

The floor of the filter bed is concrete, resting on a layer of clay puddle.
Upon this floor is laid a series of small drains ; in the case of the first two filters,
of brick ; in the case of the two last, of square clay pipes, not perforated
all over, but with one hole in the centre of each, over which a cup is placed,
perforated with a dozen small holes of about 3–16th inch opening. These square
pipes are in three-feet lengths, the size inside being not quite 4 by 5 inches ;
they have sockets, and when laid constitute a series of collecting drains about
five feet apart, c, c ; their ends on either side opening into large collecting conduits, whence the filtered water is delivered into storage reservoirs in communication with the city mains. Each of the clay pipe drains is connected with a
vertical air pipe.

Between and over the series of clay pipe drains gravel is placed, the depth
of gravel not being carried to more than three inches over the pipes. Upon
this is laid 17 inches of the carbide of iron mixed with fine sand, about half and
half. This carbide of iron forms the purifying material of the filter. Over the
layer of carbide of iron there is a layer of fine sand, of from 15 to 18 inches in
thickness. The sand, as I understand the process, is mainly depended on to
clarify the water from anything held in mechanical suspension, so to say, but
the carbide of iron destroys the noxious gases and offensive coloring belonging
to any water contaminated as this is with a large proportion of sewerage and of
the refuse of factories ; and this it is said to do usually very thoroughly, for the
water after passing through the filters presents nothing offensive to the taste or
smell, and is used unstintingly by the citizens ; but at the time of my visit the
discoloration was not perfect. The amount of water used in this hot season, and
its abnormal character in the river as regards appearance, had evidently taxed
the filters beyond their capacity. Of the four filter beds, one has to be cleansed
off every day, removing about ¾ inch of sand, which is washed and cleansed for
renewal. There are, therefore, during a large portion of the 24 hours, but three
filter beds in use.

The walls of the filters are vertical, or nearly so. In the absence of a correct diagram of these, which I could not obtain, my notes give the approximate area of the four filters as equal to 16,400 square feet; three of them, therefore, would contain about 12,300 square feet.

The consumption during the day of 24 hours was stated to average generally 750,000 imperial gallons. Taking the average day rate at 50,000 gallons per hour, we have a flow through the filters of four gallons per square foot per hour, which would not be considered extreme on the London filters; but we are to consider, that a very slow rate of filtration may be necessary here as compared with the Thames or the sea, to enable the material specially provided in this case to produce its effect upon a water so very much more objectionable than these others as regards discoloration and exposure to offensive contaminations.

The carbide of iron, which forms the purifying element of Mr. Spencer's patent process of filtration, was described to me by Dr. Statter as being prepared from red hematite iron ore, by mixing that ore with sawdust in equal portions and roasting it in an iron retort. The result is crushed to the size of fine gravel, pea size, and mixed for use with equal parts of fine sand. It costs, delivered at the works, five pounds sterling per ton. On the two first filters, it has been in use without change or addition four years, and is said not to be in any way deteriorated. The filtered water is drawn into two small storage reservoirs, having a joint capacity of 2,750,000 imperial gallons. It is thence delivered to the city by two pipe mains of 12 and 15 inches diameter respectively.

I am indebted to Dr. Statter, the Chairman of the Water Company, for permission to visit the works.

I learned from Mr. Filliter, the Engineer of the Leeds Water Works, that the process of Mr. Spencer was in use at Southport, and also at Wisbeach, applied to waters that are not contaminated with sewerage, but objectionable in color from other causes. At Wisbeach, the water comes from a moor tract of country, and is discolored by peat; at Southport, the water, which is drawn from wells, is tainted with iron rust. In both cases, the action of the new process was said to be successful in removing the objectionable features.

APPENDIX.

APPENDIX.

COPY OF INSTRUCTIONS.

OFFICE OF BOARD OF WATER COMMISSIONERS,
ST. LOUIS, Dec. 11th, 1865.

JAMES P. KIRKWOOD, Esq., *Chief Engineer.*

DEAR SIR,—At a meeting held this day at the rooms of the Commissioners, there were present His Hon. the Mayor, J. S. Thomas; Philip Wiegel, and Dwight Durkee, *President.* Mayor Thomas offered the following resolution, to wit:

"*Resolved*, That James P. Kirkwood, Esq., our Chief Engineer, be requested to proceed at once to Europe, and there inform himself in regard to the best process in use for the clarifying river waters used for the supply of cities, whether by deposition alone, or by deposition and filtration combined, making such an examination in each instance as will enable him to report to this Board the general dimensions and special characteristics of the specific works visited by him, so that this Board may be able to appreciate how far the same mechanisms, and the same or similar combinations of materials, are likely to be adaptable to the purifying of the Mississippi water at St. Louis. The following cities which are supplied by river water, and which possess works for the cleansing of that water when turbid, are indicated as points to be visited, to wit: In England—London, Norwich, Preston, Nottingham, and Southampton; Scotland—Paisley and Perth; in Ireland—Dublin; in France—Lyons, Tours, Toulouse, Marseilles; in Germany—Berlin, Hamburgh, Brunswick; in Italy—Leghorn; and that such other cities not above mentioned as may be ascertained to possess works of this class, deserving of examination, be visited also. Provided, however, that Mr. Kirkwood shall so arrange his movements as to return to St. Louis by the first day of May, 1866, at the furthest.

21

"*Resolved*, That Mr. Kirkwood be, and he is hereby, empowered to employ such assistance or interpreter when in Europe, and particularly where foreign languages are spoken, as may be necessary to enable him to get all the information needed."

Above I hand you copy of resolutions, and, to enable you to carry them out, I enclose herein my individual check, No. 30,009, on National Bank of North America, New York, for $2,700, which, I trust, will be sufficient for the whole trip.

I have to request that you will advise me of the receipt of this, also what day you sail, and any other particulars you choose ; and, further, that you will report your arrival on the other side, with such observations as your time and inclination will permit. With the hope that an overruling Providence will guide and protect you,

I remain very truly yours,

(Signed)   DWIGHT DURKEE,

President.

Table of Equivalents of certain Measures mentioned in the preceding Descriptions.

NAME OF MEASURE.	ITS EQUIVALENT IN						
	U. S. Gallons.	Imp. Gallons.	Litres.	Cubic Foot.	Cubic Metres.	Cubic Inches.	Pounds Avoirdupois.
1 U. S. Gallon........	1.	.833111	3.785203	.133081	.0037852	231.	8.3388822
1 Imp. Gallon........	1.20032	1.	4.543457	.160459	.0045434	277.274	10.
1 Litre..............	.2641866	.220097	1.	.035317	.001	61.0271	2.204737
1 Cub. Foot.........	7.480152	6.232102	28.315280	1.	.028315	1728.	62.37916
1 Cub. Metre........	264.18657	220.096714	1000.	35.316609	1.	61027.0963	2204.737
1 Cub. Inch.........	....	....	....	....	....	....	.036099

Weight of a cubic inch of water, English standard, .036065 lbs. avoir.; U. S. standard, .036099 lbs. avoir.; French standard, .036127 lbs. avoir.

The "Ordnance Manual of the U. S. Army, 1861," and the "Engineer's Pocket-Book," by C. H. Haswell, give 8.3388822 lbs. avoirdupois as the weight (U. S. standard) of a gallon of water, from which, in the above table, the weight of a cubic foot and a cubic inch are calculated.

The same works give 61.0270963 cubic inches in a litre, and 2.204737 lbs. avoirdupois as the weight (French standard) of the same.

The "Engineer's Pocket-Book," London, 1869, and "Beardmore's Manual of Hydrology," give 61.028 cubic inches in a litre, and a weight of 2.2055 lbs. avoirdupois for the same.

"Beardmore's Manual of Hydrology" gives 10.003 lbs. avoirdupois as the weight of an imperial gallon. "Agenda Opperman," Paris, 1869, gives 4.543458 litres in an imperial gallon.

All of the above works give 277.274 cubic inches in an imperial gallon, as also does Francis, in his "Lowell Hydraulic Experiments."

LONDON PUMPING ENGINES.

I will here condense in a tabular form some of the information in regard to pumping engines which is scattered over the descriptions of the London Works. These works afford fair specimens of the different kinds of pumping engines and pumps in use in England and elsewhere. The greater number of them are found to give very satisfactory results, whether as regards economy, endurance, or ease of action, and of some of these engines it may safely be said that they have not been anywhere surpassed in these respects.

Two types of pumping engines are more especially esteemed by the generality of English Hydraulic Engineers, opinions being much divided as to which should have the preference. These are : the single-acting engine with the plunger pump, usually called the Cornish engine ; and the two-cylinder double-acting engine, with the plunger and bucket pump, which may be called the Simpson engine. The fuel economy of the one has proved to be as good as that of the other ; but the cost of maintenance, the wear and tear, we have no means of comparing. The current expenses of some of the Cornish engines have been very faithfully given by the Engineers of the East London Water Works, but the corresponding expenses of the double-cylinder engines have not been made public. We are rather left to infer, therefore, that the cost of maintenance and repairs is in favor of the Cornish engine. The double-cylinder engine is a safer engine, the crank controlling and limiting the stroke, which in the Cornish engine is loose, and dependent to some extent on the watchfulness of the engine-man. The double-cylinder engine admits of a higher degree of expansion being used than on the other, with much less strain or harshness of action on the machine. In this respect it has the advantage of any description of single-cylinder engine, an advantage which renders the double-cylinder engine specially valuable as a pumping machine.

The following are the results of test trials made on these two classes of engines, to ascertain the rate of expenditure of fuel, or the "duty," so called.

The "duty" in England for pumping engines means the lbs. of work or lbs. of load raised one foot high by one cwt. of coal (112 lbs.).

In the United States it has been referred to the simpler measure of

100 lbs. The English results have, therefore, been reduced to meet this last unit.

	lbs., raised 1 foot high.
The four double-cylinder engines at Lambeth were tested by Mr. Joshua Field during 24 hours without stopping, and for every 100 lbs. of coal consumed gave a duty in foot lbs. of	86,665,075

The fuel was Welsh coal of good average quality.

The New River engines (double-cylinder), tested soon after completion, gave a result on an eight hours' run of	100,892,847

Using Welsh coal, we presume of best quality.

The Chelsea (double-cylinder) engines, tested by Mr. Field during 24 hours, gave a result of	92,765,972

Using Welsh coal.

The Chelsea engines, under a four days' trial by Mr. Cowper (11th to 15th June, 1861), gave a result of	77,796,656

The three tests first given above, and all short tests, are of little account, except as affording some indication of the capability of the engine, when compared with other tests of about the same duration.

The last-mentioned test of four days approximates more nearly to the ordinary work of these engines throughout the year, as stated by Mr. Simpson, the Engineer of the Chelsea and Lambeth Companies.

The "duty" statistics of work of the Cornish engines are for longer periods, and therefore more satisfactory.

	lbs., raised 1 foot high.
During a five days' trial of the 80-inch Cornish engine at Old Ford, by Mr. Wicksteed, using the best small Newcastle coal, the result was	86,737,739
During 11½ years' work of the same engine, using ordinary small Newcastle coal, the steam cut off at ½, the duty was	69,093,852
With the best Newcastle coal, according to Mr. Wicksteed, it would have been	82,637,205
The Wicksteed engine (90-inch) at Old Ford, during three years work, 1848, 1849, and 1850, steam cut off at ¼, gave a result of..	73,079,032
Mr. Greaves, the Engineer of the work, stated that, using the "commonest coal that could be bought in 1862," the East London Cornish engines gave a duty result of..............	62,500,000

Mr. Morris, the Engineer of the Kent Water Works, where, however, the single-acting engine uses a different form of pump from the Cornish plunger, stated as the result of 14 years' ex-

lbs.,
raised 1 foot high.

perience, using the best coal at 25 shillings per ton, that these
engines had shown a duty of   75,892,222
At present (1863), using inferior coal, at ten shillings per ton,
he got a duty of but.................................   66,964,000
At the Kew Bridge station of the Grand Junction Water Works,
there are five Cornish engines. Mr. Fraser states that the
usual duty maintained there "throughout the year," using small
coal, costing 13 shillings per ton, is   65,178,477

The above statements show sufficiently that the double-cylinder crank and
fly-wheel engine can be relied on to afford as good an economy of fuel as the
Cornish engine; the short trials given above show indeed a higher "duty" for
the double-cylinder engine than for the Cornish engines; but I assume that for
a long period of time, and using the same quality of fuel, they would not exceed
the Cornish rates.

The following table brings together the leading engines of the London
Works (the Kent Works excepted), with the view of indicating the relation of
the pump load to that of the cylinder. This is a mere blocking out, so to say,
of the question, for the friction of the engine is not added, as it should be, to
give the actual work done at the steam end; but the results are significant,
nevertheless, and of value, we think, so far as they go. The addition for friction would have been in most cases a guess which the reader can as well make
for himself. The data on which the table is founded are not given as severely
correct, though all received at the several stations from the persons in charge
there, and from personal observation. They will most of them be found, I
trust, to be near approximations. Some errors have evidently crept in, and
the publication of the table may lead to their correction.

ENGINE TABLE.

Name of Works.	Character of Engine.	Steam Cylinder. Diam. (Inches)	Stroke (Feet)	Effect of Pump Load on Piston. (Lbs. per Sq. Inch.)	Character of Pumps.	Pump. Diam. (Inches)	Stroke (Feet)	Strokes per Minute.	Area of Pump. (Square Inch.)	Load of Pump. Pressure by Gauge. (Feet)	Lbs. per Square Inch.	Total Load. (Lbs.)
Southwark and Vauxhall, at Battersea	Single-acting beam engine	64	10.6	19.05	Plunger	33	11.6	8	855.30	165	71.49	61415.
Southwark and Vauxhall, at Battersea	Do.	112	10.	17.10	Do.	50	10.	8	1963.49	175	65.82	168506.
Southwark and Vauxhall, at Battersea	Do.	68	10.	16.84	Do.	33	10.	7½	855.30	165	71.49	61145.
Southwark and Vauxhall, at Battersea	Do.	55	8.	17.16	Double-acting pump	14½	8.	12 to 14	165.13	285	123.48	20390.
Southwark and Vauxhall, at Battersea	Do.	55	8.	22.	do.	16	8.	10	201.06	300	129.98	26133.
Grand Junction at Kew	Do.	90	11.	15.30	Plunger	38	11.	6	1134.11	175	85.82	97329.
Do. do.	Do.	64	8.	10.05	Do.	24	8.	11	452.39	165	71.49	32341.
Do. do.	Do.	63	8.	10.37	Do.	24	8.	11	452.39	165	71.49	32341.
Do. do.	Do.	65	8.	13.53	Do.	24	8.	9	452.39	212	91.85	41552.
West Middlesex, at Hammersmith	Do.	54	8.	13.50	Two lifting pumps	{ 20, 15 }	{ 8., 6. }	{ 14 to 16, 14 to 16 }	{ 314.16, 176.71 }	160, 160	69.32, 69.32	21777, 12240.
West Middlesex, at Hammersmith	Do.	54	8.	.....	Double-acting pump	20	8.	..	314.16	.....	.....	.....
West Middlesex, at Hammersmith	Do.	64	8.	14.54	Do.	23	8.	..	415.47	130	56.32	28399.
West Middlesex, at Hammersmith	Do.	72	10.	.....	Do.	23	10.	..	415.47	.....	.....	.....
West Middlesex, at Hammersmith	Do.	80	10.	13.64	Do.	24	10.	..	452.39	162	70.19	31753.
New River, at Hornsey	Do.	44	10.	15.10	Plunger	15	9.	11	176.71	300	129.98	22963.
New River, at New River Head	Do.	49	8.	17.30	Two lifting pumps	{ 29, 18 }	{ 8., 6. }	14	{ 660.52, 254.47 }	85	36.82	{ 24390, 5369.6 }
Do. do.	Do.	48	8.	17.30	Do. do.	{ 29, 18 }	{ 8., 6. }	.....	{ 660.52, 254.47 }	.....	36.82	.....

ENGINE TABLE—*Continued.*

Name of Work	Character of Engine	Steam Cylinder Diam. (inches)	Steam Cylinder Stroke (feet)	Effect of Pump Load on Piston (Lbs. per Sq. Inch)	Character of Pump	Pump Diam. (inches)	Pump Stroke (feet)	Strokes per Minute	Area of Pump (Square Inch)	Pressure by Gauge (Feet)	Load per Square Inch (Lbs.)	Total Load (Lbs.)
East London, at Lea Bridge	Single-acting beam engine	100	11.	10.20	Plunger	50	11.	7 to 8	1963.49	96	41.16	80817.
Do. do.	Do. two new, 1868	84	..	.....	Do.	...	...	8 to 9	1452.20	..	.....	.....
Do. at Old Ford	Do. do.	85	10.	11.88	Do.	43	9.	8	1452.20	96	41.16	59772.
Do. do.	Do. do.	80	10.	9.2	Do.	41	9.	8 to 9	1017.88	85	36.82	37478.
Do. do.	Do. do.	72	10.	8.90	Do.	36	10.	8½	1017.88	81 to 88	37.26	56654.
Do. do.	Do. do.	90	11.	20.97	Plunger or pole.	44	11.	10	1520.53	130	56.32	78026.
Southwark and Vauxhall, at Hampton	Single-acting "bull engine"	70	10.	19.66	Do. do.	43	10.	10	1385.44	130	56.32	67270.3
Southwark and Vauxhall, at Hampton	Do. do.	66	10.	.....	Do. do.	39	10.	...	1194.59	..	.....	.....
Southwark and Vauxhall, at Hampton	Do. do.	60	10.	16.88	Do. do.	35	10.	8 to 9	962.11	155	71.49	61145.4
Southwark and Vauxhall, at Battersea	Do. do.	70	10.	19.31	Do. do.	33	10.	14	855.30	91	39.42	54614.
Grand Junction, at Hampton	Do. do.	60	10.	19.31	Do. do.	42	10.	14	1385.44	91	39.42	54614.
Do. do.	Do. do.	70	10.	13.73	Do. do.	42	10.	10 to 11	1385.44	175	85.82	52843.
Do. at Kew	Do. do.	70	10.	9.63	Do. do.	28	10.	10	615.75	100	43.33	37060.
Do. at Camden Hill	Do. do.	70	10.	9.63	Do. do.	33	10.	10	855.30	100	43.33	37060.
Do. do.	Do. do.	70	10.	13.99	Do. do.	33	10.	...	855.30	65	28.16	44786.
West Middlesex, at Hampton	Do. do.	64	10.	13.22	Do. do.	45	10.	6¼	1590.43	65	28.16	44786.
Do. do.	Do. do.	64	10.	.....	Do. do.	45	10.	6¼	1590.43	...	95.32	21560.
Chelsea, at Thames Ditton	Rotary double cylinder, two engines coupled to one fly-wheel. There are three pair of engines here of same size and pattern.	28 / 46	5.6 / 8.	12.97	Plunger and bucket.	24 / 17½	7.1	12 to 14	226.19	220	95.32	21560.

ENGINE TABLE—*Continued.*

NAME OF WORKS	CHARACTER OF ENGINE	STEAM CYLINDER		EFFECT OF PUMP LOAD ON PISTON	CHARACTER OF PUMP	PUMP			AREA OF PUMP	LOAD OR PUMP		
		Diam. Inches.	Stroke. Feet.	Lbs. per Sq. Inch.		Diam. Inches.	Stroke. Feet.	Strokes per Minute.	Square Inch.	Pressure by Gauge. Feet.	Lbs. per Square Inch.	Total Load. Lbs.
Lambeth, at Thames Ditton	Double cylinder, rotary, two engines coupled to one fly-wheel........ Three pair of these engines or six double cylinder engines of same size and pattern.	28 46	5.6 8.	11.20	Plunger and bucket.	24 17½	6.11	13 to 15	452.39	190	82.32	18620.
New River, at Stoke Newington........	Double cylinder rotary, two engines coupled to one fly-wheel.	28 46	5.6½ 8.	10.07	Plunger and bucket (night service)...	27 20	6.11	14	......	135	58.49	16744.
New River, at Stoke Newington........	Double cylinder, rotary, two engines coupled to one fly-wheel.	28 46	5.6½ 8.	10.07	Plunger and bucket (night service)...	27 20	6.11	14	......	135	......	......
New River, at Stoke Newington........	Two single cylinder rotary engines coupled to one fly-wheel.	60	8.	10.15	Two plungers and bucket pumps to each engine......	31½ 22 43 30½	7. 6.9	14 to 14½ ..	......	60 67	26. 37.70	10130. 27374.

22

The following table in regard to boilers was prepared in the hope that it would expose some uniformity of opinion and practice among the London Engineers, as respects the boiler capacity which should be provided for a given capacity or area of steam piston. The batteries of all the engines indicated in this table are composed of Cornish boilers. They are all of very nearly the same general dimensions, and they are all worked under about the same pressure of steam.

The engines too are mostly single-acting Cornish engines; the rotary engines given in the table are served by the same class of boilers, and worked under very nearly the same average of load per square inch of piston. Their action is more rapid in the proportion say of 8 to 12, and they would therefore use more steam per minute for any unit agreed upon, than the other class of engines. By referring to the first table given above, the reader can make such correction for variations in velocity as his judgment may dictate. I prefer to give this table in its crude state, without attempting the nicety of correction due to the various modifying influences of each case.

The capacity of boiler understood here refers to the gross size of the boiler without deduction for fire space or flues ; these last bear about the same proportion to each other in each case, and have therefore been disregarded. The unit at the steam cylinder to which the boiler capacity is applied, has been taken as one square foot of the area of the steam piston. This unit would correctly represent the case, were the velocities of the pistons of the different engines the same ; these velocities, however, vary even in the same class of engines, and to that extent the proportionate boiler capacities given in the table will be felt to be unsatisfactory. But as the variations in velocity are variations of practice rather than of principle, and each Cornish pumping engine is probably designed with reference to a conventional velocity for that class of machine, the capacity of boilers provided should in reality bear some uniform relation to the engine as it may be supposed to have been designed, rather than as it happens to be actuated. This kind of uniformity, however, is not found to exist. The boiler power varies considerably, as will be perceived at the different stations, and to an extent that is not easily explainable.

The table indicates a provision of boiler of from 100 to 140 cubic feet of boiler space to 1 square foot of piston area for the single-acting Cornish engines; and for the rotary engines, a provision of from 200 to 250 cubic feet of boiler space for each square foot of the steam piston area. The rotary engine, in other words, should have at least double the boiler capacity per square foot of its piston area, which would be requisite in the single-acting engine ; the steam in the rotary engine being used on both sides of the piston and the velocity of motion being usually greater.

The first Belleville engine (Cornish) of the Jersey Water Works was provided with a boiler capacity (4) in gross, equivalent to 150 cubic feet of boiler space to each square foot of piston area, and it was usually worked from a boiler capacity (3) equivalent to 112 cubic feet of boiler space to the square foot of piston area. At this time, 1869, there are six Cornish boilers to two engines, and the relations of these give 112½ cubic feet of boiler provided for each square foot of piston, and yet, when but one engine is in use it is usually served now by four boilers. This is sufficiently accounted for by the rate at which the engine is worked since the erection of a stand-pipe,—9 and 10 strokes per minute, as compared with the old rate of 6 and 7 strokes per minute.

Statement illustrative of the General Relations of Boilers to Engines on the London Pumping Works.

Name of Works and Station.	LEADING ENGINES AND THE BATTERIES PROVIDED FOR THEM AT UNDERMENTIONED STATIONS.					NUMBER OF ENGINES AND BOILERS OBSERVED AT WORK AT THE GIVEN DATES.					
	Number of Engines and Character.	Aggregate Power, Area.	Number of Boilers.	Gross Capacity of Boilers.	Boiler Capacity to One Square Foot of Piston.	Date of Observation.	Number of Engines at Work and Character.	Aggregate Power, Area.	Number of Boilers at Work.	Gross Capacity of Boilers at Work.	Boiler Space at Work for each Square Foot of Piston.
		Sq. Feet.		Cub. Feet.	Cub. Feet.			Sq. Feet.		Cub. Feet.	Cub. Feet.
Chelsea, at Thames Ditton............	6 rotary...	69.24	20	16409.	237.	24th July, 1868	{2 rotary, 2 rotary}	23.08, 23.08	6, 5	4310.5, 4270.	208.4, 185.2
Lambeth, at Thames Ditton............	6 rotary...	69.24	19	16653.	240.5	7th Aug., 1868	4 rotary..	46.16	12	10517.9	227.8
Southwark and Vauxhall, at Hampton......	3 Cornish	70.12	9	6734.7	96.	5th Aug., 1868	3 Cornish	70.12	9	6734.7	96.
Do. do. at Battersea.........	6 Cornish	175.70	25	21205.5	120.6	6th Aug., 1868	6 Cornish	175.07	20	16961.4	96.5
Do. do. at Hampton (new).....	2 Cornish	69.81	11	8291.3	119.	....	....	....	:	....	......
Grand Junction, at Hampton......	2 Cornish	39.27	9	7125.	181.4	5th Aug., 1868	2 Cornish	39.27	7	5541.7	141.1
Do. at Kew.........	5 Cornish	136.	12	8740.	63.3	29th July, 1868	4 Cornish	111.23	11	7958.3	71.8
Do. at Camden Hill......	2 Cornish	53.44	9	7634.	142.8	30th July, 1868	2 Cornish	53.44	7	5937.5	111.1
West Middlesex, at Hampton......	2 Cornish	44.68	9	6544.1	146.4	5th Aug., 1868	2 Cornish	44.68	6	4363.1	97.6
Do. at Hammersmith......	3 single-acting..	54.06	9	6361.6	117.6	31st July, 1868	2 single-acting.	38.25	8	5654.8	147.8
Do. do.	2 single-acting..	63.27	12	8626.3	139.5	31st July, 1868	1 single-acting.	34.91	9	6619.7	169.5
New River, at Greenlanes...........	6 rotary...	85.41	18	15776.9	184.6	8th Aug., 1868	2 rotary..	39.27	12	10517.9	267.8
East London, at Lea Bridge.........	1 Cornish	54.54	8	7032.1	128.9	July, 1866	1 Cornish	54.51	6	5374.0	96.7
Do. at Old Ford............	4 Cornish	146.76	16	14964.16	95.8	4th Aug., 1868	3 Cornish	118.49	10	8790.1	74.2

INDEX.

178   INDEX.

ST. LOUIS

PROPOSED FORM O

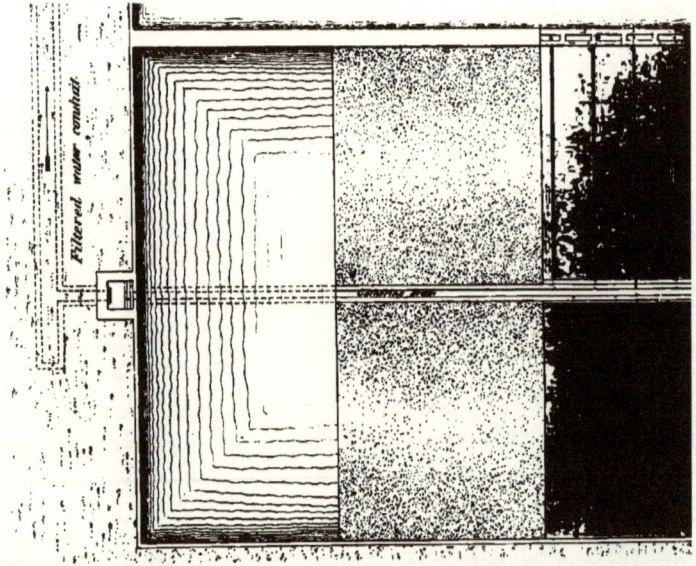

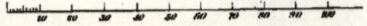

Filtered water conduit

CROSSING DRAIN

Section of Reservoir through centre of gate

LTERING RESERVOIR

Unfiltered water

Settling Reservoir

Transverse section of Filtering Reservoir

150 Feet

drain

ST. LOUIS WATER WORKS

DETAIL OF THE FILTERING RESERVOIRS

Section through the center.

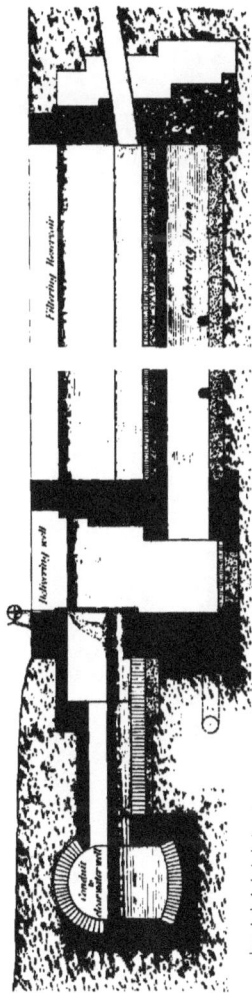

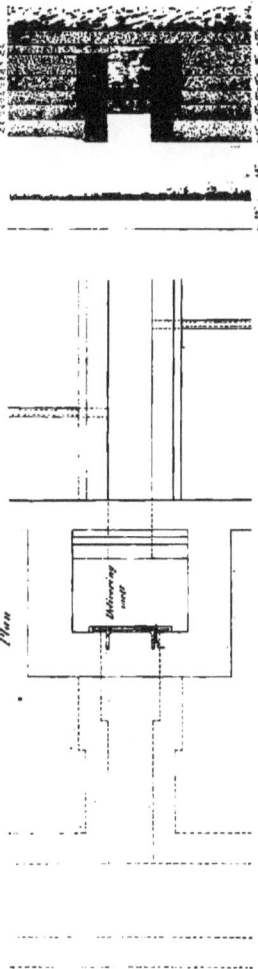

Section across the gathering drain.

Plan.

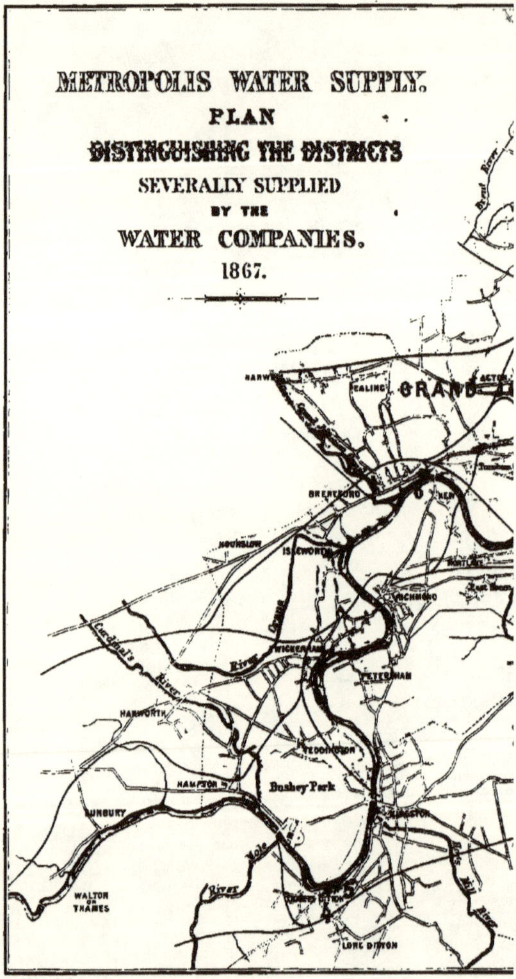

METROPOLIS WATER SUPPLY.
PLAN
DISTINGUISHING THE DISTRICTS
SEVERALLY SUPPLIED
BY THE
WATER COMPANIES.
1867.
EALING
GRAND
HOUNSLOW
PETERSHAM
Bushey Park
SUNBURY
WALTON
ON
THAMES
LONG DITTON
Cardinal's River
River Mole

PLATE II

N. The figures show the positions
of the principal stations of the
several water companies viz:

Pumping station of Chelsea w. works   4
Do   Lambeth   5
Do   Southwark   6
Do   Vauxhall
Do   Grand Junction   8
Do   West Middlesex   9
Do   New River   10
Do   East London   11

SCALE.

LONDON

CHELSEA WATER WORKS

FILTER BEDS

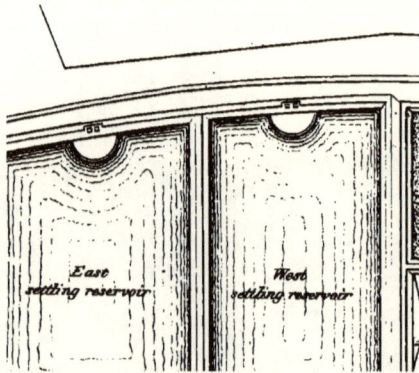

East settling reservoir *West settling reservoir*

A

Engine House

shaft

Coal store

50   100   150   200 Feet

from London to Esher &c.

steam under road

pumping engine

New

Filter Beds

street water engine

Coal Landing

R I V E R   T H A M E S

B

UNIVERSITY OF CALIFORNIA
DEPARTMENT OF CIVIL ENGINEERING
BERKELEY, CALIFORNIA

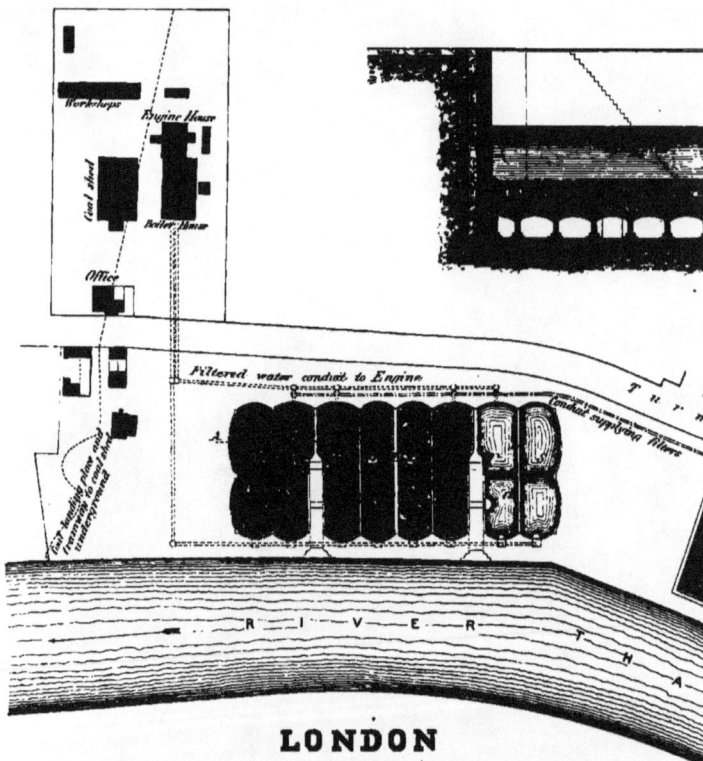

Workshops

Engine House

Coal shed

Boiler House

Office

Filtered water conduit to Engine

A

Combined supplying filters

Tur

Pipe leading from dip trench to underground channel

R I V E R   T H A

LONDON

LAMBETH WATER WORKS

RESERVOIRS AND FILTERS AT

DITTON

August 1808

PLATE V.

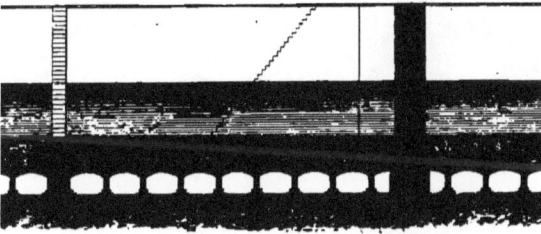

n of filter through A.B

The arches of the filters are in lengths of
2 feet 3 inches each, and there is a space
of 1 inch between them

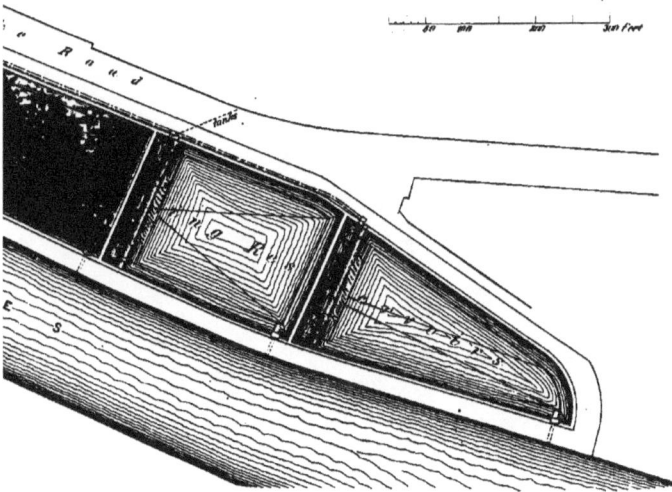

LONDON

SOUTHWARK & VAUXHALL WATER COMPANY

FILTERING WORKS AT

BATTERSEA

RIVER THAMES

Filter Bed
area 96,000 sq. ft.
C^5

Filter Bed
free 100,000 sq. ft.
C^3

Settling Reservoir
Area 270,000 sq. ft.
B^1

Settling Reservoir
area 145,000 sq. ft.
B^2

C^1

C^4

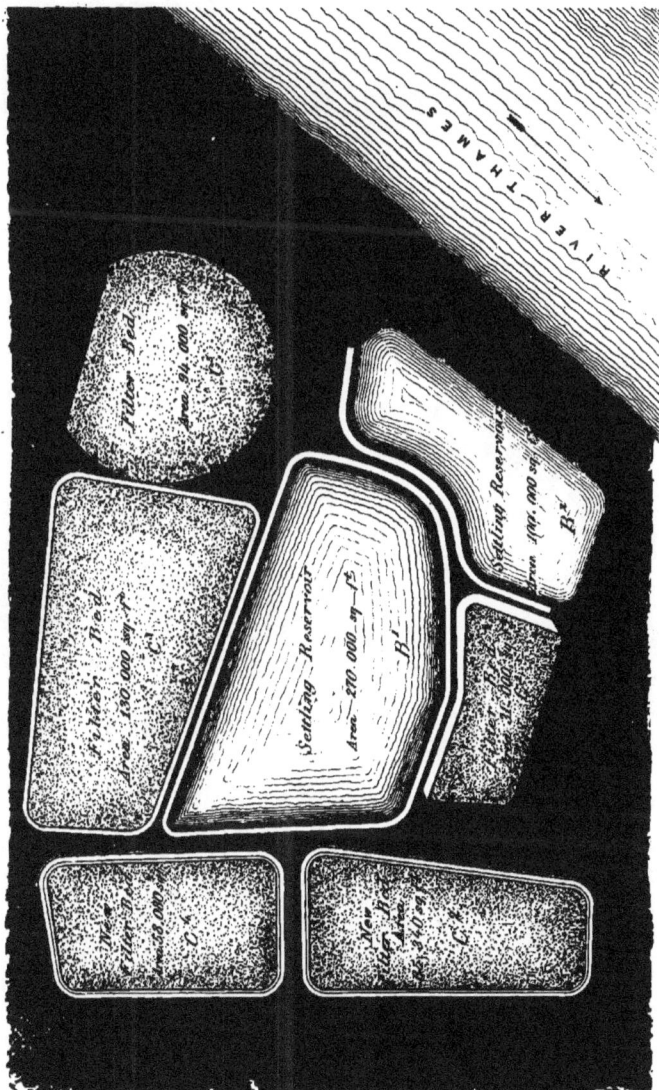

PLATE VII

LONDON

SOUTHWARK & VAUXHALL WATER WORKS

NEW WORKS IN CONSTRUCTION AT

HAMPTON.

August 5.ᵗʰ 1868

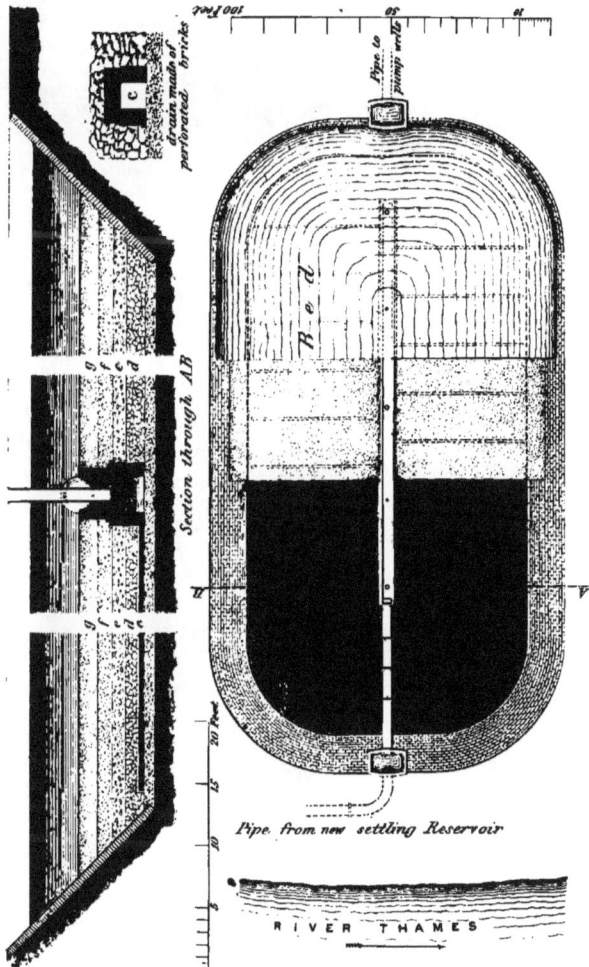

Section through A.B

drain mouth of perforated bricks

Bed

Pipe to pump wells

Pipe from new settling Reservoir

RIVER THAMES

100 Feet
50
10

20 Feet
15
10
5

PLATE VII

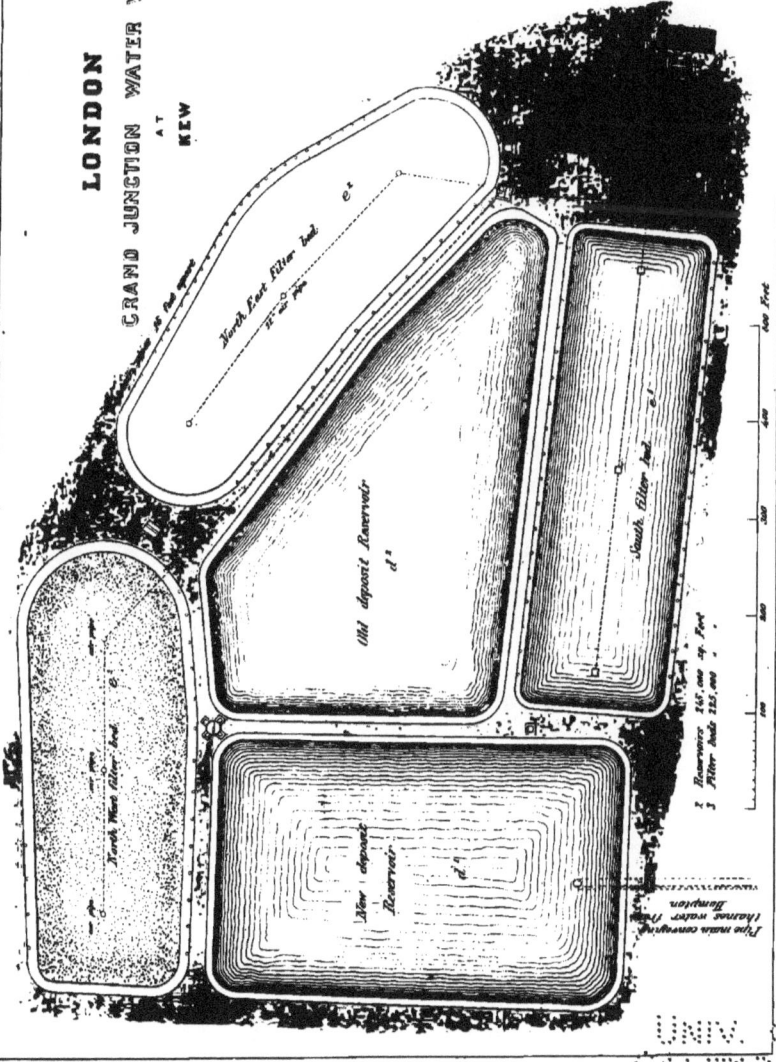

LONDON

GRAND JUNCTION WATER WORKS

AT

KEW

North East Filter bed e²

Old deposit Reservoir d²

South filter bed e¹

North West filter bed e

New deposit Reservoir d¹

Pipe main conveying Thames water from Hampton.

2 Reservoirs 265,000 sq. Feet
3 Filter beds 125,000 "

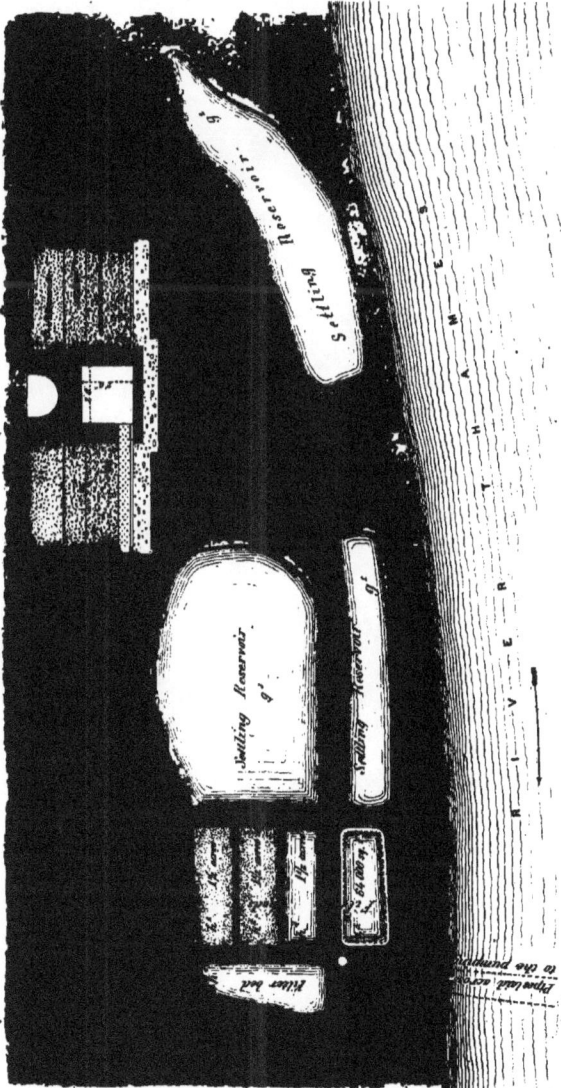

LONDON

WEST MIDDLESEX WATER WORKS

Sketch of

FILTER BEDS & SETTLING RESERVOIRS

Settling Reservoir 9

Settling

Settling Reservoir 9²

Settling Reservoir 9²

Filter bed

Filter bed

THAMES RIVER

Pipe leads on to the pump

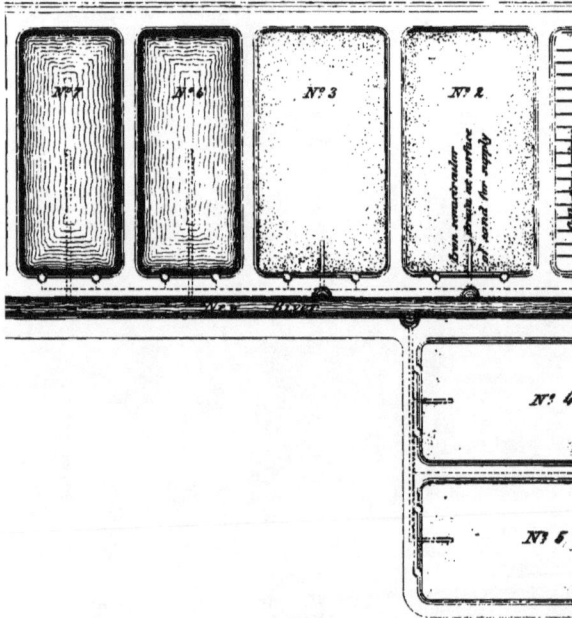

Green lanes Road

Settling Reservoir

m'

m'

m'

Sluice way

Engine House
yards

Clear water well

40 pipe
24 pipe

Well connected
with the
different pumps

v.7'

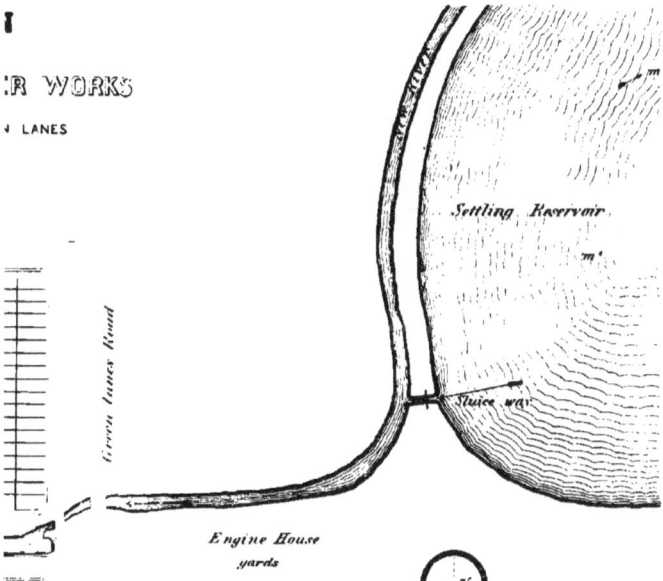

fig 3
Form of clay pipe

Bricks laid dry
Bricks on edge
laid in mortar
Puddle

fig 2
Dry brick collecting drains

UNIVERSITY OF CALIFORNIA
DEPARTMENT OF CIVIL ENGINEERING
BERKELEY, CALIFORNIA

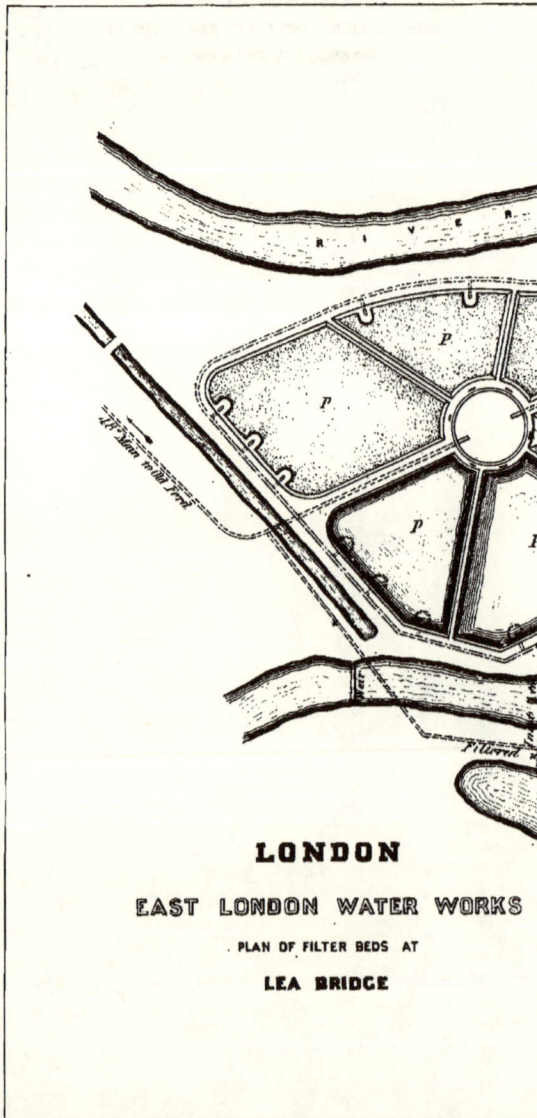

LONDON

EAST LONDON WATER WORKS

PLAN OF FILTER BEDS AT

LEA BRIDGE

PLATE XI

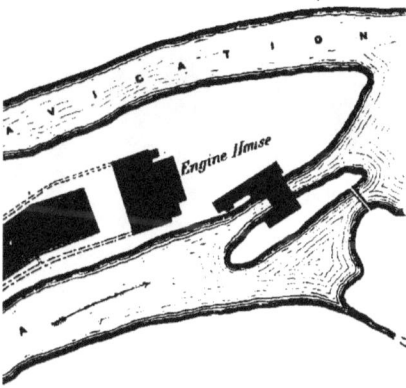

Mode of delivering the water upon the filters P.P.P

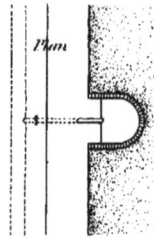

Section

Plan

Fig 2
Sketch of the settling reservoirs at Waltham Stowe

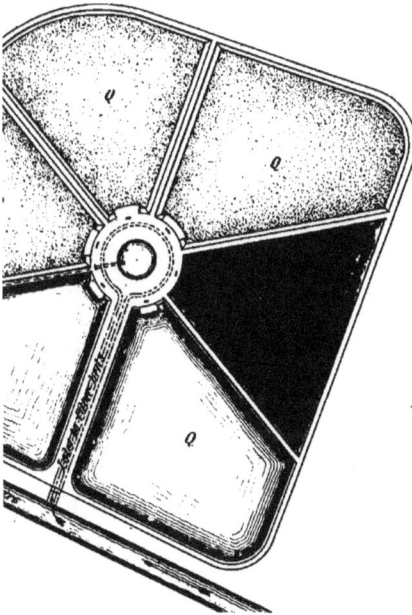

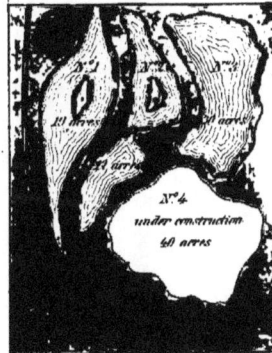

No 4
under construction
40 acres

Engine House

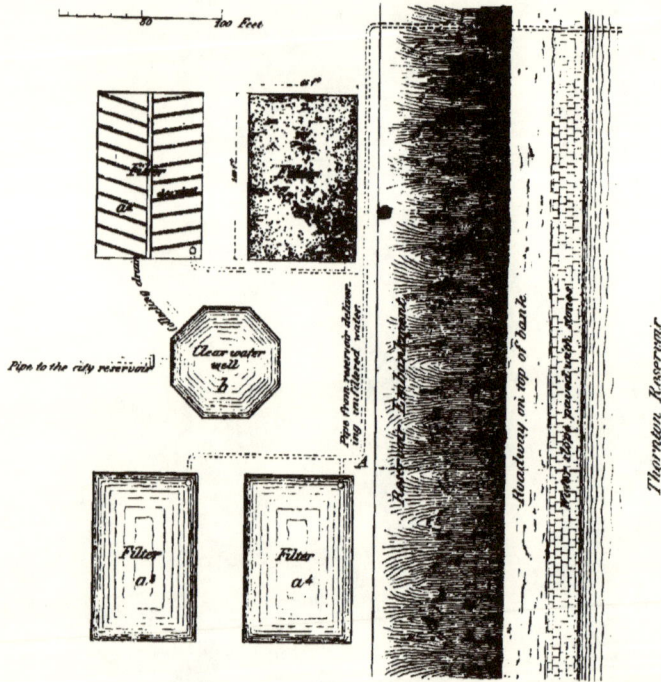

80   100 Feet

Filter *a²*

Filter *a¹*

Clear water well *B*

Pipe to the city reservoir

Pipe from reservoir delivering unfiltered water

Filter *a³*

Filter *a⁴*

Thornton Reservoir

Roadway on top of bank

LEICESTER WATER WORKS

SKETCH OF
FILTER BEDS AND RESERVOIRS

Section through AB

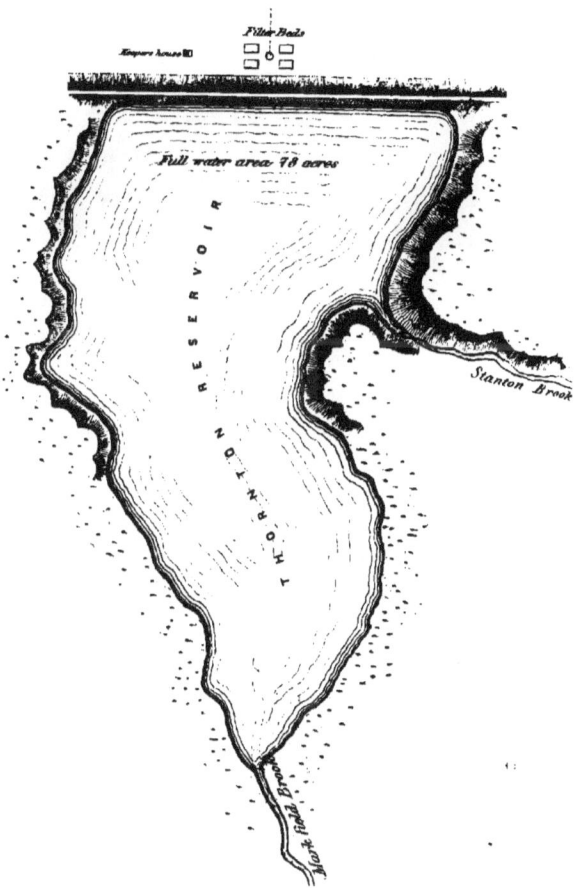

Filter Beds

Keepers house

Full water area 78 acres

THORNTON RESERVOIR

Stanton Brook

Mark Field Brook

Section through Filter at A.B

YORK WATER WORKS

FILTER BEDS

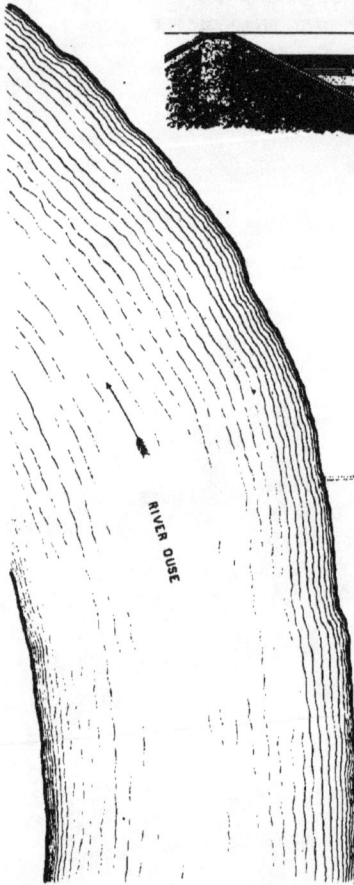

RIVER OUSE

21" River main

Road

24" Main. leading to high service reservoir

Settling reservoir

Settling reservoir

Engine House

18" pipe to filters

15" pipe filtered water to well

New filter bed to be built

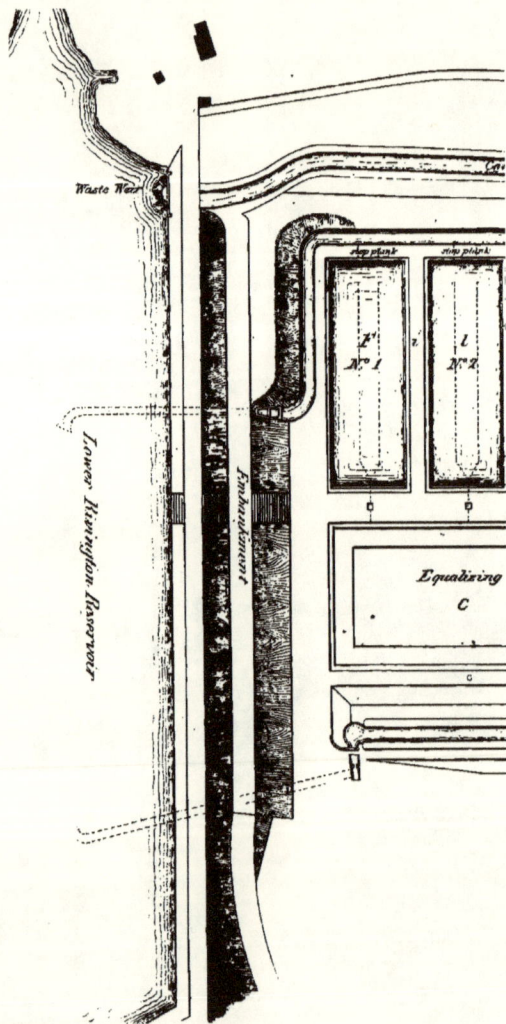

Waste Weir

Lower Rivington Reservoir

Embankment

stop plank

I
N°1

z

I
N°2

Equalizing
C

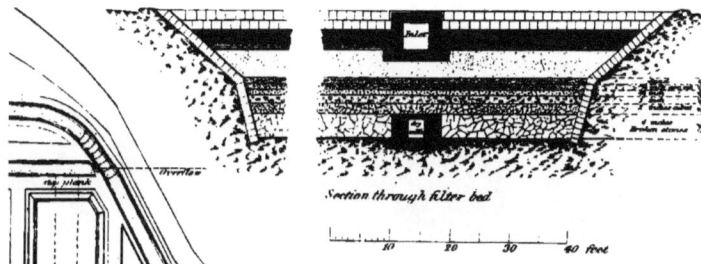

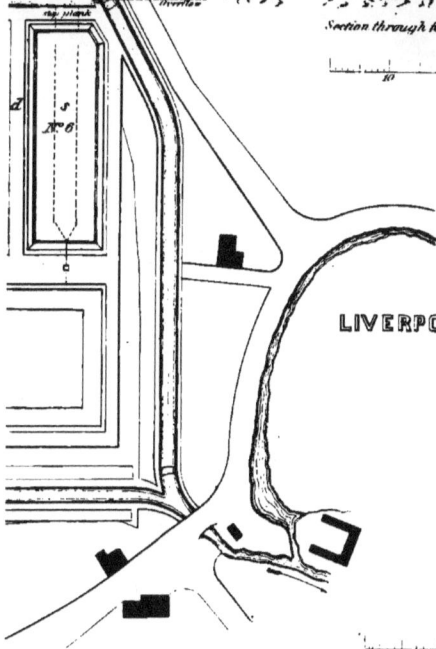

Section through filter bed

LIVERPOOL WATER WORKS

FILTER BEDS AT

RIVINGTON

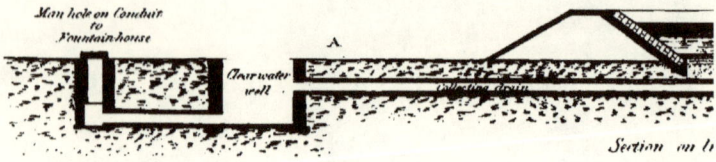

Man hole on Conduit
to
Fountain house

Clear water
well

A

Collecting drain

Section on l

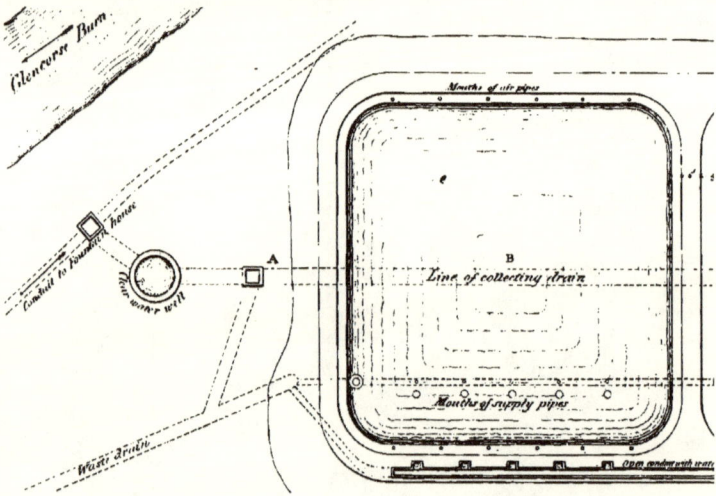

Glencorse Burn

Conduit to Fountain house

Clear water well

A

Mouths of air pipes

e

B

Line of collecting drain

Mouths of supply pipes

Water Froth

Open gutter with wate

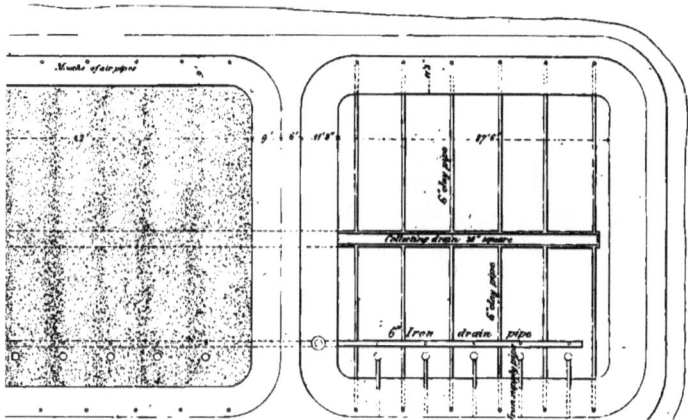

Mouths of air pipes

13'

9' 6"   11'6"   17'6"

6' clay pipe

Collecting drain 18" square

6' clay pipe

6" Iron drain pipe

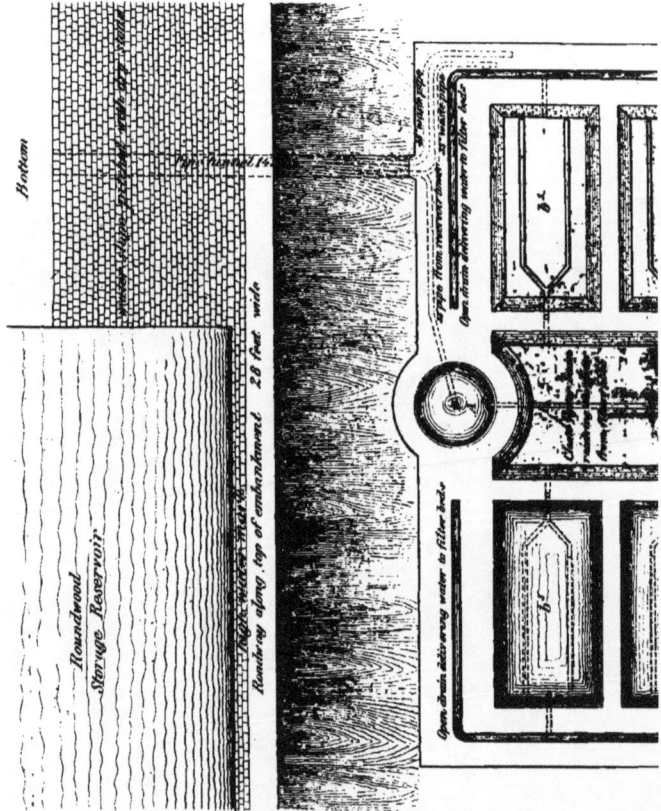

DUBLIN WATE[R]

FILTER BEDS

Bottom

Roundwood Storage Reservoir

Roadway along top of embankment   28 feet wide

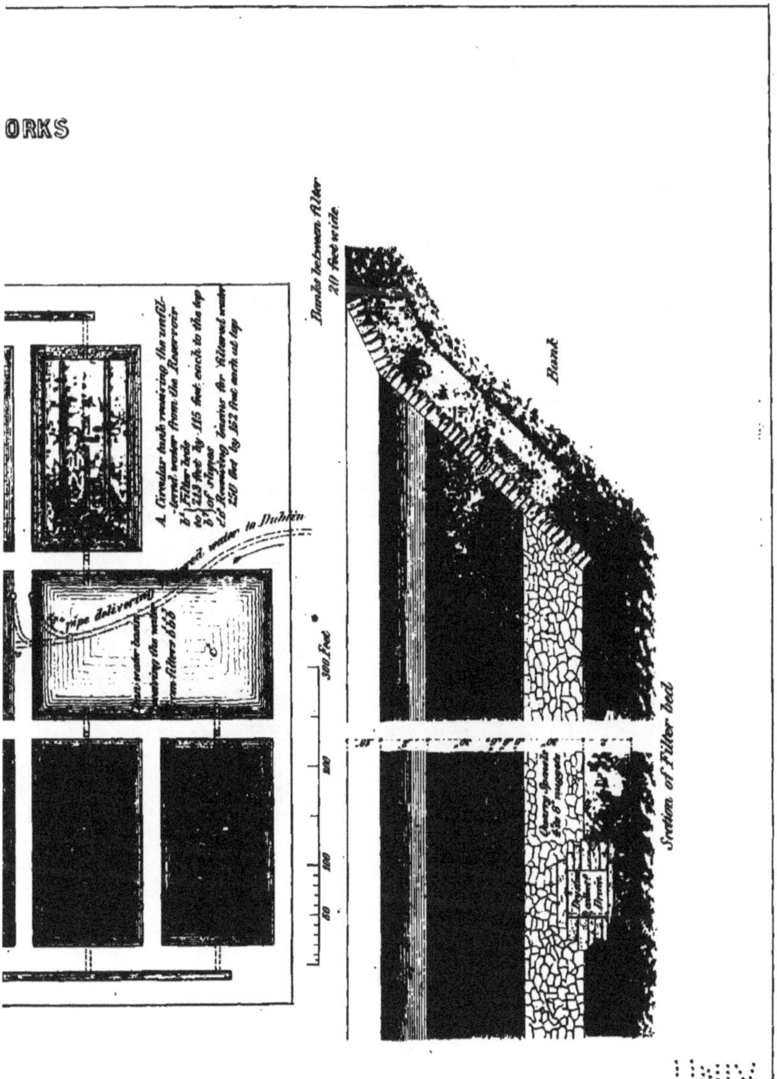

PLATE XVI.

ORKS

Section of Filter bed

Banks between Filter 20 feet wide

Bank

A. Circular tank receiving the unfiltered water from the Reservoir
B. Filter beds
C. Receiving basins for filtered water

pipe delivered

water to Dublin

300 Feet

200

100

50

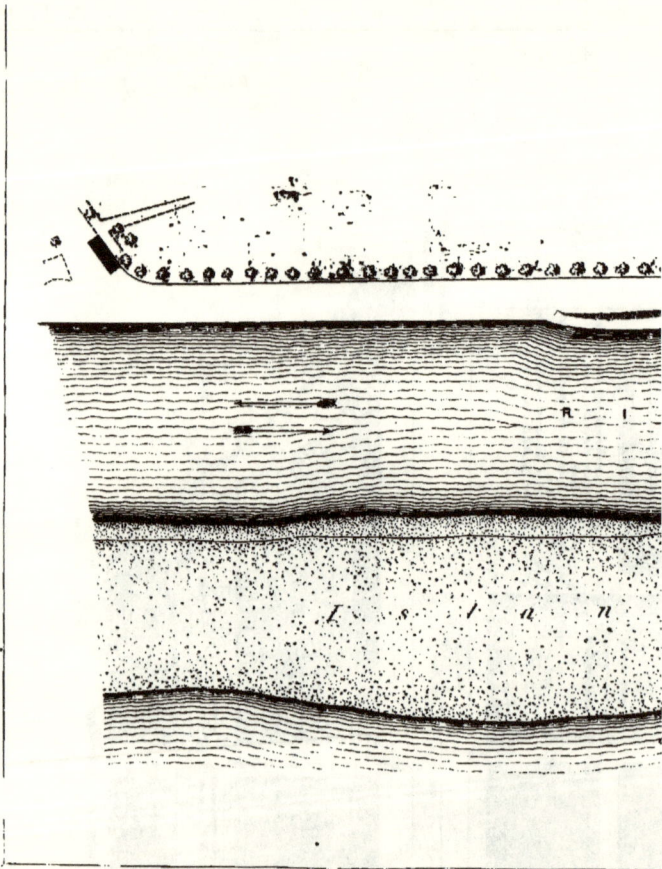

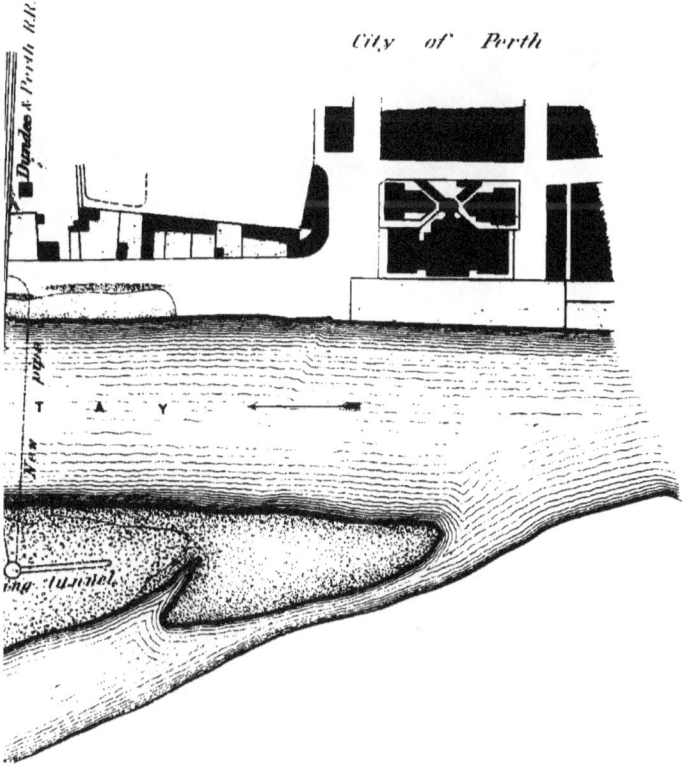

BERLIN WATER W

FILTER BEDS

Section on line M N

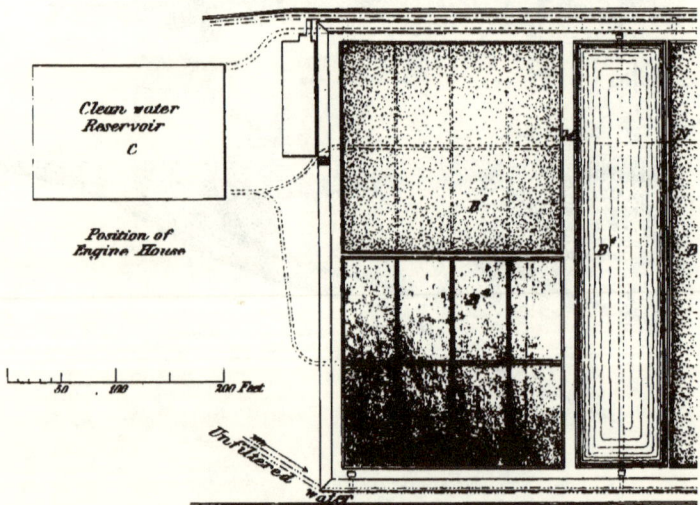

Clean water
Reservoir
C

Position of
Engine House

Unfiltered water

50   100   200 Feet

PLATE XVII

KS

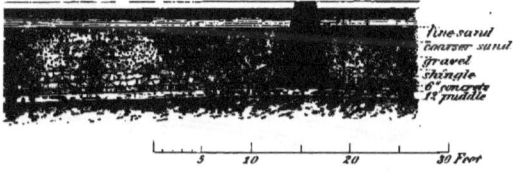

fine sand
coarser sand
gravel
shingle
6" concrete
12" puddle

5   10   20   30 Feet

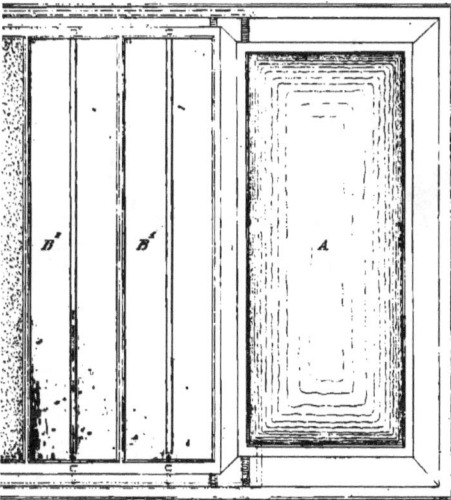

B^2 B^1 A

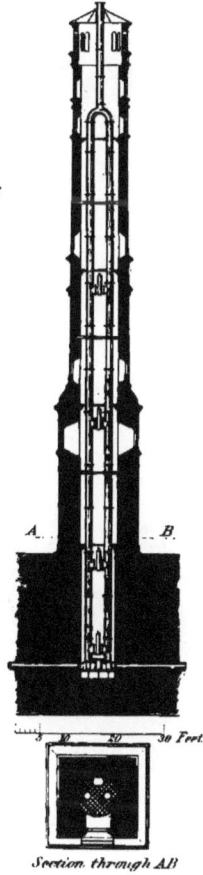

A.   B.

5   10   20   30 Feet

Section through AB

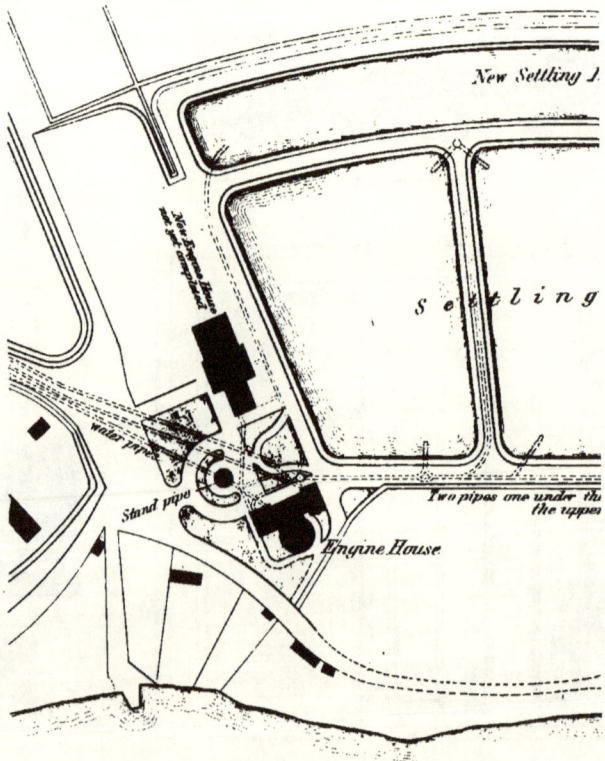

HAMBURGH WA

SETTLING RES

1866.

New Settling I

New Pumping House
and for extensions

Settling

water pipe

Stand pipe

Engine House

Two pipes one under th
the upper

N O R T H

HELIO. ENGR. & PRINT

PLATE XIX

WORKS

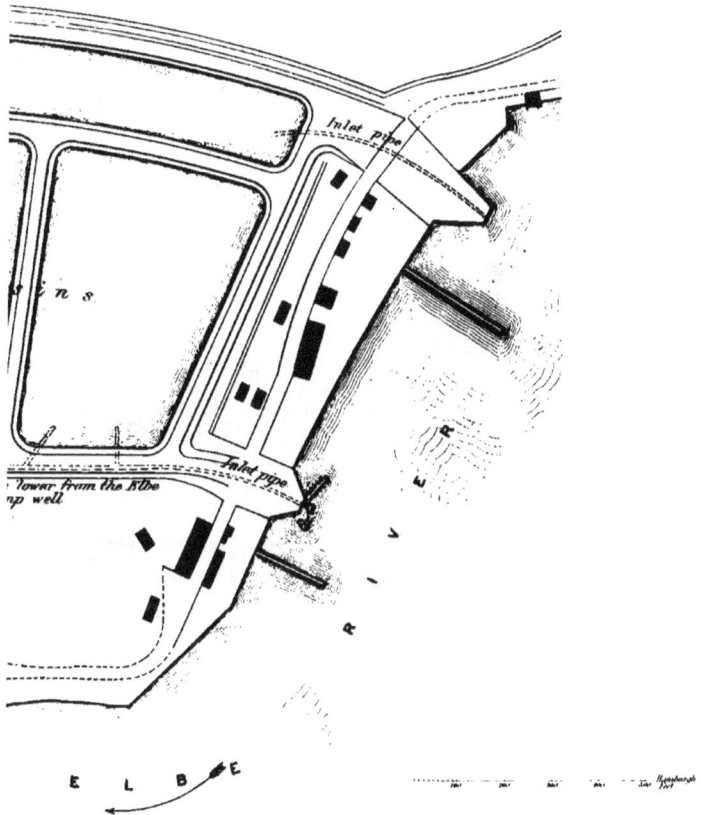

Inlet pipe

Inlet pipe

Tower from the Elbe
mp well

R I V E R

E L B E

The Hammerworth
Port

ALTONA WATER WORKS

SETTLING BASINS AND FILTER BEDS

A T

BLANKENESE

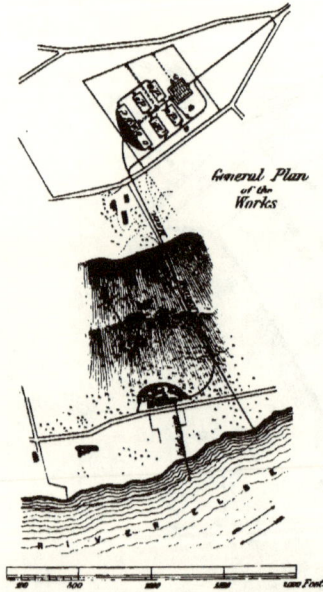

General Plan of the Works

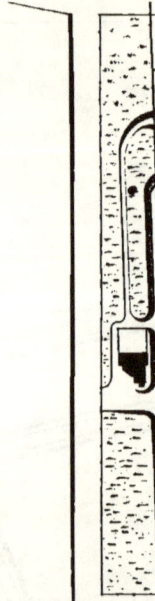

PLATE XX

a Small receiving Basin
b } Strainers or small stones
b'
cc Settling Basins
d,d,d,d Filter Beds
e Clear water

50   100   200   300 Feet

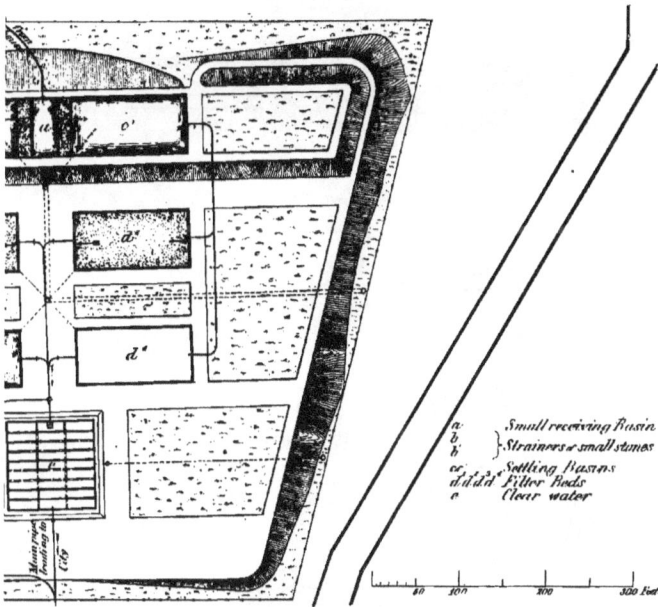

Section of Basins

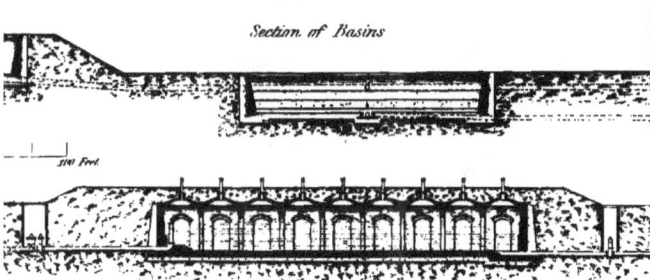

100 Feet

TOURS WATER WORKS

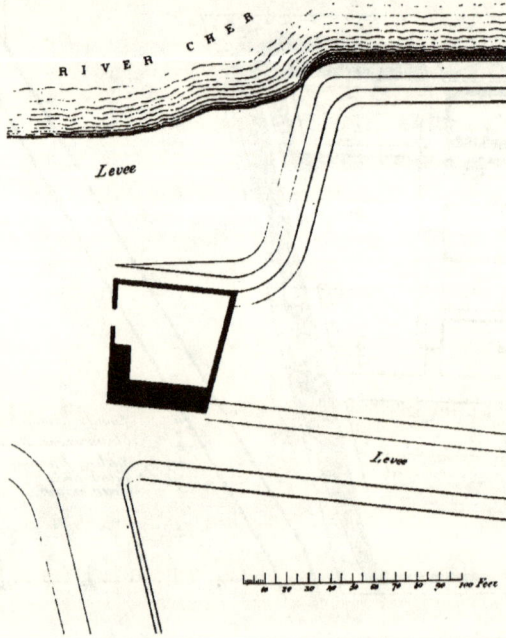

RIVER CHER

Levee

Levee

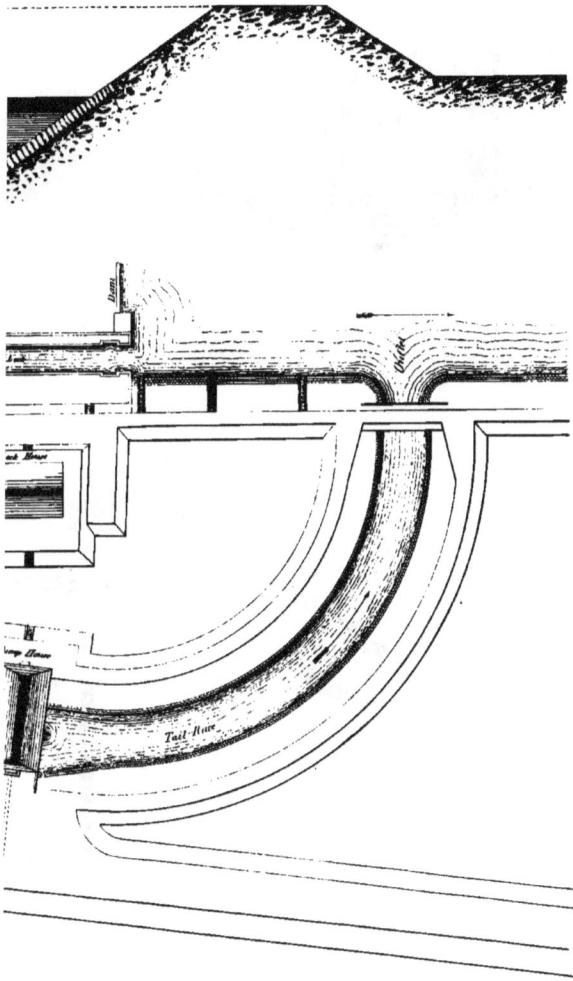

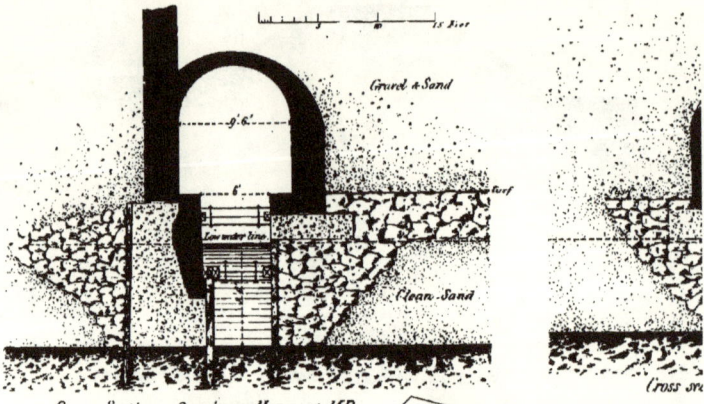

Gravel & Sand

9'.6'.

6'

Surf

Low water line

Clean Sand

Cross Section of main gallery at MD

Cross se

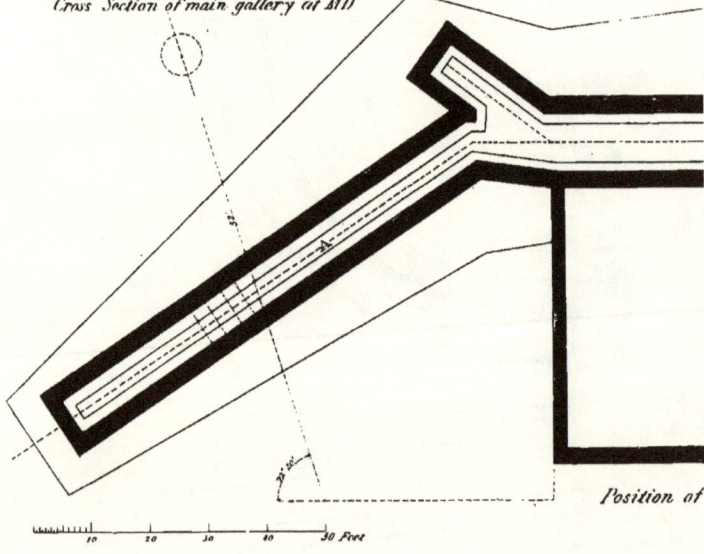

A

25° 25'

Position of

10   20   30   40   50 Feet

Gravel and Sand

Low water line

Sand

galleries A. B.

Gravel sand & shingle

Low water line

Sand

Cross section of Gallery C

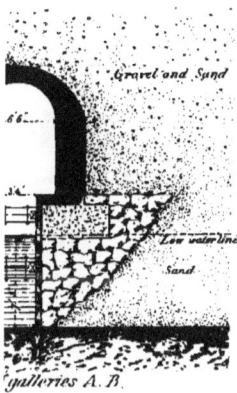

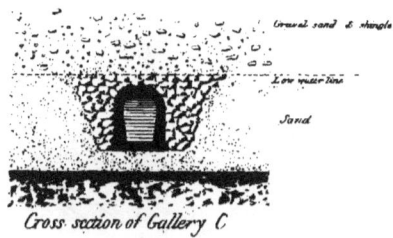

ANGERS WATER WORKS

FILTERING GALLERIES

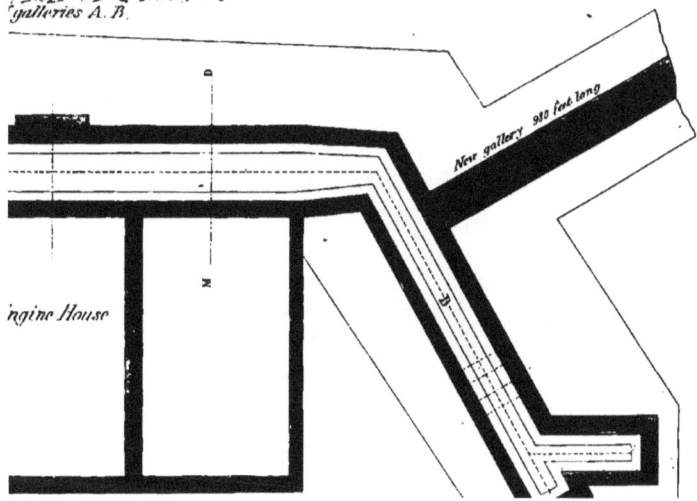

D

New gallery 980 feet long

Engine House

N

D

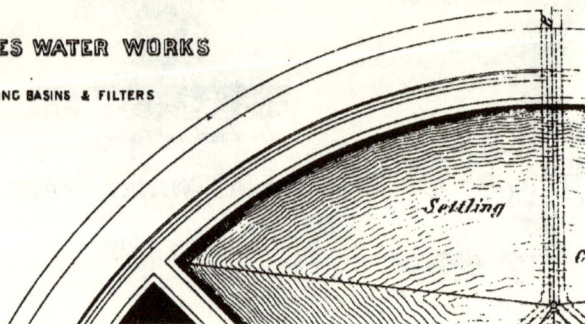

NANTES WATER WORKS

SETTLING BASINS & FILTERS

Settling

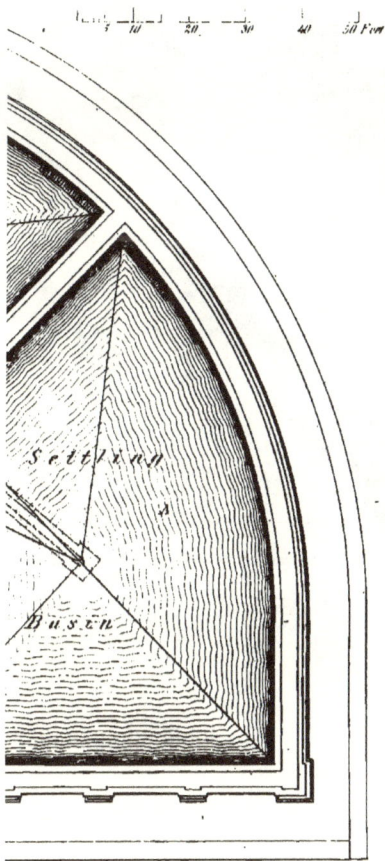

Section Through D E

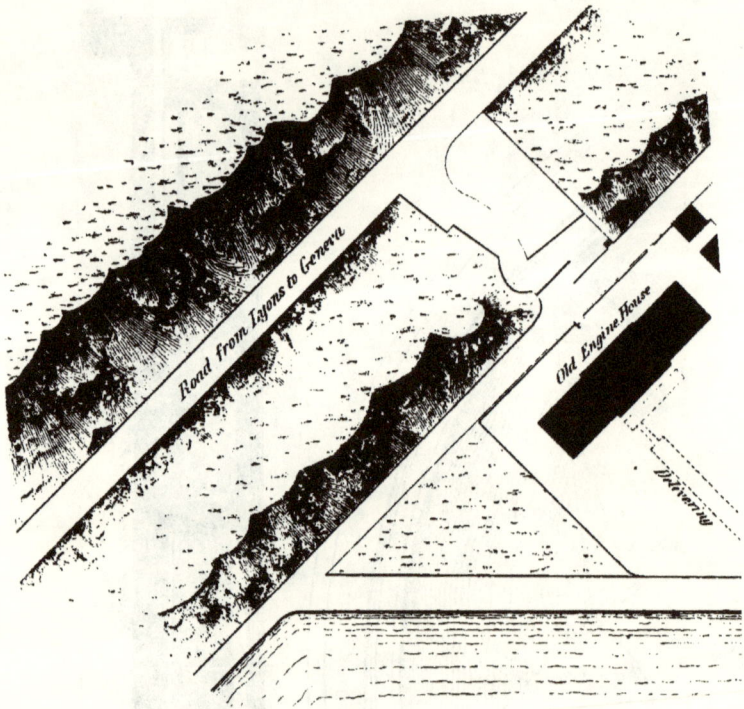

Road from Lyons to Geneva

Old Engine House

LYONS WATER WORKS

FILTERING GALLERIES AND BASINS

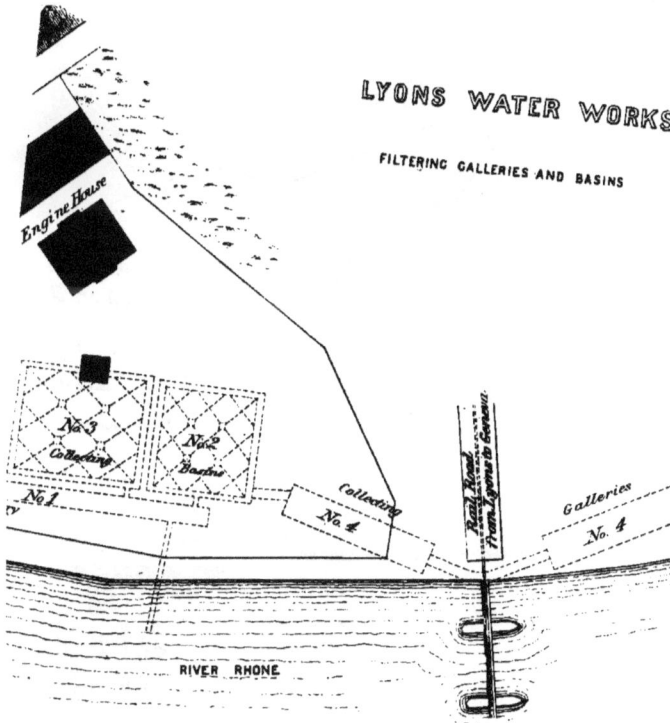

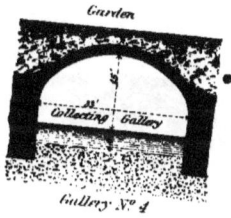

Engine House

No 3
Collecting
Basins

No 2
New
Basins

No 1

Collecting
No 4

Road
From Lyons to Geneva

Galleries
No. 4

RIVER RHONE

Garden

N.
Collecting Gallery

Gallery No 4

Dillon Road

Gravel Plain

Filter

GARONNE RIVER

Quay

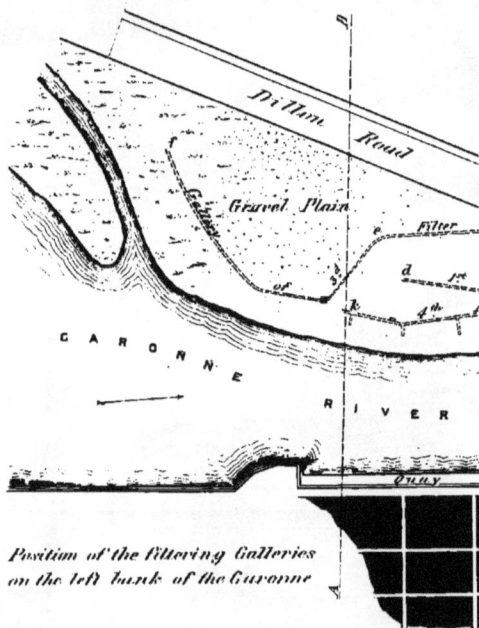

Position of the filtering Galleries
on the left bank of the Garonne

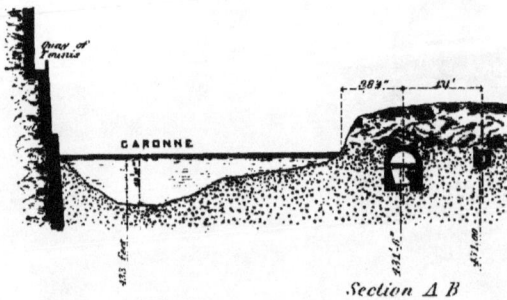

Quay of Toms

GARONNE

Section A B

PLATE XXV

WORKS.

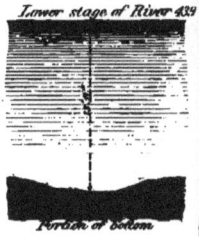

Lower stage of River 439

Portion of bottom

Cross section of new gallery Nº 4

Cross section of the branches
of new Gallery

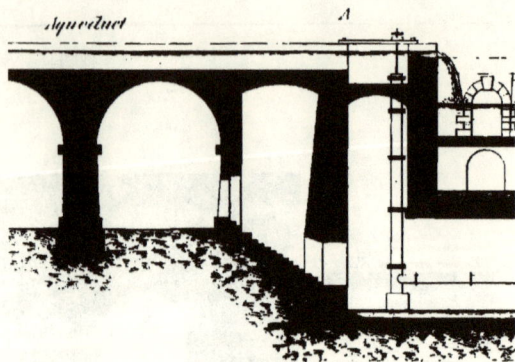

Aquæduct.   A.

angchamp Garden

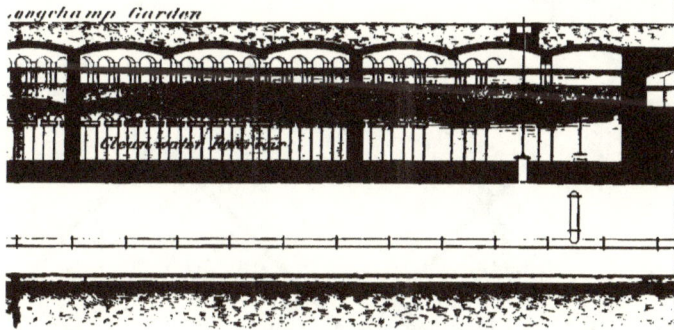

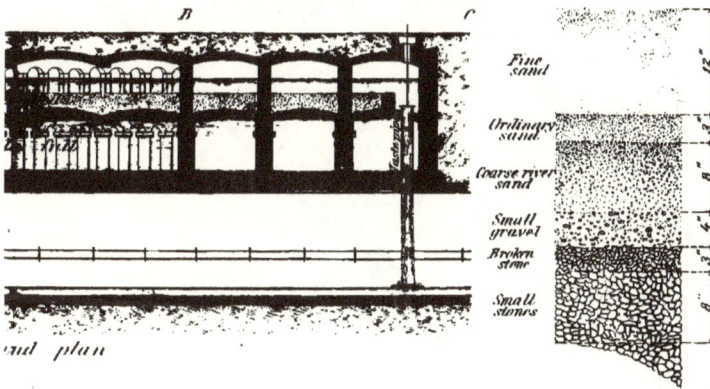

B   C

Fine
sand

Ordinary
sand

Coarse river
sand

Small
gravel

Broken
stone

Small
stones

nd plan

50 Feet

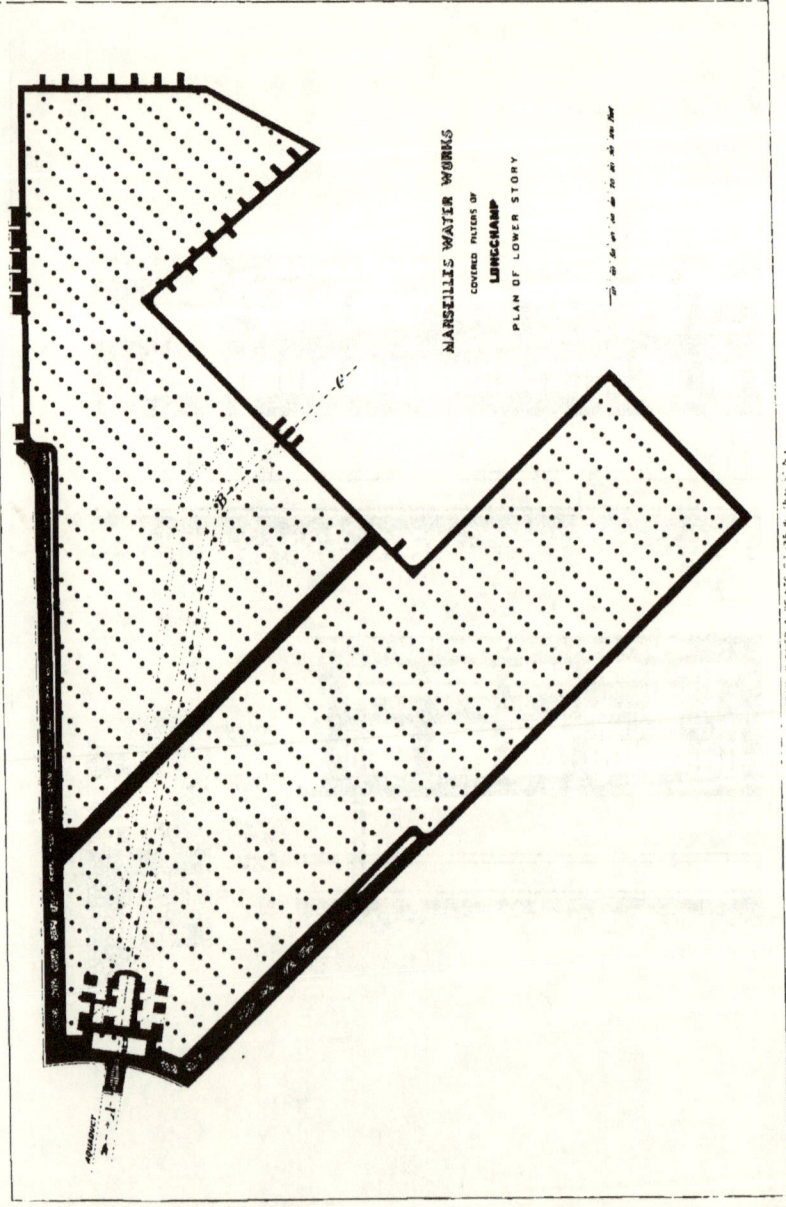

MARSEILLIS WATER WORKS

COVERED FILTERS OF

LONGCHAMP

PLAN OF LOWER STORY

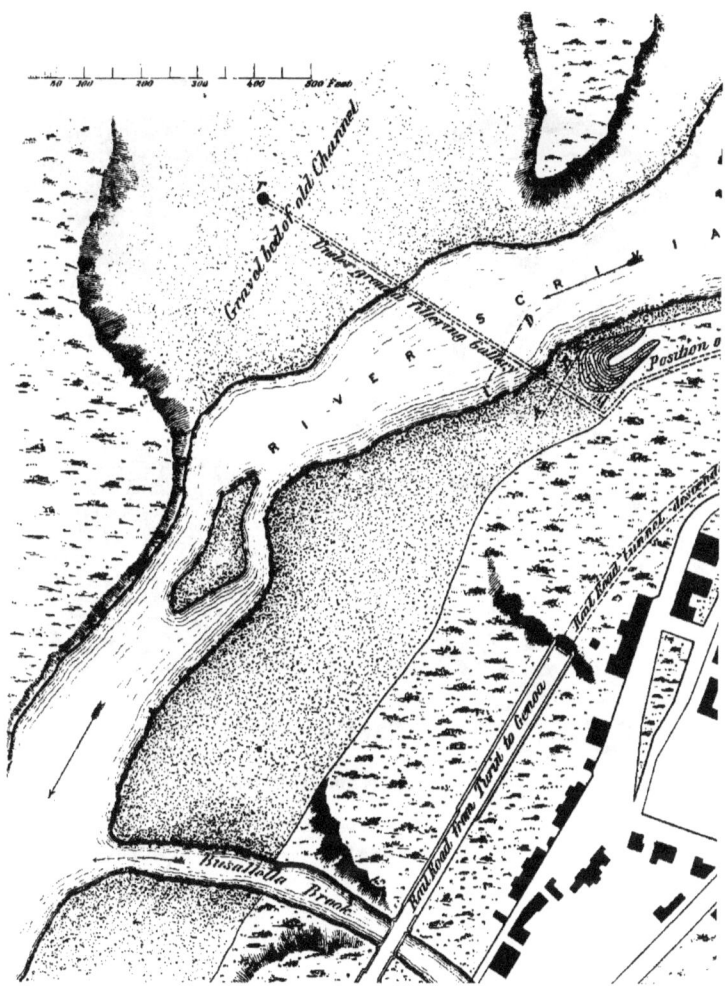

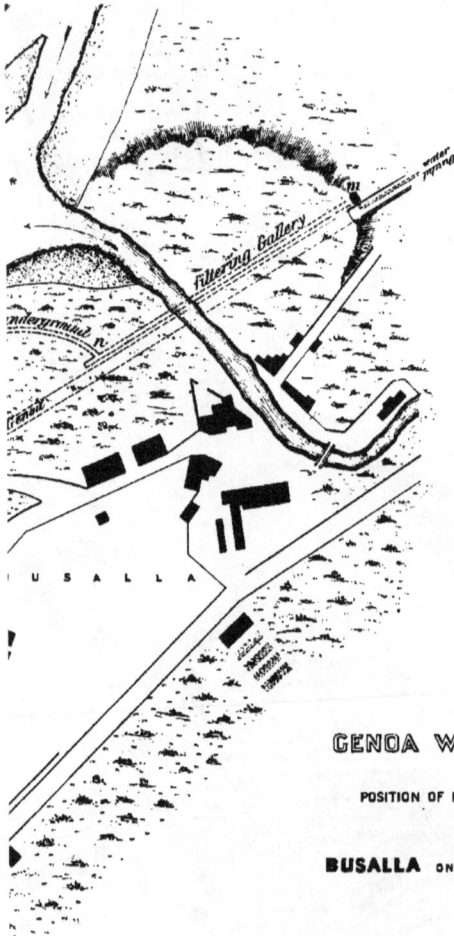

SECTIONS
OF THE
Filtering Gallery

Section CD
under the bed of Scrivia river

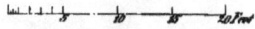

Section AB
in Gravel bed bordering river channel

GENOA WATER WORKS

POSITION OF FILTERING GALLERIES

AT

BUSALLA ON THE RIVER SCRIVIA

LEGHORN WATER WORKS

FILTER HOUSE
OF THE
PIAN DI ROTA

Pipe to the City

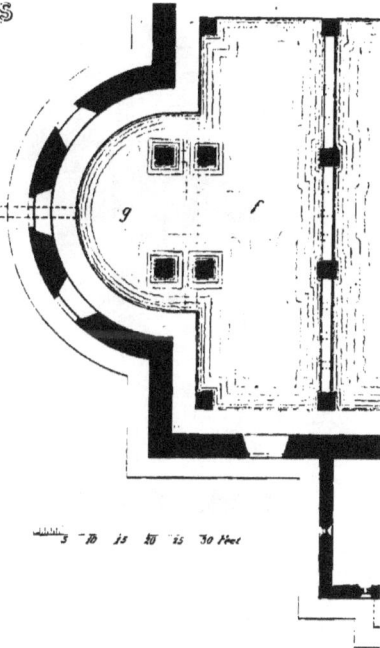

g

f

7 feet

Form of Aquaduct in tunnel

Surface of the ground

Form of Aquaduct in earth

5   10   15   20   25   30 Feet

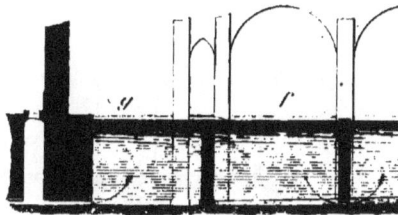

g

f

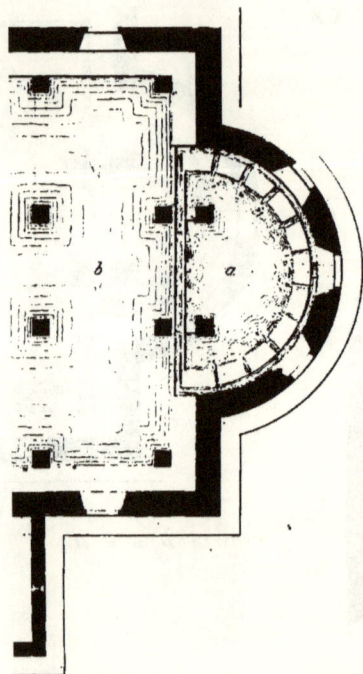

Aquaduct from
the springs

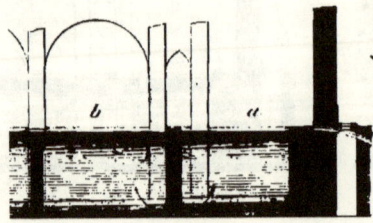

Arrangement of filtering material

Gravel   Charcoal   Gravel   small gravel

PLATE XXX.

LEGHORN

CITY CISTERN

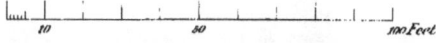

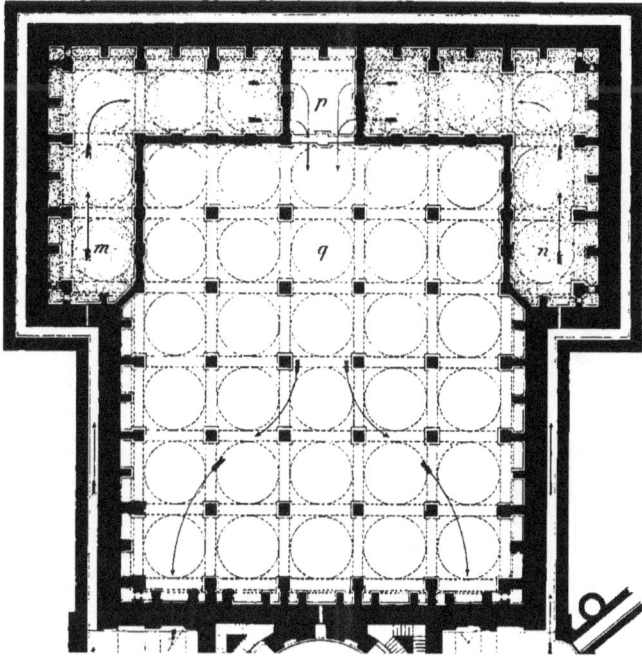

www.ingramcontent.com/pod-product-compliance
Lightning Source LLC
Chambersburg PA
CBHW020847270326
41928CB00006B/589